SECOND THOUGHTS AND THE EPISTEMOLOGICAL ENTERPRISE

What happens when we have second thoughts about the epistemic standing of our beliefs, when we stop to check on beliefs which we have already formed or hypotheses which we have under consideration? In the essays collected in this volume, Hilary Kornblith considers this and other questions about self-knowledge and the nature of human reason. The essays draw extensively on work in social psychology to illuminate traditional epistemological issues: in contrast with traditional Cartesian approaches to these issues, Kornblith engages with empirically motivated skeptical problems, and shows how they may be constructively addressed in practical and theoretical terms. As well as bringing together ten previously published essays, the volume contains two entirely new pieces that engage with ideas of self and rational nature. Kornblith's approach lays the foundations for further development in epistemology that will benefit from advances in our understanding of human psychology.

HILARY KORNBLITH is Distinguished Professor of Philosophy at the University of Massachusetts, Amherst. He has written widely on topics in epistemology, philosophy of mind, and related areas, and is the author of *Inductive Inference and Its Natural Ground* (1993), *Knowledge and Its Place in Nature* (2002), *On Reflection* (2012), and *A Naturalistic Epistemology: Selected Papers* (2014).

SECOND THOUGHTS AND THE EPISTEMOLOGICAL ENTERPRISE

HILARY KORNBLITH
University of Massachusetts, Amherst

CAMBRIDGE
UNIVERSITY PRESS

University Printing House, Cambridge CB2 8BS, United Kingdom

One Liberty Plaza, 20th Floor, New York, NY 10006, USA

477 Williamstown Road, Port Melbourne, VIC 3207, Australia

314-321, 3rd Floor, Plot 3, Splendor Forum, Jasola District Centre, New Delhi - 110025, India

79 Anson Road, #06-04/06, Singapore 079906

Cambridge University Press is part of the University of Cambridge.

It furthers the University's mission by disseminating knowledge in the pursuit of education, learning and research at the highest international levels of excellence.

www.cambridge.org
Information on this title: www.cambridge.org/9781108724128
DOI: 10.1017/9781108682688

© Hilary Kornblith 2019

This publication is in copyright. Subject to statutory exception and to the provisions of relevant collective licensing agreements, no reproduction of any part may take place without the written permission of Cambridge University Press.

First published 2019
First paperback edition 2021

A catalogue record for this publication is available from the British Library

ISBN 978-1-108-49851-7 Hardback
ISBN 978-1-108-72412-8 Paperback

Cambridge University Press has no responsibility for the persistence or accuracy of URLs for external or third-party internet websites referred to in this publication, and does not guarantee that any content on such websites is, or will remain, accurate or appropriate.

Will not a tiny speck very close to our vision blot out the glory of the world, and leave only a margin by which we see the blot? I know no speck so troublesome as self.

– George Eliot, *Middlemarch*

Contents

Acknowledgments		*page* viii
Introduction		1
1	Introspection and Misdirection	17
2	What Is It like to Be Me?	32
3	Distrusting Reason	49
4	The Impurity of Reason	69
5	What Reflective Endorsement Cannot Do	94
6	Belief in the Face of Controversy	113
7	Naturalism vs. the First-Person Perspective	136
8	Is There Room for Armchair Theorizing in Epistemology?	156
9	The Role of Reasons in Epistemology	181
10	Doxastic Justification Is Fundamental	201
11	Our Sense of Self	221
12	Our Rational Nature	243
Index		262

Acknowledgments

Chapters 11 and 12 are new to this volume. The remaining chapters originally appeared in the following locations. Permission to reprint these essays is gratefully acknowledged.

1. "Introspection and Misdirection," *Australasian Journal of Philosophy*, 67(1989), 410–422.
2. "What Is It like to Be Me?," *Australasian Journal of Philosophy*, 76 (1998), 48–60.
3. "Distrusting Reason," *Midwest Studies in Philosophy*, 23(1999), 181–196.
4. "The Impurity of Reason," *Pacific Philosophical Quarterly*, 81(2000), 67–89.
5. "What Reflective Endorsement Cannot Do," *Philosophy and Phenomenological Research*, 80(2010), 1–19.
6. "Belief in the Face of Controversy," in T. Warfield and R. Feldman, eds., *Disagreement*, Oxford University Press, 2010, 29–52.
7. "Naturalism vs. the First-Person Perspective," *Proceedings and Addresses of the American Philosophical Association*, Romanell Lecture, 87(2013), 107–126.
8. "Is There Room for Armchair Theorizing in Epistemology?," in M. Haug, ed., *Philosophical Methods: The Armchair or the Laboratory?*, Routledge, 2014, 195–216.
9. "The Role of Reasons in Epistemology," *Episteme*, 12(2015), 225–239.
10. "Doxastic Justification Is Fundamental," *Philosophical Topics*, 45 (2017), 63–80.

Introduction

This volume collects a dozen essays of mine written over the past thirty years, two of which are new to this volume. The essays cluster around a common theme, which I explain here.

Most of our beliefs are unreflectively arrived at. We go about our daily affairs, rarely stopping to reflect upon the epistemic status of our beliefs. When I am awakened by my alarm clock, I get dressed and ready for work with no thought at all about the epistemic status of my beliefs. Getting dressed and eating breakfast inevitably involves taking in an extraordinary amount of information about my environment: the location of the hot and cold water taps, where my clothing is, the height of each step on the stairway, what is in the refrigerator, and so on. All of this information is registered in me passively without a thought given to whether the beliefs produced within me are justified. My focus is not on epistemological matters; it is on getting dressed, eating breakfast, and getting to work.

And so it is with others as well, of course. Reflecting on our beliefs and their epistemic status is the exception rather than the rule. Non-human animals and very young children never engage in such reflection. The supremely overconfident do it far less than they should. And those crippled by self-doubt may engage in it to a pathological degree. But normal human adults do, at times, stop to reflect about whether they are believing as they should. Even if most of our beliefs, at most times, are not given a second thought, it does seem that the capacity for such reflective thinking, and the actual practice of engaging in it, is an important part of human intellectual life. The essays in this volume address just such second thoughts.

We give matters a second thought, in many cases, quite involuntarily. My wife was recently enjoying a pleasant stroll in Central Park, barely noticing the passersby, when she did a double take. Was that Leonardo DiCaprio who just walked by? The second thought was triggered in her, not something she chose to do as part of a carefully managed inquiry. But freely chosen or not, this second thought involved a reflective examination of the epistemic credentials of her tentative identification. At other times, our second thoughts are very much a matter of choice. We purposefully stop to check upon beliefs already formed or hypotheses under consideration. We engage in epistemological investigation with the explicit goal of making sure that our beliefs are appropriately responsive to the facts.

Second thoughts about the epistemic standing of one's beliefs are the starting point of much epistemology. My focus here, however, is somewhat non-standard. For many epistemologists, much as they may agonize over the status of our beliefs about the physical world, about the future, about the past, and about other minds, they regard certain classes of our beliefs as especially resistant to the sort of doubt and second thoughts mentioned here. In the Cartesian tradition, beliefs about one's current mental states enjoy a special resistance to doubt. And for many epistemologists, beliefs which are a priori justified, including beliefs about the nature of good reason itself, enjoy a similarly special status. Such beliefs may, of course, be reflectively examined; one may give any belief a second thought. But if certain Cartesian views about these matters are correct, these beliefs will always stand up to such reflective scrutiny. Unlike other beliefs, reflective examination of this special class – certain beliefs about the self and about good reason – have an epistemic standing which assures that they need no correction, and so need no further reflective scrutiny. My focus in this volume is on just such beliefs. Where others would exempt such beliefs from doubt, or severely limit the scope of such doubt, I argue that such beliefs should be a matter of special concern.

My doubts do not come from thinking about the possibility of evil demons plotting against us, seeking to deceive us at every turn, nor from considering the possibility that we might be brains in vats, subject to direct electrical stimulation of our gray matter supervised by the twenty-first-century descendants of those evil demons. Such wild hypothetical cases raise concerns about global skepticism, and, for better or for worse, global skepticism is not my concern here. My worries stem from the more homely results of work in social psychology. These doubts, while far less global, are also, in my view, far more pressing. And they target the very kinds of beliefs which more traditional epistemologists have thought most immune to the kind of correction which second thought might provide.

As I see it, there is a great deal of work in epistemology which is prompted by the phenomenon of reflective scrutiny, regarding it as emblematic of the epistemological enterprise. The phenomenon of deliberation about what to believe, or whether to believe, is seen as offering an entree to understanding epistemological matters generally: the nature of inference, rationality, and justification. More than this, deliberation, and thus the epistemological matters which it is thought to illuminate, is then investigated from a first-person point of view. We understand deliberation, it is thought, when we examine it from the point of view of the deliberator.

My own view is that this is a mistake, and that we can only understand epistemological matters, and even deliberation itself, when we engage in the kind of third-person examination of such phenomena which is found in experimental psychology. The first-person point of view deeply distorts our understanding of ourselves and of deliberation, but we can only come to see that this is so if we engage with the psychological literature on these matters. Far too much epistemological theorizing, especially about deliberation and reflective thought generally, never departs from the first-person point of view.

The result of these essays, taken collectively, is a kind of reversal of the Cartesian picture: where others see beliefs about oneself and about the a priori as especially resistant to doubt, and beliefs about the physical world as especially precarious, my own view is just the mirror image of this picture: I see our beliefs about much of the physical world as especially secure, and beliefs about the self, and the nature of reason, as far more precarious. I hope that bringing these essays together helps to make the case for this way of thinking.

Chapter 1, "Introspection and Misdirection," lays out a central strand in my challenge to the Cartesian picture. Descartes viewed a special kind of reflective self-evaluation as absolutely essential for achieving *scientia*, a kind of high-grade knowledge. More recent analytic epistemologists sympathetic with the big Cartesian picture have translated this into a contemporary idiom. On this way of viewing things, reflective examination of the epistemic credentials of a belief is a prerequisite for justified belief, and a necessary condition for knowledge. The prescribed process of reflective self-examination achieves two things simultaneously: it lays out standards for justified belief, and it gives guidance to the concerned epistemic agent. In this essay, I look at the advice offered by two paradigmatic Cartesian epistemologists: Roderick Chisholm's foundationalist prescriptions, and the coherentist demands laid out by Laurence BonJour. Although the advice presented by these philosophers differs from one another quite dramatically, they betray a common faith in the powers of reflective self-examination to improve an agent's epistemic position. This raises the question of whether the kind of introspective self-scrutiny which Cartesian philosophers endorse does, in fact, achieve the desired result.

There is a wealth of material available in the social psychology literature which bears on this question, and it does not bode well for Cartesian epistemology. As I argue here, when we stop to reflect on the epistemic credentials of beliefs we hold in order to determine whether we hold those beliefs for good reasons, we are subject to a powerful illusion. We seem to have direct access to the reasons for which we hold our beliefs. In fact, however, our understanding of these reasons is a product of confabulation: we engage in a bit of sub-conscious inference in an attempt to explain how it is that we must have arrived at the beliefs we have. As I argue, this does not make our beliefs about our reasons unreliable: inference to an explanation, at least given suitable background information, can be quite reliable. But when we understand how this inference works, we see that it is especially ill suited to the task which Cartesian epistemologists wish to put it. We engage in reflective self-examination in an attempt to locate and correct our errors. The thought is that unreflective belief may easily go wrong, and it would thus be irresponsible simply to trust to luck that such believing operates as it should. We therefore engage in reflection to provide a check on our beliefs: reflection is recruited to serve the purpose of error-detection. Unfortunately, the way in which confabulation works makes it especially unsuited to this role. As I argue, the errors we make in arriving at our beliefs are not likely to be corrected by way of reflection. Instead, we are liable to emerge more confident than we were before we stopped to reflect, but no more reliable. The process of reflective self-examination gives us the illusion that we have subjected our beliefs to a rigorous screening that will improve our epistemic position. In fact, however, it achieves no such thing.

Chapter 2, "What Is It like to Be Me?," further develops the anti-Cartesian views of Chapter 1. On Descartes' view, we have infallible introspective access to our current mental states. More than this, our infallibility is not, according to Descartes, merely a matter of contingent psychological law. In order to do the work it does in his foundationalist epistemology, the infallibility of introspection must be something Descartes can be assured of prior to and independent of any experimental investigations. These extremely strong claims about the epistemic status of beliefs about our mental states are rarely held anymore, but they provide a useful starting point for challenging even the more qualified Cartesian views which are still very much a part of the current philosophical landscape.

I begin by presenting an extended discussion of an example of an individual suffering from paranoid personality disorder. This is not, of course, the kind of case which inspires Cartesian intuitions about self-knowledge, but, as I argue, it has implications even for far more typical cases. The paranoid individual regularly makes judgments about his own mental states – about the extent to which he is defensive, about whether he is angry, jealous, or insecure – which are horribly inaccurate. It is not that these beliefs are inaccurate because they are insufficiently reflective. Further reflection on these issues would not lead to greater accuracy; indeed, quite the opposite. The belief-forming processes which go to work when the paranoid individual introspectively examines the various features of his mental life are extremely unreliable, and they are unreliable because of the ways in which his paranoia distorts his judgment. Our mental states form a complex causally interconnected system, and reflective processes of self-examination may be facilitated, or, as they are in this case, distorted, by the ways in which our various mental states interact.

When the paranoid individual introspects and examines his emotional state, he may come to believe that he is not angry even though, in fact, he is. His introspective evidence does not alert him to the fact that he is angry. But now you and I may introspect and come to believe, on that basis, that we ourselves are not angry. If we do so because our introspective evidence provides no reason to think that we are angry, then, in that respect, we are no different from the paranoid individual. For this reason, it seems that our introspective evidence, by itself, cannot give us adequate reason to believe that we are not angry.

Now paranoid personality disorder is not a common condition, and one may think that this is sufficient reason to justify ignoring this worry. That may well be. But, as I argue, there are many mental conditions which are extremely common, and which lead to similar sorts of distortions: they lead individuals who suffer from these conditions to misjudge their mental states on the basis of their introspective evidence. The fact that these conditions are very common suggests that you and I cannot reasonably ignore the possibility that we are subject to them, absent specific evidence that speaks to that issue. But then our introspective evidence of our current mental state, which is no different from that of those who suffer from these common mental conditions, and which distorts their view of what their mental state really is, cannot, by itself, justify our beliefs about our current mental states.

I therefore argue for a mitigated skepticism about self-knowledge. The skepticism is empirically based, and the breadth of this skepticism is entirely dependent on the extent to which there are common mental conditions which distort the introspective view of those who suffer from these conditions on particular subjects. Some mental states may elude this argument if there are no common conditions which distort subjects' views of these particular states. But, as I argue, there are many very common mental conditions which distort subjects' views about many mental states about which all of us have a great many opinions. This is compatible with the suggestion that we may, nevertheless, come to know that we are, or are not, in these mental states, as long as we have the relevant non-introspective evidence that we are not subject to the distorting mental condition. But it does mean that we cannot have knowledge or justified belief about whether we are in these mental states by introspection alone. And it means as well that since many people are in no position to know whether they suffer from the relevant mental condition, that they may not be in a position to know, or even be justified in believing, whether they are in a great many different mental states about which their introspective evidence seems, on its face, to be decisive.

Chapter 3, "Distrusting Reason," addresses a different part of the Cartesian picture. On Descartes' view, it is not just our view of our own current mental states which occupies a privileged epistemic position; our view of the truths of reason are epistemically privileged as well. More recent epistemological views put this point in slightly different terms: it is widely held that the manner in which we should reason is knowable a priori, and thus resistant to many of the sources of challenge which our empirical beliefs are subject to. In this essay, I examine one particular sort of challenge to this view, one according to which it might be wise to be especially distrustful of appeals to reason.

Certain Marxists, Freudians, feminists, and deconstructionists have urged that we should be especially distrustful of explicit appeals to reason. Without seeking to align myself with any of these views, or attempting to reconstruct the arguments such philosophers give for this distrust, I argue that there is a view here which is not only worthy of serious consideration, but which offers an account of explicit appeals to reasons which is superior to the traditional a priorist account. I approach this by considering the ways in which appeals to reason and argumentation play a role in public discussion.

It is often held that when someone publicly defends a claim with which we disagree, we should consider the reasons which are offered in favor of the claim and carefully evaluate whether the reasons offered do, indeed, support the claim at issue. Sincerely engaging with the reasons offered is part of what it is to be open-minded, and it would be unreasonable to reject such a claim out of hand simply because our own belief on the matter is different.[1] It is true, of course, that in attempting to evaluate the claim, we may miss something important, or we may be biased in certain respects so that we fail to see the relevance of certain issues which are, in

---

[1] For a very useful recent discussion of these issues, see Jeremy Fantl, *The Limitations of the Open Mind*, Oxford University Press, 2018.

fact, relevant. But if there is a public discussion of the claim at issue, then it seems that, should we all approach the matter in the manner recommended, these concerns are likely to be of vanishingly little significance. The speaker may be biased or ignorant in some ways, as may you or I. But if we all focus on the reasons as best we can, our biases and areas of ignorance are likely to cancel one another out. You are likely to notice the ways in which I am biased and you are not, or areas in which I am ignorant and you are not, and vice versa. Since we can each recognize one another's shortcomings in these respects precisely by focusing on the reasons for and against a particular claim, the public discussion of reason is likely to be especially epistemically useful. We should, as a result, be especially trusting of the public discussion of reason.

I think that considerations of this sort are very much at work in explaining the confidence that is often placed in the public discussion of reason, and I believe as well that, in certain sorts of situations, considerations such as these count in favor of such confidence. But this defense of the practice of trusting the public discussion of reason makes certain presuppositions about the distribution of bias which cannot always be counted upon. If the sources of bias are many and idiosyncratic, then the kind of argument just given provides reason for thinking that the public discussion of reason will allow us to transcend our individual biases, since the group is likely to be able to correct the various idiosyncratic biases of the individuals which compose it. But if there is some common source of bias which the members of the group are all, or almost all, subject to, then the public discussion of reasons will not uncover it, but, instead, merely entrench it further. As I argue, the idea that there should be such widespread biases is not at all far-fetched. There are certain subjects on which, indeed, this is exactly what we should expect. And here, the public discussion of reasons will be epistemically counterproductive.

This does not, I argue, count in favor of a blanket skepticism about reason, or simply opting out of the public discussion of reasons across the board. But neither is it a reason to simply ignore the problem and hope for the best. We must, instead, take seriously various hypotheses about the distribution of bias, and investigate the extent to which these various hypotheses are likely to be true. We need, as well, to undertake various steps necessary to ameliorate the common sources of bias, biases which are, epistemically, far more pernicious than the idiosyncratic biases which are often a focus of our attention.

Chapter 4, "The Impurity of Reason," takes on the issue of the a priori far more directly, and whether the manner in which we ought to reason is a priori knowable. Laurence BonJour has provided one of the most detailed and compelling defenses of the a priori in his book *In Defense of Pure Reason*.[2] He famously argues that a complete rejection of the a priori amounts to "intellectual suicide," for it would undermine all legitimate inference.[3] I examine BonJour's arguments in detail here, and defend a view on which the issue of whether we have a priori knowledge turns on certain empirical questions about human psychology, questions which cannot be settled by way of introspection or reflection.

I defend a largely Quinean view of the a priori, although my own presentation of the Quinean argument does not depend on any sort of skepticism about intentional notions, or the alleged indeterminacy of translation or inscrutability of reference. Instead, I focus exclusively on Quine's holistic view of confirmation, and his invocation of various examples from the history of science to illustrate the claim that some of the most paradigmatic examples of apparently a priori knowledge turned out to be false. Claims which at one time seemed not only obviously true, but which seemed immune from the possibility of empirical refutation, gave way in the face of large changes in theory, changes which themselves were justified by surprising empirical evidence of a sort not previously conceived of.[4] This argument, as I see it, undermines one of the central motivations for the a priori.

Unlike Quine, however, I argue that these considerations still leave room for a priori knowledge, but whether we have such knowledge depends on the fate of a controversial empirical claim. Here I follow Georges Rey,[5] Alvin Goldman,[6] and Louise Antony.[7] Should it turn out that we have certain native psychological processes which take no empirical input, and yet reliably produce true beliefs – for example, in the way that would occur were certain theorem-proving inferential tendencies built right in to our cognitive systems – then we should allow that there is, indeed, a priori knowledge. This is just what certain mental logicians, such as Lance Rips, have argued is in fact the case.[8] Even if this were true, however, a priori knowledge so understood could not do many of the

---

[2] Cambridge University Press, 1998.   [3] Ibid., 5.
[4] I take this to be the force of the very brief and suggestive remarks in section 6 of "Two Dogmas of Empiricism," reprinted in Quine's *From a Logical Point of View*, Harper Torchbooks, 1961.
[5] "The Unavailability of What We Mean I: A Reply to Quine, Fodor and LePore," in Jerry Fodor and Ernest LePore, eds., *Holism: A Consumer Update. Grazer Philosophische Studien* 46(1993), 61–101; and "A Naturalistic A Priori," *Philosophical Studies* 92(1998), 25–43.
[6] "A Priori Warrant and Naturalistic Epistemology," *Philosophical Perspectives* 13(1999), 1–28.
[7] "A Naturalized Approach to the A Priori," *Philosophical Issues* 14(2004), 1–17.
[8] *The Psychology of Proof: Deductive Reasoning in Human Thinking*, MIT Press, 1994.

things which it has traditionally been called upon to do. More than this, there is good reason, as I argue here, for thinking that even on this controversial empirical supposition, the a priori would not play anything like the very fundamental role in grounding inference generally which BonJour, and many other epistemologists in the Cartesian tradition, have supposed.

Chapter 5, "What Reflective Endorsement Cannot Do," examines the role which reflection has played in three different philosophical projects. Ernest Sosa has argued that there are two fundamentally different sorts of knowledge, animal knowledge and reflective knowledge, and reflective knowledge is, in important ways, epistemically superior to mere animal knowledge.[9] Reflective knowledge, on Sosa's view, requires not only that we hold a belief as a result of a reliable competence, but that we reflectively endorse holding the belief. A number of philosophers have argued that the nature of inference is best understood by appealing to the role that reflection plays in deliberating about what to believe.[10] On this view, what it is to infer q from p crucially involves believing that p provides reason to believe that q, a mediating belief which reflection provides in the course of deliberation. On this view, inferring q from p requires not only that one's believing p brought about one's belief that q; it requires that one reflectively endorse the transition from p to q. Harry Frankfurt has argued that reflection provides the key to understanding the nature of freedom of the will.[11] Freedom of the will, on Frankfurt's account, requires not only that one's behavior be caused by the interaction between one's beliefs and desires, but, in addition, that one reflectively endorse acting on the basis of the desire which moves one. And finally, Christine Korsgaard has argued that reflective endorsement holds the key to understanding the source of normativity.[12] The normative standards which govern both belief and action carry the force they do as a result of our reflective endorsements.

I argue that in each of these cases, reflection not only does not do the kind of work which these philosophers require it to do, but that it could

---

[9] See, among others, "Knowledge and Intellectual Virtue," reprinted in Sosa's *Knowledge in Perspective: Selected Essays in Epistemology*, Cambridge University Press, 1991, 225–244; "Reflective Knowledge in the Best Circles," *Journal of Philosophy* 94(1997), 410–430; "Two False Dichotomies: Foundationalism/Coherentism and Internalism/Externalism," in W. Sinnott-Armstrong, ed., *Pyrrhonian Scepticism*, Oxford University Press, 2004, 146–160.
[10] See, for example, Sydney Shoemaker, "On Knowing One's Own Mind," reprinted in his *The First-Person Perspective and Other Essays*, Cambridge University Press, 1996, 25–49.
[11] "Freedom of the Will and the Concept of a Person," reprinted in his *The Importance of What We Care About: Philosophical Essays*, Cambridge University Press, 1988, 11–25.
[12] *The Source of Normativity*, Cambridge University Press, 1996.

not possibly do the work they assign to it. Each of these philosophers, as I argue, has a view of first-order psychological processes which underplay their importance, while pairing that view with an account of reflective processes which give them powers which no psychological process could possibly have. What is needed for understanding the phenomena which these philosophers seek to understand is an account of reflection which demystifies it.[13]

Chapter 6, "Belief in the Face of Controversy," argues that we should dramatically reduce the confidence we have in our own beliefs when we find that our epistemic peers hold views which conflict with our own. Here, too, this is part and parcel of the anti-Cartesian theme which is the backbone of this volume. As the Cartesian sees it, when we hold beliefs which, by our own lights, are well supported by reasons, the fact that some other party sees matters differently should not weigh heavily with us. Our private reasons carry a kind of epistemic weight that the contrary opinions of others cannot significantly diminish. The defense of a kind of epistemic humility which emerges from this essay is an important part of both the attack on Cartesian ways of thinking about epistemological issues and the alternative I offer, which are the central theme of this collection of essays.

Chapter 7, "Naturalism vs. the First-Person Perspective," attempts to provide at least the beginnings of the demystified view of reflection which I argued, in Chapter 5, is so badly needed. A great deal of work not only in epistemology, but in philosophy generally, takes the first-person perspective at face value. Internalists in epistemology, following in the footsteps of Descartes, see the first-person perspective on belief acquisition and revision as the key to understanding the nature of justified belief. Accordingly, they focus on deliberation about what to believe as the natural route to understanding fundamental epistemological issues, and they examine such deliberation from the perspective of the deliberator, that is, from the first-person perspective. Surprisingly, as I show in this essay, even a number of self-described externalists in epistemology have focused much of their attention on the perspective of the deliberator, seeing this perspective as revealing of important features of our epistemic situation. But important as an investigation of deliberation is for understanding our epistemic lives, it need not be conducted from the perspective of the deliberator. Social psychologists have examined the deliberative process in detail, and any attempt to understand deliberation and reflective self-examination cannot

---

[13] I examine all four of these philosophical projects in far greater detail in *On Reflection*, Oxford University Press, 2012.

ignore the important results which this third-personal and scientific perspective reveals. This essay thus further develops the ideas introduced in Chapter 1.

The first-person perspective presents a vivid picture of what we are doing when we deliberate, and it provides us with a powerful impression that the act of deliberation allows us to take charge of the psychological processes by which our beliefs are produced and revised. Beliefs are often produced in us unreflectively, but when we stop to reflect on what we ought to believe, it seems, we intervene in the processes which would otherwise produce beliefs in us unwittingly; we are able to survey the considerations which count for and against various beliefs; and we are able, on the basis of those very considerations, to adopt beliefs which best answer to our reasons.

Compelling as this picture is when we reflect on our beliefs, the scientific investigation of the deliberative process reveals it to be largely an illusion. The process of deliberation is often epiphenomenal to the acquisition and revision of our beliefs. It often provides us with after-the-fact rationalizations for our beliefs, rather than reasons on the basis of which our beliefs are actually acquired. Even when the act of deliberation does play a causal role in influencing our beliefs, that role is often far less beneficial than it seems from the first-person perspective. The act of reflecting on our beliefs, and deliberating about what to believe, can make us less reliable in the beliefs we form than we would otherwise be, rather than more reliable. Just as the processes which go to work in us in forming and revising our beliefs when we fail to reflect are sometimes very reliable and sometimes very unreliable, the processes which go to work in us when we stop to reflect – contrary to how they seem from the first-person perspective – are a mixed bag: they are sometimes reliable; they are sometimes inefficacious; and they are sometimes very unreliable. We should not see reflection as offering us a variety of psychological processes which are different in kind from those which operate in us when we fail to reflect. The processes involved in reflection are very much of a piece with the processes which operate in us unreflectively.

Chapter 8, "Is There Room for Armchair Theorizing in Epistemology?," critically examines the role which reflection plays in one widely defended view of philosophical methodology, namely, armchair theorizing, with special focus on the application of this methodology to epistemological issues. Many philosophers have a view of philosophy and proper philosophical method which makes it different in kind from investigations in the empirical sciences. On the purest version of this view, philosophical claims are a priori knowable, and the results of scientific investigations, accordingly, are just irrelevant to philosophical issues. On a slightly weaker version of this view, philosophical investigations are properly conducted "from the armchair," that is, without the aid that esoteric scientific information might provide. Philosophical research, on this view, may draw on the kind of commonsense information available to the folk, information which informs our everyday view of the world, and, to be sure, this means that, strictly speaking, our philosophical views may not be a matter of a priori knowledge. Nevertheless, such armchair methods are different in kind from the empirical sciences and do not require their input. Finally, Timothy Williamson, who denies that philosophical methodology is "exceptional," that is, different in kind from scientific methodology, nevertheless himself defends the legitimacy of armchair methods in philosophy.[14] My examination and, ultimately, rejection of armchair methods in epistemology thus has a broad target.

I begin by arguing that an armchair approach to understanding how the mind works will be seriously defective. This is not, of course, a difficult case to make. Since the advent of scientific psychology at the end of the nineteenth century, it has been quite clear that our everyday views of the workings of the mind are not only incomplete, but often quite inaccurate as well. Modern-day work in the cognitive sciences has only deepened our understanding of the gap between our folk view of the mental and a proper scientific account. It is equally clear, as I argue, that work in the philosophy of mind must draw on such a scientific account if it is to be remotely informative. Analyzing our ordinary concepts of various mental phenomena, when these concepts build in substantive misunderstandings of the phenomena they are concepts of, cannot form the basis of any worthwhile philosophical investigation. Since the middle of the last century, the philosophical study of the mind has been ever more enriched by contact with the empirical literature in psychology. A philosophy of mind confined to the armchair would be seriously impoverished.

Although there is certainly an important body of work in epistemology which draws on empirical studies, the field of epistemology, to my mind, has lagged behind the philosophy of mind in its recognition of the extent to which the scientific study of the mind is relevant to philosophical concerns. But many of the same points which can be made about philosophy of mind apply equally to epistemology. Just as a philosophical study of our mental concepts cannot illuminate actual mental phenomena when

---

[14] *The Philosophy of Philosophy*, Blackwell, 2007.

our concepts build in substantive misunderstandings about the mind – as they often do – a philosophical study of important epistemological notions cannot illuminate actual epistemological phenomena when our epistemological concepts build in substantive misunderstandings of how the mind actually works. As I argue here, such misunderstandings about the workings of the mind have played a deleterious effect in epistemological theorizing, and the only available corrective is to allow epistemological theorizing to be informed by empirical work in psychology. Armchair reflection, unaided by such empirical work, does not provide a defensible methodology for epistemology.

Chapter 9, "The Role of Reasons in Epistemology," examines the extent to which an epistemological theory ought to appeal to the notion of a reason for belief. Understandably, many epistemological theories make talk of reasons a centerpiece in their theorizing. Many commonsense philosophical distinctions, and many important epistemological phenomena, are very naturally explained in terms of reasons. Interestingly, however, a reliabilist account of justified belief makes no such explicit appeal, and this raises the question of whether reliabilists, or indeed, any epistemologist, genuinely need to introduce the notion of a reason into their epistemological theorizing. Now the fact that the standard reliabilist account of justified belief makes no appeal to reasons does not even assure that reliabilists should seek to defend a view of epistemology which eschews all talk of reasons. The notion of a reason might play an important role in explicating various epistemological phenomena other than justified belief. In addition, even if it is possible to offer an account of justified belief which makes no reference to reasons, it may be that there is a very natural reliabilist account of what reasons are, and thus it may well be that reliabilists should seek to explicate the notion of a reason rather than eliminate it. But all of this suggests that the question of whether an epistemological theory should appeal to talk of reasons, or, instead, bypass such talk in favor of other notions, is deserving of exploration. This essay undertakes just such a project.

I argue that the commonsense appeal of the notion of a reason for belief, and the ways in which we regularly make use of it, not only in folk epistemological practice, but in a good deal of epistemological theorizing, is aided and abetted by certain illusions we are subject to when we stop to reflect on the question of what we ought to believe and engage in deliberation. These are just the illusions discussed in Chapters 1, 7, and 8. This, by itself, does not mean that we should, automatically, dispense with talk of reasons, but I do believe that it makes the prospect of such an eliminativist approach to reasons less foreboding than it would otherwise be. More importantly, it serves to undermine one of the most important motivations for appealing to reasons in explaining epistemological phenomena.

In the end, I do not argue for eliminationism about reasons. I am not sure where we should stand on this important issue. I do, however, seek to identify an empirical question about human psychology which would help to resolve the issue even if, at the present time, I do not believe that there is sufficient evidence to confidently place our bets on one particular answer rather than another.

Chapter 10, "Doxastic Justification Is Fundamental," certainly looks, on its face, as if it addresses an issue in epistemology which is entirely independent of the focus of this volume. Epistemologists distinguish between two different notions of justification: propositional justification and doxastic justification. A claim is said to be propositionally justified for a person when that person has good reasons to hold that claim to be true, whether or not the person does hold such a belief, and, even assuming that such a belief is held, whether or not it is held for those reasons. A belief is said to be doxastically justified for a person when that person holds the belief in question and holds it on the basis of the very reasons which make it propositionally justified. As these notions are typically explained, and as I just explained them, propositional justification is presented as the more fundamental notion, and doxastic justification is explained in terms of it. In this essay, I argue, following Alvin Goldman,[15] that the order of explanation should be reversed: doxastic justification should be seen as the more fundamental notion, and propositional justification should be explained in terms of it.

This reversal of the order of explanation has surprising consequences. In particular, I argue that viewing the matter in this way allows us to see why the principles of proper reasoning are not knowable a priori, and can only be known through an empirical investigation of the psychological processes by which our beliefs are formed, processes which we cannot become aware of simply by way of reflection. This essay thus expands on issues which are raised in Chapters 3, 4, and 9. If I am right about this, this essay provides an important underpinning for one of the central themes of this volume.

Chapter 11, "Our Sense of Self," addresses questions about the many features of our selves which provide us with a sense of who we are, and the extent to which our views on these matters are likely to be accurate. My point of departure is an essay by David Velleman, "Family Matters," which

---

[15] "What Is Justified Belief?," in George Pappas, ed., *Justification and Knowledge*, Reidel, 1979, 1–23.

provides a very vivid account of the nature of this sense of self, and the extent to which it plays an important role in our lives.[16] But Velleman is not concerned merely to articulate what our sense of self amounts to, or how it is important to us. Velleman argues that our sense of self is deeply bound up with our understanding of our biological family history, that is, the history of the individuals to whom we are biologically related. And because Velleman attaches such tremendous importance to our understanding of biological family history and the way in which it informs our sense of self, he argues that those couples who would have children by way of gamete donation, leaving those children biologically unrelated to the parents who raise them, are doing those children a terrible disservice. Indeed, he argues that having children in this way is immoral.

The main focus of this essay is on our sense of self, and the extent to which the beliefs we have which help to constitute it are plausibly seen as embodying self-knowledge. Velleman is right, I believe, to think that our sense of self is typically of great importance to us, and he is right, as well, I believe, in thinking that our beliefs about our biological family history often play an important role in shaping our sense of our own identity. But issues of self-knowledge are not the focus of Velleman's essay, and I believe that bringing them to the fore casts a very different light on these issues than can be found in Velleman's essay. The considerations I raise present still further reasons for thinking that a good deal of philosophical theorizing, and a good deal of folk thought as well, gives us credit for far more self-knowledge than we actually have.

Chapter 12, "Our Rational Nature," addresses the question of what it is in virtue of which we count as rational. Many philosophers, following Aristotle, speak of humans as rational animals, and in doing so, they not only commit themselves to the idea that human beings have the capacity to act and believe rationally, but they have in mind, as well, that this is something *distinctively* human, that is, that other animals are not rational in the relevant sense. Now some of these philosophers hold the view that non-human animals do not even have mental states which are properly regarded as beliefs or desires, and it is an easy task to show that, absent mental states of this sort, no animal could rightly be thought of as rational. But many philosophers who think that at least some other animals have beliefs and desires – certainly apes, and almost certainly many other mammals, arguably even certain other animals as well – nevertheless think that only humans are rightly regarded as genuinely rational. Why should that be?

---

[16] *Philosophical Papers* 34(2005), 357–378.

Here the distinction between beliefs and actions arrived at unreflectively and those arrived at as a result of deliberation comes into play. The capacity to deliberate, that is, to engage in reflection on what one ought to believe or what one ought to do, seems to be something which human beings have and other animals lack. And the suggestion is that it is the capacity to engage in such reflection which earns us the title of rational animals. Other animals may be built by natural selection to pick up information about their environments in a reliable manner; they may be such that they typically act so as to satisfy their desires. But we humans do not just register information passively and unreflectively in the way that other animals do, and we do not merely behave without reflective engagement with the reasons we have to behave one way or another. We can reflect on our reasons for belief or action, and it is in this capacity that our rationality is to be found. Reflective engagement with reasons is the home of rationality.

This essay critically examines this view of the nature of rationality and argues that it fundamentally misunderstands both reflective and unreflective belief and action. Reflective judgment and behavior is not the unique home of rationality, although it does certainly lend human thought and action a degree of complexity which is not to be found in other animals. We should not view this added complexity, however, as a basis for regarding reflective belief and action as different in kind from belief and action which is not the product of reflection; we should certainly not view this added complexity as a reason for thinking that only in virtue of the capacity for reflection should any animal be regarded as rational.

Taken together, these essays provide a substantial challenge, and a substantial alternative, to Cartesian ways of thinking about self-knowledge, about reflection, about the nature of reasons, a priority, and rationality. It is my hope that having these essays together in one volume helps to make the case for this anti-Cartesian view of these topics, and that the different strands of this view lend it a degree of strength which the individual essays, by themselves, could not possibly have.

I

*Introspection and Misdirection**

One of the motivations for engaging in epistemological theorizing is the desire to improve one's epistemic performance. We would all prefer to be more successful than we are at believing truths and avoiding falsehoods. Accordingly, some epistemologists offer epistemic advice to truth-seeking agents, advice which is designed to improve their epistemic performance. Historically, the faculty of introspection has played a significant role in such advice. I do not believe that introspection is well-suited to play such a role. I will argue that introspection should not play a large role in the project of epistemic self-improvement, and that in many cases, it will worsen an agent's epistemic situation. Indeed, the value of introspection is inversely proportional to the need for such improvement. Those who are most in need of epistemic improvement will be harmed most by seeking aid from introspection. Introspection is unlikely to improve an agent's epistemic position, but it is likely to make a bad situation worse. Or so I shall argue.

I will begin, accordingly, by making plain the role of introspection in Descartes' epistemic project, for it is in Descartes' epistemology that introspection is called upon to do the greatest work. My concerns here, however, are not primarily historical. I will argue that many of those who reject much of what Descartes has to offer nevertheless allow introspection to play a very prominent role in their epistemological views. Indeed, if we divide current epistemologists into two camps, the internalists and the externalists, we find that externalists largely refrain from offering epistemic advice, while internalists allow introspection to play a central role in the advice they offer. Thus, those who are concerned to offer any epistemic advice at all seem to

---

* I have benefited from reading Fred Schmitt's "Epistemic Luck" (manuscript). Anyone who reads Schmitt's paper will see that I owe him a great debt. I have received helpful comments from Lynne Baker, Richard Grandy, Steven Luper-Foy, Mark Kaplan, William Mann, Sydney Shoemaker, and, especially, Derk Pereboom and William Wilcox. I have also received helpful stylistic suggestions from Leslie Weiger. Work on this essay was in part supported by a generous grant from the National Endowment for the Humanities.

continue to appeal to the powers of introspection. This will raise, in an urgent form, the question of the value of introspection in the project of epistemic self-improvement. And, as I have said, I will argue that it is likely to be harmful in those cases where it has any effect at all.

In Section I, I briefly lay out the relevant features of Descartes' epistemic project. In Section II, I introduce the distinction between internalists and externalists, and I argue that current externalists refrain from offering epistemic advice, while current internalists allow introspection to play a central role in the advice they offer. In Section III, I present a prima facie case for the view that introspection is powerless to detect our epistemic shortcomings, and in Section IV, I attempt to strengthen that case. Section V presents a hypothesis about the way in which introspection works which, if correct, provides still further support for my claims about the limitations of introspection. I close with a brief suggestion about the project of epistemic self-improvement.

I

Introspection plays two distinct roles in leading an agent to improve his epistemic situation, according to Descartes. First, introspection is called upon to reveal the defects of the unreflective agent's position. Second, introspection is called upon to remedy those defects. Let us examine each of these roles.

In *Meditation I*, Descartes reveals that his current epistemic situation is defective. He realizes that he has had many false beliefs in the past, and that many of his current beliefs, being arrived at on the basis of past beliefs, are thus likely to be false. All of this is revealed by way of introspection. Moreover, once Descartes introduces the method of doubt, that he will suspend belief in everything about which it is possible to be mistaken, nothing more than introspection is required to see that everything can be doubted. Descartes accordingly resolves to suspend all belief, and that he has succeeded in doing this can be determined by introspection as well. The negative part of Descartes' program, described in *Meditation I*, is carried out under the aegis of the faculty of introspection.

Likewise, the positive part of Descartes' program is supervised by introspection. On Descartes' view, belief is now to be achieved by acts of will, which are clearly introspectable, and these acts of will are to be exerted in virtue of the recognition of the clarity and distinctness of certain ideas. The entire process of belief acquisition is thus certified by the faculty of introspection.

Descartes' theory of justification is a historical theory: he believes that the justificatory status of a belief is dependent upon its ancestry. Only those beliefs which are arrived at in the appropriate way are to count as justified. By choosing our beliefs on the basis of the appropriate introspectable features of our minds, we may certify, by introspection, that our beliefs do indeed meet the appropriate standards.

Introspection is thus called upon to reveal the defects of our current epistemic situation, to provide the will with the appropriate materials with which to remedy the situation, and to certify that those defects have been remedied.

Whatever other defects this procedure may have, and it has a great many, there is one practical difficulty it faces. It is obvious that this procedure is very slow. Any agent who seeks to arrive at all of his beliefs in this way will have very few beliefs. There can be little doubt that Descartes was interested in giving epistemic advice which was practical, and so someone who was otherwise completely untroubled by Descartes' description of the proper way to acquire beliefs would at least have to concern himself with this practical difficulty. Let me suggest some shortcuts, then, for the impatient Cartesian. I will not suggest that Descartes would have endorsed these shortcuts, but I will argue below that many contemporary epistemologists would.

Consider the negative part of Descartes' program: rejecting all of those beliefs about which it is possible to be wrong. Descartes is aware that this is not easy.[1] There are habits of belief acquisition which are deeply ingrained in us and are very hard to overcome. If one were to take Descartes seriously, in his suggestion that we must begin by giving up all of these habits of belief acquisition, we might never get to the positive part of Descartes' program. It may not, however, be necessary to overcome all of these habits, for if prior to ridding ourselves of our habits of belief acquisition, we simply determine which of them are defective, we might be able to spend our time better. Many of our current unreflective belief-acquisition procedures may, after all, turn out to be adequate as they stand. Those which are adequate may be left in place with no harm done; those which are not will have to be weeded out. This will save us the time involved in first giving up certain habits and then, perhaps, attempting to acquire those very same habits again.

---

[1] *The Philosophical Works of Descartes*, E. S. Haldane and G. R. T. Ross, eds., Cambridge University Press, 1931, see esp. vol. I, 148.

My impatient Cartesian will think that all of this can be accomplished by way of introspection, just as Descartes allowed his project to be supervised under the aegis of introspection. One might even attempt to enlist Descartes' support. Descartes did, after all, claim that "I can affirm with certainty that there is nothing in me of which I am not in any way conscious."[2] If the mind is, in this way, wholly transparent to introspection, my program for the impatient Cartesian should be one which Descartes himself would endorse. On this account, the method of doubt is nothing more than a literary device for making vivid the possibility of error.

II

I wish to argue that my program for the impatient Cartesian is one which is accepted by many contemporary epistemologists. I will need to begin by distinguishing between internalists and externalists about justification. I will then argue that current internalists favor the impatient Cartesian program.

David Armstrong introduced the term "externalist" in *Belief, Truth and Knowledge*:

> According to "Externalist" accounts of non-inferential knowledge, what makes a true non-inferential belief a case of *knowledge* is some natural relation between the belief-state ... and the situation which makes the belief true.[3]

Armstrong contrasts externalist accounts with what he calls Cartesian accounts, because the natural relation which externalists appeal to need not be available to introspection; on Cartesian accounts, those features of a true belief which make it a case of knowledge are available to introspection. Amending Armstrong's usage slightly, I will say that an account of justified belief is "externalist" if the features of a belief which make it justified need not be accessible to introspection; while an account of justified belief on which those features of a belief which make it justified must be accessible to introspection I will call "internalist."

As Armstrong notes, the most prominent externalist accounts are causal and reliability accounts. One interesting feature of such accounts, however, is that they refrain from offering epistemic advice. Although one might naturally assume that an account of justified belief will issue directly in a

---

[2] Ibid., vol. II, 13.
[3] David Armstrong, *Belief, Truth and Knowledge*, Cambridge University Press, 1973, 157.

set of prescriptions for the truth-seeking agent, the prescriptions which externalist theories offer are no better than the stockbroker's advice to buy low and sell high. "Arrive at your beliefs by reliable processes" or "Have your beliefs caused by the facts" are not the kinds of advice truth-seeking agents are looking for; this kind of advice does not tell them what to do. Externalists simply are not in the business of offering doxastic advice of the sort such agents seek.

Internalists, on the other hand, are in the business of offering such advice. I will examine two different kinds of internalist advice, foundationalist and coherentist. Because it is impossible to canvas all such accounts, I will choose two representative philosophers, Roderick Chisholm and Laurence BonJour. In each case, I will examine the extent to which introspection is implicated in their epistemic advice. I will argue that it plays a very prominent role.

According to Chisholm, if we wish to know whether a particular belief is justified, we must engage in Socratic questioning. If I want to know whether my belief that p is justified, I must ask myself, "What justification do I have for thinking that this is true?"[4] I am thus to ask myself what my reasons are for holding the belief, and I am to answer this question by introspecting. Similarly, when I find that my reason for believing that p is that q, I am to ask myself the same question about my belief that q. I am to continue this process until I reach some proposition which is directly evident. That a proposition is directly evident is recognizable through introspection.

Chisholm proceeds to elaborate the connection which must obtain between directly evident propositions and those which are only indirectly evident if the latter are to be justified at all. That these conditions obtain can be recognized by introspection.[5]

Thus, unlike Descartes, Chisholm does not require that we begin the epistemological project by rejecting all of our beliefs. Instead, we may examine the beliefs we currently have and see whether they meet the appropriate standards. Only those which fail to meet these standards need to be rejected. All of this is accomplished by means of introspection. In short, Chisholm adopts the program of the impatient Cartesian.

Similarly, consider Laurence BonJour's coherentist account of justification.[6] According to BonJour, a belief is justified for an agent just in case it

---

[4] *Theory of Knowledge*, 2nd ed., Prentice-Hall, 1977, 17.   [5] Ibid., 62–86.
[6] *The Structure of Empirical Knowledge*, Cambridge University Press, 1985.

coheres with the rest of the agent's beliefs. BonJour is at great pains to argue that both an agent's beliefs and the coherence relation itself are available to introspection.[7]

> It would be possible, of course to adopt an externalist version of coherentism. Such a view would hold that the person whose belief is justified need himself have no cognitive access to the fact of coherence, that his belief is justified whether or not such coherence is cognitively accessible to him (or, presumably, to anyone). But such a view is unacceptable.[8]

As BonJour makes abundantly clear, the question about cognitive accessibility is a question about the faculty of introspection.[9]

BonJour is thus offering the truth-seeking agent a certain bit of epistemic advice. We are to introspect and determine whether our beliefs cohere; those which do not are to be rejected, while those which do cohere are to be retained. Although BonJour does not believe that the faculty of introspection is infallible, he does, like Descartes, call on this faculty to locate our cognitive errors, to provide the materials for correcting those errors, and to certify that the correction has taken place. BonJour too adopts the program of the impatient Cartesian.

I cannot examine all current foundationalist and coherentist views here. I do believe, however, that Chisholm and BonJour are not idiosyncratic in this respect: current foundationalists and coherentists are all impatient Cartesians. All of these philosophers are committed to embarking on the project of epistemic self-improvement in a way which gives introspection a very central role. It is thus well worth asking whether introspection is well-suited to play this role. If we allow introspection to play the role which internalists advise, what will the likely results be?

III

Let me begin with an account of a study conducted by Nisbett and Wilson.

> passers-by in a shopping mall were invited to examine an array of consumer goods (four nightgowns in one study, four identical nylon pantyhose in another) and to rate their quality. There was a pronounced position effect on evaluations, such that the right-most garments were heavily preferred to the left-most garments. When questioned about the effect of the garments' position on their choices, virtually all subjects denied such an

---

[7] See especially ibid., 101–106.   [8] Ibid., 101.   [9] Ibid., 137–138.

influence (usually with a tone of annoyance or of concern for the experimenter's sanity).[10]

This is an interesting case to begin with because the position effect presents a strong prima facie case of faulty inference. In evaluating various consumer goods, we should not be influenced by their relative position; nevertheless, it seems that we are. Subjects in this study, however, are unaware that their judgments are affected by the relative position of the goods being evaluated. Moreover, it seems quite clear that asking these subjects to introspect more carefully – "Are you sure you weren't influenced by the fact that the garment you chose was on the right?" – would not make them better acquainted with the source of their judgments. Here then is a case in which we might hope that the concerned truth-seeker would notice his faulty pattern of inference and come to reject it; but introspection is no help here. On introspecting, subjects believe that they are evaluating these goods in just the way they ought to. Unreflective agents are thus influenced by the position effect. Agents who are asked to introspect and determine the reliability of the process by which their judgment is reached will not notice that they are so influenced, and will thus conclude that they have reasoned correctly. Far from helping in the process of self-correction, introspection here merely results in a more confident, though no less misguided, agent. One should not think that an unusually responsible or circumspect agent would be affected differently here. Especially responsible agents may be more willing than most to recognize their own mistakes when they are pointed out. There is no reason, however, to think that responsible agents are less susceptible to this illusion.

Consider, in particular, how agents in the situation described would proceed if they were to follow the advice offered by Chisholm or by BonJour. Chisholm suggests that agents ask themselves why it is reasonable to think some particular belief to be true. In order to answer this question, they are instructed to introspect. Now consider the agent who believes, in the situation described, that the nightgown on the right is the best. She is supposed to ask herself what reason she has for thinking this true. What the experiment tells us is that she will take herself to have objectively good reasons for her belief; she will take herself to have noticed features of the nightgown on the right which make it the best of the lot. Now I do not pretend to have a Chisholmian deduction from directly

---

[10] Richard Nisbett and Lee Ross, *Human Inference: Strategies and Shortcomings of Social Judgment*, Prentice-Hall, 1980, 207.

evident propositions here, but if the Chisholmian system can ever show evaluative propositions to be justified, it will show this proposition to be justified. The agent here will take herself to have just the kind of evidence she has in the standard case. Chisholm's advice will thus lead her to the conclusion that she is justified in this case, and that she should therefore continue to hold the belief.

BonJour's advice does no better. The agent, according to BonJour, should ask herself whether her belief that the nightgown on the right is best coheres with the rest of her beliefs. Now I'm not at all sure how an agent is supposed to go about answering this question, but this much is clear: the case for coherence in this case is as good as it ever gets in evaluative judgments. When the agent checks to see how well this belief coheres with the rest of her other beliefs, she will find that it passes the test; she should thus continue to hold the belief.

Thus, in both the case of the advice offered by Chisholm and that offered by BonJour, we find that agents who arrive at their beliefs as a result of the position effect will come to believe after taking the proffered advice that they are in fact justified in their beliefs. Introspection here is powerless to detect the error made, and when called into service as a source of epistemic improvement, it merely serves to certify a misguided process of belief acquisition. Agents who do not seek out the advice of Chisholm and BonJour will arrive at their beliefs in a mistaken fashion. Those who do seek out their advice will continue to err, but will add to their stock of beliefs the belief that they are fully justified in their judgments.

This case is not unusual or atypical. Consider Tversky and Kahneman's work on the anchoring effect.[11] Subjects were asked the number of African members of the United Nations. A roulette wheel was spun, and subjects were asked whether the number which turned up was too high or too low. In those cases where the roulette wheel provided an anchor of 10, the mean estimate was 25; where the anchor was 65, the mean estimate was 45. It is quite clear that subjects were influenced in their judgment by the result of the spin of the roulette wheel. None of the subjects, however, showed any awareness of this influence; nor is there reason to think that asking the subjects to introspect more carefully here would provide much assistance. Once again, the suggestion that introspection may provide us with a valuable check on the reliability of our inference is shown to fail. It

---

[11] Amos Tversky and Daniel Kahneman, "Judgment under Uncertainty: Heuristics and Biases," reprinted in Kahneman, Slovic, and Tversky, eds., *Judgment under Uncertainty: Heuristics and Biases*, Cambridge University Press, 1982, 14.

is clear that the advice which foundationalists and coherentists offer here would only add the mistake of further confidence to an already misguided agent.

Both of these cases thus far described involve subjects' failures to detect factors influencing their judgments. These are not, however, the only kinds of errors subjects make in attempting to discover the source of their judgments by introspection. Factors which influence our judgments may be overlooked, but, in addition, factors we believe to influence our judgments may have little or no influence on us. Nisbett and Ross had subjects read a passage describing a baby's accidental drowning; subjects were then asked to pick out those portions of the passage which they thought were most responsible for its emotional impact. The portions which were indicated by the subjects were just the ones which Nisbett and Ross thought were most responsible for its dramatic effect. When the same passage was given to a different group of subjects with the indicated passages removed, however, they rated it as having the very same emotional impact as the first group.[12] Subjects in the first group, as well as Nisbett and Ross themselves, thus believed that the source of their emotional reaction could be traced to certain portions of the passage, but they were mistaken. Introspection simply does not provide us with accurate information about the etiology of our mental states. This kind of mistake is especially important to the Chisholmian program, for there introspection is supposed to inform the agent as to his reasons for belief. The information introspection gives in this case is mistaken. Even in the coherentist case, however, the mistaken belief about the source of one's judgment will have a deleterious effect, for it will help to smooth the coherence relations of the belief in question with the remainder of one's body of beliefs. Here too then introspection adds nothing more than misguided confidence to the errors which are already being made.

Mistakes of this sort also occur in perceptual cases. Passengers on a plane are able to tell when the plane is headed up or down, right or left. This is something, it seems, that one detects visually. The orientation of the plane, however, is not detected by visual means at all, as is revealed by noticing that the very same effect occurs even on night flights where there is no possible visual source of information about the plane's orientation. Information about the orientation of the plane is conveyed not visually, but kinesthetically; one detects the orientation of the plane by detecting the orientation of one's body. Careful introspection is powerless to detect the

---

[12] Op. cit., 209.

source of this information. The illusion that the orientation of the plane is detected visually persists even when one knows that it is detected kinesthetically.

There is, then, an important range of cases in which introspection systematically misleads subjects about the sources of their beliefs. Subjects who undertake the project of epistemic self-evaluation by attempting to introspect the source of their beliefs will, at least in the kinds of cases described, misdiagnose their reasons for belief. The project of self-evaluation and self-correction thus gets off on the wrong foot. In some cases, such as the mistaken belief about the source of information about an airplane's orientation, the mistake is harmless. In this case, subjects mistakenly believe that their information is obtained visually, but they are not mistaken in their belief that they can reliably detect the orientation of the plane. In other cases, however, the mistake is more significant. Processes which are in fact unreliable are not recognized as such. Factors which should not influence a subject's judgment are not recognized as influential. In cases such as these, introspection is not only powerless to detect the errors we make, but in misdiagnosing the source of our judgments and our reasons for believing, the reliance on introspection as a tool for self-evaluation merely instills a false sense of confidence in an already misguided agent.

IV

It may be objected that the cases I have described thus far show nothing more than that introspection is not infallible. Once one acknowledges that introspection is not infallible, one will expect that there should be cases, like those described, in which introspective reports on the nature of one's mental processes will be mistaken. It is one thing to claim that introspection is fallible; it is quite another, however, to claim that introspection is unreliable.

I wish to argue that the cases described, and others like them, support the stronger thesis that introspective reports of mental processes are unreliable and misleading. The cases thus far described are not ones where there is interference with an otherwise reliable process; nor are these cases where circumstances are created in the psychological laboratory which are unlike those encountered in the ordinary course of events. Rather, the cases described are ones where introspection is allowed to work as it would in ordinary circumstances, and yet the typical result is a mistaken belief about the agent's process of belief acquisition or retention. For an agent to be mistaken about such a process is to be mistaken about his reason for belief.

These cases shift the burden of proof onto those who would defend introspection as the touchstone for epistemic advice.

Indeed, I wish to argue that the situation is even worse than this. Introspection is not merely unreliable; it does not merely fail to give us accurate information about our reasons for belief. A tendency to rely on introspection in pursuing the project of epistemic self-improvement will most likely lull the agent into a false sense of security. Introspecting in order to check on the justificatory status of one's processes of belief acquisition will likely lead to the belief that these processes are justified, regardless of their reliability. In order to see why this is so, we need to look at studies on features of belief acquisition in general.

In studies of hypothesis testing in a variety of situations, two kinds of confirmation bias have been detected. First, subjects seeking to test a hypothesis tend to seek out confirming instances and do not attempt to check for disconfirming information. Second, when disconfirming information is nevertheless encountered, it tends to be taken far less seriously than confirming information, even when the hypothesis being tested was not antecedently believed.

Peter Wason[13] gave subjects a sequence of three numbers and told them that the sequence conformed to some general rule. Subjects were asked to try to discover this rule by proposing three number sequences which, they would be told, either conformed or failed to conform to the rule. Subjects were then asked to explain, as they proposed each sequence, what it was they were doing. Typical subjects had a hypothesis in mind which they were testing, but tested the hypothesis by examining only confirming instances of it. When a number of confirming instances were piled up, they would announce that they had discovered the rule governing the initial sequence. Strangely, when subjects were told that they had not discovered the rule, in more than half the cases the next sequence tested was an instance of the very rule they had just been told was incorrect.

Lord, Ross, and Lepper[14] studied confirmation bias in a somewhat more naturalistic setting. Subjects were recruited in two groups; one group believed that capital punishment has deterrent effects, while the other group believed that it does not. Each group read summaries of two studies,

---

[13] "On the Failure to Eliminate Hypotheses in a Conceptual Task," *Quarterly Journal of Experimental Psychology* 12(196), 129–140; also reported in Peter Wason and Philip Johnson-Laird, *Psychology of Reasoning: Structure and Content*, Harvard University Press, 1972, 204–214.

[14] "Biased Assimilation and Attitude Polarization: The Effects of Prior Theories on Subsequently Considered Evidence," *Journal of Personality and Social Psychology* 34(1979); also reported in Nisbett and Ross, op. cit., 170–172.

one of which supported the claim that capital punishment has deterrent effects, the other supporting the claim that it does not. The methods of the studies varied. One study compared a given state at two different times, with and without capital punishment. The other study compared different states, with and without capital punishment, at the same times.

Subjects found the studies which supported their previously held views to be well conducted and convincing, while those supporting the contrary view were found to have significant methodological flaws. Those subjects who read a study which ran contrary to their own view first were not significantly affected by it. Those who read a study which supported their opinion first were even more convinced that they were correct. After both groups read one study supporting each view, each group was more strongly convinced that the view they held before walking in to the experiment was correct.

Nisbett and Ross comment,

> Before the advent of modern social science, many questions, like the issue of the deterrent value of capital punishment, were ones for which there really was no empirical evidence ... One might expect, though, that once genuine empirical evidence for such questions became available, that evidence would sway opinion to whichever side it supported or, if the evidence were mixed, that it would serve to moderate opposing views. Instead, the effect of introducing mixed evidence may be to *polarize* public opinion.[15]

The existence of confirmation bias provides a global reason for thinking that responsible agents are unlikely to discover, at least by way of introspection, the extent of their epistemic shortcomings. Most agents think of themselves as tolerably reliable in their acquisition of belief, and with good reason. Once this belief is in place, however, our natural confirmation bias will serve to insulate it from disconfirming evidence. Especially in the case of an agent's belief in his own reliability, this discounting of disconfirming evidence will not seem at all strained. Everyone, after all, makes mistakes; that an agent discovers he has made a mistake on a particular occasion should not, it seems, lead to general doubts about the reliability of his inferences. Precisely because this is so, one's mistakes will not, ordinarily, take on any special salience because they are not especially salient, they will not be remembered as well.[16] Thus, when an agent becomes unusually reflective and tries to survey his past performance, the performance he is able to remember further confirms his earlier assessment of his own reliability. Our natural confirmation bias thus not only hides its own

---

[15] Op. cit., 171.   [16] See, e.g., Nisbett and Ross, op. cit., 180–183.

workings from us; it serves to make our inferential shortcomings in general more difficult to detect. Thus, those who introspect in order to check on the reliability of their processes of belief acquisition are liable to find that they pass the test with flying colors.

Some will object here that I have been conflating questions about justification with questions about the reliability of belief-acquisition processes. Chisholm and BonJour attempt to give agents advice which will result in justified belief. Neither of them, however, equate justified belief with reliably produced belief. All I have shown, it will be argued, is that following their advice will fail to improve our reliability. I have not shown, however, that following their advice will fail to lead to justified belief.

It is possible to divorce one's concept of justification from reliability in this way. I certainly do not wish to presuppose a reliabilist account of justification here. On the other hand, the proposed defense of Chisholm and BonJour is not without cost. If one does so divorce one's concept of justification from that of reliability, it becomes very hard to say why one should care to have justified beliefs. I began this essay by assuming that the truth-seeking agent is looking to improve his epistemic performance, and that Chisholm and BonJour mean to offer this agent just such advice. If we now say that following their advice will not aid in getting at the truth, then the project of achieving justified beliefs seems pointless.

Like Descartes, I assume that the responsible epistemic agent is truth-seeking and that in attempting to improve his epistemic situation he is attempting to improve his reliability; he wishes to be more effective in getting at the truth. If Chisholm and BonJour respond to the examples I have cited by allowing that justification does not help in getting at the truth, then they have conceded my point.

V

Descartes held that the mind is wholly transparent to introspection. Such a view of the mind is obviously incompatible with the data. Most importantly, those features of our beliefs in virtue of which they are either justified, or unjustified, are not transparent to introspection, so long as we are working with a concept of justification which is worth caring about. In light of the currently available data, what view should we have of the powers and the workings of introspection?

The first point to make is that our processes of belief acquisition, and indeed mental processes in general, are largely unavailable to introspection. Were this not so, cognitive psychology would be easy; but it is not easy. It has been known for quite some time that the factors which influence our perceptual beliefs are ones of which we are largely unaware through introspection. Now that a good deal of data on inference has begun to become available, it seems that, in the case of inference just as much as perception, introspection reveals very little about the nature of our mental processes.

Our introspective reports on mental processes involve a good deal of rational reconstruction, as Daniel Dennett has suggested.[17] Moreover, as the experimental data reveal, this rational reconstruction involves heavy reliance on the presupposition of our own reliability. In attempting to figure out what process is responsible for one of our beliefs, we typically begin by assuming our own rationality[18] and then try to figure out what a rational person would have done. This is not to say, of course, that this process of rational reconstruction occurs consciously. Nevertheless, we must posit such inferences to make sense of the experimental data. How else could we possibly explain that those who are influenced by the position effect in judging the quality of consumer goods explain the source of their judgments as lying in objective features of the goods whose quality they judge?

It is for precisely this reason that introspection is so ill-suited to the task of providing agents with epistemic advice. Even if one thought that this process of rational reconstruction involving heavy reliance on the assumption of rationality were reliable, perhaps because we are, after all, quite reliable in our processes of belief acquisition, one would still be forced to the conclusion that introspection is badly suited for the project of epistemic self-improvement. What is needed for the epistemic project to work is the ability to recognize our epistemic shortcomings. But whatever success we have in recognizing our processes of belief acquisition is due to our reliance on the assumption of rationality, and it is precisely our reliance on this assumption that makes it difficult for us to recognize our mistakes. Here, as elsewhere, our epistemic successes and failures are to be explained as products of one and the same underlying process. In this case, however, the pattern of our failures is of profound epistemic importance. It blinds us to exactly those areas in which our performance most needs improvement.

---

[17] *Brainstorms*, Bradford Books, 1978, 88.
[18] Some may argue that the assumption of rationality is indispensable, for without such an assumption, we cannot even think of ourselves as believers. Although it is certainly true that some degree of rationality is required if a subject is to have beliefs at all, the above examples make abundantly clear that far less rationality is required for belief attribution than is actually assumed by agents in reconstructing their own inference patterns.

I have argued that introspection is ill-suited to play the central role in epistemic self-improvement which it has been thought to play at least since Descartes. This is not because I believe the project of self-improvement to be pointless, but rather because I believe that project to require a more subtle understanding of our processes of belief acquisition and retention than mere introspection can provide. The moral of my story is obvious. The very important project of epistemic self-improvement can only succeed with the help of cognitive psychology. We should accept no substitutes.

2

What Is It like to Be Me?

I wish to present an anti-Cartesian account of self-knowledge for I believe that the powers of introspection have been vastly overestimated. First, I argue that it is not a conceptual truth that our introspective judgments are infallible, or even mostly true. Second, I argue that a wide range of introspective judgments are false; the mechanisms by which introspective judgments are produced may not be very reliable. These two points are developed at length in Sections I through IV. Third, I argue that introspection alone is often insufficient to ground claims to know the contents of one's own mental states. And finally, fourth, I argue that in many cases, we lack sufficient evidence from any source to ground claims to know the contents of our own mental states. These last two points are developed in Section V. Section VI presents some concluding remarks.

My skeptical conclusions about self-knowledge are not part of a more general skeptical view; indeed, quite the opposite. I wish to defend an inversion of the typical Cartesian order: we are in a better position to know things about the external world, by and large, than we are about ourselves.

I

Imagine Descartes asking himself the question, "What is it like to be me?" This question would not have been a source of puzzlement to Descartes, for its answer, on his view, is immediately present to introspection. Descartes held that the mind is fully transparent to introspection. What it is like to be me is, on Descartes' view, something I cannot fail to know.

Now there is an important tension between Descartes' realism about mental phenomena and his view that our mental states are transparent to introspection. To be a realist about the mental is to believe that mental phenomena are what they are independent of what anyone might believe about them. There is no incompatibility between being a realist of this sort and believing that mental states are de facto transparent to us. That is, one might believe that, as a matter of causal law, each mental state always produces in us the recognition that we are in it.[1] This kind of de facto transparency, however, would need to be discovered, and could not serve as a foundation for knowledge of the sort Descartes wanted. Those who wish not only to claim that our mental states are transparent to us, but put this claim about transparency to epistemological work, are making a claim about the mental which does not sit well with realism. The epistemological claim is that there is a conceptual tie between being in a mental state and believing that one is in it;[2] the realistic claim is simply that mental states are radically independent of beliefs about them. It is precisely this tension which we find in Descartes.

We are thus left with a choice: we must give up either Descartes' realism about the mental or his claim that there is a conceptual relationship between our being in a mental state and our recognition of that fact. It is the second of these possibilities which I will explore here. It is here, I believe, that the truth is to be found. Interestingly, it is precisely here, Thomas Nagel argues in "What Is It like to Be a Bat?,"[3] that attempts to give a realistic account of the mind run into difficulties:

> Very little work has been done on the basic question . . . whether any sense can be made of experiences having an objective character at all. Does it make sense, in other words, to ask what my experiences are really like, as opposed to how they appear to me? We cannot genuinely understand the hypothesis that their nature is captured in a physical description unless we understand the more fundamental idea that they have an objective nature. (448)

Notice that Nagel insists simply that we be able to "make sense" of the idea that we are mistaken about our mental states; he does not insist, in the

---

[1] This view is, however, extremely implausible. Once one gives up the conceptual claim of transparency, one is forced to take the empirical evidence seriously; and the evidence is overwhelmingly against any kind of transparency at all. See, e.g., Richard Nisbett and T. D. Wilson, "Telling More than We Can Know: Verbal Reports on Mental Processes," *Psychological Review* 84(1977), 231–259; T. D. Wilson, "Self-Deception without Repression: Limits on Access to Mental States," in Mike Martin, ed., *Self-Deception and Self-Understanding: New Essays in Philosophy and Psychology*, University Press of Kansas, 1985, 95–116. For a discussion of the importance of these results for traditional epistemological projects, see my "Introspection and Misdirection," Chapter 1.
[2] This conceptual claim can come in degrees. Descartes' version is maximally strong, but one might claim that the conceptual connection between mental states and beliefs about them is weaker. Thus, Sydney Shoemaker argues for a weaker, but still conceptual, connection between mental states and beliefs about them. See "On Knowing One's Own Mind," *Philosophical Perspectives*, 2(1988), 183–209. I do not directly address Shoemaker's position in the text, but the view I present supposes no conceptual connection whatsoever between mental states and beliefs about them. See also Note 8 below on Shoemaker.
[3] *Philosophical Review* 83(1974), 435–450.

end, that we ever actually be mistaken. Realists about the mental must explain how there can be an appearance–reality gap even when it comes to mental states.[4]

Contra Nagel, this is a challenge which realists have lived up to, at least since Freud.[5]

There is no difficulty in giving an account of our mental life which leaves room for the possibility of a gap between our mental states and our beliefs about them.

Let us turn, then, to a post-Freudian look at the question, "What is it like to be me?"

II

I know a great deal about myself. My wife, my siblings, my friends also know a great deal about me. Consider my motivations. I cannot help but have beliefs about my reasons for acting. I believe that I am sometimes moved by kindness; I believe I have other motivations as well. I also know that there are times when I am mistaken in the accounts I give of my motivations. I have seen others deceive themselves about their motivations, and I believe that I am not immune to such self-deception. There are also cases of mistaken beliefs about oneself which are not rightly called self-deceptive; or at least there are cases of such mistaken beliefs which are not motivationally driven.[6] I have seen such things in others, and I am quite sure that I am susceptible to them as well. I have certain views about what kind of person I am, but I know that my view of myself could not possibly be correct in every detail. I believe this is the view which any circumspect agent must have of him- or herself.

These post-Freudian truisms presuppose a realistic view about the mental; they presuppose that there are objective facts about what I am like, and that I am, at times, mistaken about these facts. These truisms are embedded in a theory of our mental lives. This theory views our mental states as exhibiting a complex causal structure, and our processes of belief

---

[4] This simply reiterates the point made by David Armstrong and John Mackie in 1963. Armstrong, "Is Introspective Knowledge Incorrigible?," *Philosophical Review* 72(1963), 417–432; Mackie, "Are There Any Incorrigible Empirical Statements?," *Australasian Journal of Philosophy* 41(1963), 12–28.

[5] I do not mean to suggest that there was no awareness of the possibility of error in descriptions of one's own mental states prior to Freud. There can be little doubt, however, that Freud greatly contributed to the integration of this point into the commonsense conception of the mental.

[6] See, e.g., Richard Nisbett and Lee Ross, *Human Inference: Strategies and Shortcomings of Social Judgment*, Prentice-Hall, 1980, ch. 9.

acquisition as ones which, even when directed upon our own mental states, may go wrong. We even have some accounts of the ways in which attempts at self-knowledge do go wrong. It is part of this theory that, in some respects, I am especially poorly placed to find out the truth about myself. Precisely because my mistakes may be driven by a desire to see myself as a certain sort of person, what I am really like may be harder for me to find out than for certain well-placed others. I have no doubt that my wife knows things about me that I do not. It is not that I can't in principle know these things; it is just that I am not in a good position to see them.

Post-Freudian folk psychology thus gives very real content to the suggestion that there is a fact of the matter about what it is like to be me, and to the idea that this fact is independent of my beliefs about what I am like. What more could Nagel want? In the passage quoted earlier, Nagel focuses not on what I am like, or what it is like to be me, but on the nature of my experiences. "Very little work has been done on the basic question ... whether any sense can be made of experiences' having an objective character at all." Is there something then distinctive about the nature of experience – some essential subjectivity – which inevitably eludes objective description? Let us see.

III

Consider Jack.[7] Jack is very defensive. He is quite insecure, and he believes, incorrectly, that people are frequently talking down to him. He often misconstrues innocent remarks, taking them to contain innuendoes about his appearance, his intelligence, and his family. If people are having a quiet conversation near Jack, he assumes that it is about him, and that voices are lowered in order to prevent him from hearing the unflattering comments which, he mistakenly believes, people so often make about him. On those rare occasions when someone does make a remark to Jack which contains even a grain of criticism, the result is anger, and Jack becomes convinced that, first, the person in question has a far more negative opinion of him than that person actually does, and second, that this negative opinion is a product of jealousy, feelings of insecurity, or the like. Jack is tremendously self-involved, and he believes that he is the cause of a great deal more that goes on in the world than he is.

---

[7] Jack is a case of paranoid personality disorder. See *Diagnostic and Statistical Manual of Mental Disorders*, 3rd revised ed., American Psychiatric Association, 1987, 337–339.

Many of Jack's beliefs about the world are inaccurate. His beliefs about what people say, their tone of voice, and their facial expressions are extremely unreliable. Jack's character plays a role in the way these beliefs are acquired. It is because he is self-involved and insecure that he forms beliefs as he does. That these character traits play a role in belief acquisition, however, is not apparent to Jack. His beliefs about tone of voice, facial expression, and the like seem just as immediate to him as the beliefs which you and I form on these subjects do to us.

Now it is not merely Jack's perception of the world around him which is distorted, for Jack is not a master of self-understanding either. Jack does not believe that he is defensive, insecure, or self-involved. Jack's unreflective opinion of himself is quite different; it is terribly inaccurate. His opinion of himself is not inaccurate, however, because it is unreflective. If Jack were to reflect on the question of whether he is defensive, his opinion would be no more accurate. Indeed, the only thing which could get Jack to reflect on this question would be the request to do so, and this would surely bring into play, in a powerful way, the very mechanisms which so badly distort his understanding both of the world around him and of himself. His unreflective view of his own character is quite inaccurate, but the opinion he would form on careful reflection is even more inaccurate.

Jack's understanding of his emotions is no more accurate than his understanding of his character. I have already said that Jack becomes angry and defensive when he is criticized in any way. But Jack sincerely believes that he does not become angry when criticized, and if he is challenged on this, and his anger becomes so manifest that even he can see it for what is; he will insist that he has only become angry because his sincerity and self-understanding have been challenged, not that he was angry earlier when he was merely the object of some minor criticism. Jack's anger at the time of criticism was not apparent to him, nor would further reflection on the question have made it apparent. As with the question of his defensiveness, the only way we could get Jack to reflect on the question of his anger would be by raising that question directly, and this would only deepen his defensiveness, and thereby deepen his misunderstanding of his own emotions.

What is it like to be Jack? In order to answer this question, one might ask Jack, but this would not be a good idea. Asking Jack would prompt the very mechanisms of distortion which so deeply affect his self-understanding. So if we wish to know what it is like to be Jack, we will have to do something more subtle than we usually do in trying to understand someone else; we cannot simply take his word at face value. We will need to engage in theory construction. We will need to try to figure out, given his behavior, including his verbal behavior, what the mental life of such a person must be like. I said that this is more subtle than what we typically do in trying to understand another person, but this is not because we do not engage in such theory construction in the typical case. It is because the task of theory construction is usually a great deal easier than it is with Jack. Jack is, as a widely used euphemism would have it, a complicated person.

But even if our task of understanding what it is like to be Jack is a difficult one, surely, some will say, Jack's task of understanding what it is like to be Jack is quite easy. How, after all, could he fail to know? We have already seen quite a number of respects in which Jack does fail to know what it is like to be Jack. Jack does not begin to understand how defensive he is, how insecure, and so on. He does not understand his emotions. He does not understand the nature of his everyday interactions with others. His beliefs about his mental life are wide of the mark in important ways. Jack fails to know what it is like to be him precisely because of the kind of mental life he has.

Now all of this seems to me undeniable, but it will also be seen by those who think there is something privileged about the first-person point of view as beside the point. There are lots of things about Jack's mental life of which he is either unaware or badly mistaken. Those who wish to defend some area of first-person privilege, however, do not wish to claim that every fact about our mental life is directly accessible to introspection. Such a view would be absurd. And when people talk about the features of a person's mental life which make it the case that there is something it is like to be that person, they do not have in mind the features of Jack's personality upon which I have been dwelling. Even though Jack misunderstands those features of his mental life, it is, after all, his mental life. He has a perspective on it which others lack. And it is this perspective on which he is authoritative. Or so many would claim.

Now I agree that Jack has a perspective on his mental life which others lack. But what I deny is that Jack is authoritative even about the features of this perspective.[8] There is no level of description, I believe, at which Jack is

---

[8] My denial that Jack is authoritative on the features of his perspective is in apparent disagreement with Shoemaker, loc. cit., but Shoemaker's discussion of self-knowledge makes an explicit assumption of rationality, as he emphasizes. It might be argued that the case of Jack violates this assumption, thus leaving no disagreement between us. If Shoemaker is to respond in this way,

authoritative about his mental life. Jack's understanding of himself, at every level, must be just as mediate, corrigible, and theory-laden as our understanding of Jack. There is not even the smallest grain of truth to be found in Descartes' claim of deep epistemological asymmetry between our understanding of our own mental lives and our understanding of other things.

It is important not to confuse the fact that there is something it is like to be Jack with any claim about self-knowledge. There is something it is like to be a bat, but this does not give the bat self-knowledge, for the bat lacks the conceptual repertoire to understand its own experience. Now Jack has the conceptual repertoire to categorize his experience. So it is not only the case that there is something it is like to be Jack; Jack is in a position to have beliefs about his experience. This makes it possible, in principle, for Jack to have knowledge about what it is like to be him; and in this respect, Jack is unlike the bat. But having the experience, like the bat, and also having the conceptual repertoire, like Jack, still does not guarantee self-knowledge, even knowledge of what it is like to be oneself. When one's introspective gaze is directed at one's own experience, and when one attempts to conceptualize it so as to form beliefs about it, interfering factors may generate mistakes, as they do in Jack.[9] In such a case, while one has beliefs about what it is like to be oneself, these beliefs are often mistaken. And the experience of being oneself, without any belief about that experience, is no kind of knowledge at all.

IV

Our perspective on Jack's mental life is an external perspective. We see Jack's mental life from the outside. He sees it from the inside; he lives it. How does this help him, epistemologically, at least according to those who wish to grant some special status to the first-person perspective? In order to understand the motivation for such a view, we would do well to examine a different subject than Jack. Jack is not the kind of character to get Cartesian intuitions flowing.

So let us consider Mary, an altogether different character from Jack. Mary is emotionally well-adjusted. She has none of the defensiveness, the

---

however, this will leave relatively small scope for his argument, given the incidence of mental disorders. See Note 13 for some of the relevant figures.

[9] I do not believe that the operation of interfering factors is the only source of mistake about one's own mental states, as I argue below in Section V. It is, however, one important source of error.

insecurity, the self-involvement of Jack. Mary does not systematically misperceive others' intentions. She sees a smile as a smile, not a snarl. She does not hear others making unflattering remarks about her, unless they are. And her response to criticism is nothing like Jack's. She does not typically become angry or defensive. Mary's judgments about the world around her are quite accurate, unlike Jack's, and her level of self-understanding is quite high as well. She sees herself, to a very large degree, for what she is.

Mary has a perspective on her own mental life which we lack, and her perspective gives her a very rich and largely accurate[10] understanding of herself. Another person would have to know Mary for a long time to understand her nearly as well as she does herself. Mary is not nearly as 'complicated' as Jack, but understanding any person very well takes a good deal of time.

The fact that Mary has a first-person perspective on her mental life puts her at an advantage over others in understanding what she is like. Her understanding of her character and emotions seems direct; it is unmediated by self-conscious inference or theory construction, at least in the typical case. Mary doesn't have to think about what is going on in her mind; she can just tell. The rest of us have far less direct access to what Mary is like. Here is a straightforward case of first-person privilege. And those who are inclined to a Cartesian understanding of the epistemology of first-person access tend to think about cases like that of Mary, rather than less emotionally healthy individuals like Jack. We will not understand the epistemology of first-person access, however, if we focus only on a single kind of case.

I want to compare Mary's access to her own mental states first, with her access to the external world, and second, with Jack's access to his own mental states. These two comparisons will serve to illustrate the claims I wish to make about the epistemological status of first-person access.

So how does Mary's access to her own mental states compare with her access to the external world? From a phenomenological point of view, Mary's access to her own mental states seems simple, direct, and unmediated. In this respect, her access to her own mental states is no different from her access to various features of the external world. From a phenomenological point of view, Mary doesn't seem to infer that there is a book on the table; she can just tell about that too. Now the phenomenological level of analysis of psychological processes is not terribly deep; what seems

---

[10] Although see Section V below for some qualifications.

simple, immediate, and direct may be psychologically complex. This is surely the case with Mary's grasp of features of the external world. Mary's ability to recognize a book as a book was acquired. Mary had to learn what a book is, and what a book typically looks like, in order to gain the discriminatory capacity to recognize books. She can now do that at a glance. The process is so internalized that it has become phenomenologically simple. Much the same is true with her understanding of her own mental states.[11] Mary's ability to recognize anger as anger was also acquired. She was, as a child, taught to understand the difference between anger and fear and other unpleasant emotions. Now, as an adult, the process of recognizing her mental states is so internalized that it too has become phenomenologically simple. And like her ability to recognize various states of the external world, Mary is quite reliable on a wide range of such discriminatory tasks. Her judgments about many of her mental states, like her judgments about many states of the external world, tend to be correct. In both cases, judgments about her mental states and judgments about the world, Mary makes some mistakes. These mistakes, however, seem to be the exception rather than the rule.

How does Mary differ from Jack? Jack's judgments about both the external world and his own mental states are just as simple, direct, and unmediated, phenomenologically, as Mary's. And the psychological processes which produce Jack's beliefs, about both the external world and his own mental states, are, like the ones which produce Mary's, extraordinarily complex. Jack's judgments are not nearly so reliable as Mary's are. He tends to make a very large number of mistakes, both about the world and about his own internal states. But Jack is in no position to know about his unreliability. His errors hide themselves from him because the very processes which make his judgments so inaccurate also prevent him from becoming aware of that inaccuracy. From the inside, Jack's judgments seem just as well justified as Mary's.

Where are the advantages of the first-person perspective on one's own mental states? There certainly are epistemological advantages which Mary reaps from having a first-person perspective on her mental states. She is in a better position to know the contents of her mind than most anyone else. Indeed, when it comes to certain questions about her mental states – for example, exactly what she is thinking about at a particular instant – she is

---

[11] This point is well made by Alison Gopnik, who refers to this phenomenon as "the illusion of expertise." See her "How We Know Our Minds; The Illusion of First-Person Knowledge of Intentionality," *Behavioral and Brain Sciences* 16(1993), 1–14.

frequently the only one who is in any position to know what is going on in her mind. Moreover, she knows far more about her mental life than anyone else. These are, without a doubt, epistemological advantages of the position Mary is in vis-à-vis her mental states. But note that these advantages do not flow from the mere fact that Mary has a first-person perspective on her mental states. Jack has that perspective on his mental states as well, and his understanding of his mental life is inferior to that of others whose only access to Jack's mental life is from the outside.

It is not having a first-person perspective by itself which allows for the quality of Mary's epistemological position. What Mary has that Jack lacks is a reliable perspective on her mental states. And what she has that we lack is causal proximity to her mental states. Mary is, and we are not, always affected by her mental states, and because she is so constituted that the connection between her mental states and her beliefs about them is a reliable one, she is in a better position than anyone, most of the time, to know the contents of her own mind. But this does not make for a difference in kind between Mary's knowledge of her own mental states and our knowledge of Mary's mental states.

Because the difference between a first-person perspective and a third-person perspective is a matter of causal proximity, it is comparable to the difference between looking at a person from across a table and from across a street: closer is, frequently, better. Moreover, once we recognize that the advantages of the first-person perspective, when it does constitute an advantage, come from the causal proximity of a person to her own mental states, it becomes clear that this is not an advantage which tracks the distinction between mental and physical even in the typical case. I am in a position of epistemic advantage to others in making judgments about the state of my stomach – whether it is full or empty, for example – and even the state of my wristwatch and wedding ring – how they are oriented on my body – which is not different in kind from the epistemic advantage I have over others in making judgments about, for example, my beliefs. And when it comes to certain mental states, such as the ones involved in the early stages of perceptual processing or those involved in language acquisition and use, the first-person perspective offers no epistemic advantage over the third-person perspective. These mental states do not produce beliefs about themselves in the way that beliefs, desires, and emotions so frequently do.

The mental qua mental thus does not offer us any special epistemic advantages. There are mental states which, given certain background conditions, do tend reliably to produce beliefs about themselves, but in this respect they do not differ from certain physical states of the environment which are causally proximate to sensory receptors. The mind is so constructed that it is apt, under appropriate background conditions, to detect certain of its own states. But it enjoys this connection with much of its immediate environment as well.

V

The approach to self-understanding which I have been urging here leads, as I will argue, to two surprising conclusions. First, introspection, by itself, is almost certainly insufficient to ground claims of self-knowledge in the vast majority of cases. And second, it may well be that knowledge of one's own mental states is far less pervasive than is typically assumed.

Now this second claim is, of course, a kind of skepticism, and I am, on the whole, quite unsympathetic with skeptical argument. Most skeptical arguments, it seems to me, raise the standards for knowledge so high as either to make the claim that we lack knowledge, so construed, uninteresting, or, alternatively, to trade on premises which, although initially plausible, are cast in doubt as a result of the very fact that they lead to a skeptical conclusion. So what I need to do here, in defending a kind of mitigated skepticism about self-knowledge, is show that the argument I have in mind is not merely an instance of some general all-purpose skeptical argument.

I begin with a skeptical claim about our discriminatory capacities which, although surprising, is easily shown to be justified. I then isolate the features of the evidence for this claim which make the argument for it different than standard all-purpose skeptical arguments. Finally, I present an argument for my theses about introspection and our knowledge of our own mental states, and show that this argument has the same features as my argument about our discriminatory capacities – i.e., it is not just an instance of some all-purpose skeptical strategy.

The discriminatory capacity I have in mind is color perception, and the skeptical claim I wish to make is that many people, perhaps most, do not know whether they are color-blind. This will, I think, strike most everyone as absurd. But the evidence on this, I believe, is quite clear.

People who are color-blind do not have the same range of discriminatory capacity with respect to color that others do. But this lack of discriminatory capacity is not immediately apparent. Indeed, a very large number of people who are color-blind do not discover that they are for decades. The failure to have the relevant discriminatory powers does not come to their attention in the ordinary course of events. Now this is,

I think, surprising, because it is widely assumed that such a substantial perceptual deficit would, of necessity, come quickly to one's attention. The facts, however, are otherwise. Many people discover, only quite late in life, that they are, and always were, color-blind.

Now the fact that color blindness does not, in the ordinary course of events, come to the attention of those who are affected by it, makes me think that the majority of people probably do not know whether they are color-blind. Color blindness is not a rare condition.[12] If it were the sort of thing which affected only one person in ten million, then one might reasonably ignore the possibility that one is so affected. But color blindness is nothing like that. And so the majority of people who believe that they are not color-blind probably do not have an adequate basis for that opinion.

This does not mean that none of the people who believe that they have normal color vision can know this about themselves. First, there is a test for determining one's discriminatory capacity. And even apart from taking the test, there are certain kinds of situations which, if one were regularly in them, would bring one's color blindness to one's attention, if one had it. Painters, for example, are so often called upon to make subtle discriminations of color that it is very likely that those of them who are color-blind come to discover it fairly quickly. But those who have neither had the test for color blindness nor been subject to the special conditions of painters and the like simply have no basis for an opinion on the question of their own color blindness.

This skeptical argument is not just an instance of some all-purpose skeptical argument. First, color blindness is not merely a logically possible condition; people actually are subject to it. Second, color blindness is not a rare condition; indeed, it is quite widespread. When I point out that most people do not have evidence which counts one way or the other on the question of their color blindness, I am thus not merely pointing to some out-of-the-way possibility which they cannot exclude. In virtue of this fact, the skeptical argument presented will not serve a general skepticism. The mere logical possibility of mistake, or the extremely small likelihood of mistake, plays no role here.

How does this bear on the question of knowledge of one's own mental states? First, I want to argue that the introspective evidence we have on many of our mental states is not sufficient to rule out possibilities which

---

[12] Among Caucasian males, for example, the group in which color blindness is most prevalent, more than 8 percent of the population is afflicted. See Leo Hurvich, *Color Vision*, Sinauer Associates, 1981, 267.

are just as real as the possibility of color blindness. In these cases then, if we are to have knowledge of our own mental states, it cannot depend on introspective evidence alone. This is not sufficient for any kind of skepticism about self-knowledge, for it might be that the additional non-introspective evidence required is typically available. Unfortunately, the evidence which we would need to rule out the very real possibility of mistake may not be possessed by most people much of the time. If I am right about this, knowledge of the contents of one's own mind may be a less common phenomenon than is typically believed.

The mistakes which Jack makes about the contents of his mind go some distance toward the conclusions I wish to argue for. Jack makes many errors about his mental states. Moreover, the kind of emotional difficulties which are the source of Jack's errors are not introspectable. When Jack introspects to see whether he is defensive, insecure, or self-involved, his introspective evidence provides him with a negative answer. Thus, the fact that you and I, when we introspect, to determine whether we are defensive, insecure, or self-involved, also come up with a negative answer does not serve to distinguish us from Jack. Jack's psychological condition is not a mere logical possibility. It is anything but rare.[13]

Now I do not mean to be arguing that you and I do not have reason to believe that we fail to suffer from the same emotional difficulties as Jack. At this point, all I am arguing is that our introspective evidence is of no use in distinguishing us from Jack, and thus, if we do have adequate evidence that we do not suffer from Jack's problems, it must come from other sources. Indeed, I believe most of us do have sufficient evidence to distinguish ourselves from Jack. But before I discuss what that evidence might come to and just how much work it can do for us, I want to make a further point about the significance of the fact that our evidence that we are different from Jack, if we have evidence of that, cannot have its source in introspection.

Jack is mistaken about many of the features of his mental life. Although his introspective evidence tells him that he is not angry on occasions when

---

[13] The *Diagnostic and Statistical Manual of Mental Disorders* (or *DSM*) does not express an opinion on the prevalence of paranoid personality disorder because individuals subject to it so rarely seek treatment. There is no reason to believe, however, that it is rare. Moreover, a wide variety of personality and affective disorders, all of which give rise to similar distortions of both perception and self-understanding, are distressingly widespread. Thus, for example, the *DSM* lists borderline personality disorder as "apparently common" (347). Studies of major depression indicate that "[t]he range for females is from 9% to 26%; that for males, 5% to 12%. Studies examining the proportion of the adult population that currently has the disorder report rates ranging from 4.5% to 9.3% for females and 2.3% to 3.2% for males" (229). The comparison with color blindness thus significantly understates my case.

he is the subject of minor criticism, he is mistaken about this. Now you and I also believe that we are not angered by minor criticism. But since our introspective evidence is insufficient to distinguish us from Jack, the introspective evidence that we are not angry on such occasions is insufficient to ground any knowledge. We cannot reasonably claim to know that we are not angry solely on the basis of introspective evidence, since there are real psychological conditions, present in a non-trivial percentage of the population, which would provide us with the very same introspective evidence we have, and yet lead to false belief. For the range of mental states on which Jack tends to make errors then, we must conclude that if we are in a position to know that we are in such mental states, it cannot be solely on the basis of introspective evidence.

Now Jack's condition is not the only one which might be brought up in service of my conclusion. Indeed, many emotional and mental problems share all of the relevant features of Jack's condition. There are many such problems which (1) are not detectable introspectively, (2) are present in a non-trivial percentage of the population, and (3) give rise to misunderstandings of the subjects' character traits, motivations, emotions, desires, beliefs, and experiences. The conclusion we must draw from this is that if we know that we are not subject to these conditions, our evidence is not solely introspective. The evidence which introspection provides on these matters is not sufficient to provide us with knowledge.

Indeed, all of this actually understates the situation because it is not only facts about people with emotional and other psychological problems which serve to undermine the epistemic weight of introspective evidence. Even people who are emotionally healthy, like Mary, tend to make a wide range of errors about their mental states. While it was once the standard view among psychologists that being emotionally well-adjusted goes hand in hand with an accurate understanding of oneself and the world around one, the evidence against this claim is now quite strong.[14] People who are emotionally well adjusted tend to overestimate the success of their social interactions, have an exaggerated idea of the extent to which they have control over the course of their lives and features of the world around them, and have a degree of optimism which can, on no reasonable construal, be justified by the facts. These mistakes are part and parcel of a wide range of errors which subjects

---

[14] For a brief survey, see Shelley Taylor and Jonathan Brown, "Illusions and Well-Being: A Social Psychological Perspective on Mental Health," *Psychological Bulletin* 103(1988), 193–210. For greater detail, see Shelley Taylor, *Positive Illusions: Creative Self-Deception and the Healthy Mind*, Basic Books, 1989.

make about themselves, including their own mental states. In particular, emotionally healthy individuals tend to attribute favorable character traits, emotions, and mental abilities to themselves which do not square with the behavioral evidence. When it comes to certain topics, emotionally well-adjusted people tend to lack knowledge, not because their evidence for a true belief is insufficiently strong, but rather because their beliefs on these topics are just plain false. When the beliefs are ones about a subject's mental states, it is thus the case that the introspective evidence cannot possibly be sufficient to ground knowledge.

Let me try to clarify exactly how deeply I believe these conclusions cut. I do not believe that they show introspection to be powerless to ground any knowledge whatsoever about one's mental states. Many cases of self-knowledge will elude this argument. But I do believe that the argument has very wide scope. If a person makes a judgment about his own mental state, and if there are real psychological conditions had by a non-trivial percentage of the population which would provide people with them with the very same introspective evidence and such that, in people with those psychological conditions, the resulting judgment would be false, then the introspective evidence by itself is insufficient to ground knowledge. In order to show then that a particular judgment about a person's mental state cannot be supported by introspective evidence alone, one must find an appropriate psychological condition which would provide its subjects with the same introspective evidence, even though the resulting judgment would be false. Now I believe it is clear enough, given the extremely wide range of psychological problems to which people are susceptible, and the attendant errors in self-perception which they give rise to, that this is sufficient to undermine the epistemic weight of introspection in an extremely wide range of judgments.

But none of this is sufficient yet to justify any sort of skepticism, for it may be, for all I have said, that we typically have the relevant sort of evidence needed to justify our knowledge claims, although the evidence finds its source in perception rather than introspection. Indeed, although I do favor a mitigated skepticism about our knowledge of our own mental states, the scope of this skepticism is far narrower than the scope of my claim about the limitations of introspection alone.

I said earlier that I believe you and I do have good reason to believe that we are not in Jack's unfortunate situation, although this evidence does not come from introspection. What kind of evidence could support a person's belief that he or she is not suffering from the emotional problems I've attributed to Jack, or from the various other psychological conditions which serve as a source for skepticism about introspective access to the contents of one's mental states? There is, I believe, a wide range of evidence which grounds such beliefs. Some of the psychological conditions which are relevant here are highly heritable. Thus, if one knows that one's family has had no history of mental illness, this provides one with good reason for thinking that one is unlikely to be subject to these particular problems. Some of the psychological conditions which give rise to dramatic misunderstandings of one's own mental states would prevent one from holding down a job for an extended period of time or continuing in close personal relationships. Those experiencing no difficulties at work or who have good relationships with others thus have reason to believe that they are not subject to these conditions. The list of reasons could be extended almost indefinitely. In every case, however, the reasons are specific to the conditions involved. There are no global defeaters for these psychological conditions, no evidence one might have which will simultaneously show that one is subject to none of them. At the same time, the kind of evidence I've discussed is certainly widely possessed. To the extent that people have such evidence, then, they may have good reason to believe that a wide range of their mental states is just as they are represented to themselves in introspection. It is just that introspective evidence, by itself, is not what grounds their knowledge.

If all of this is correct, what residual reasons are there for skepticism? I believe there may be many. What I have in mind here are conditions which are like Jack's, but less extreme. Even people who are emotionally healthy can be a bit defensive at times, and this gives rise to a distorting effect on their introspective understanding. Such a distorting effect is less dramatic than in Jack's case, but it cannot be neglected either. Such people certainly do make mistakes about their own mental lives, and highly non-trivial ones. Defensiveness, of course, is not the only such distorting factor. Indeed, for each of the extreme psychological conditions one might list to show that introspective evidence is not sufficient to ground knowledge of one's own mental states, one can usually find milder versions of the same phenomenon to ground a deeper skeptical claim. This claim is deeper because it withstands challenge not only from introspective sources, but from perceptual sources as well. At the same time, however, it is narrower, for it will not take in as wide a range of first-person judgments. The milder psychological conditions, of course, give rise to a less full-blown case of self-misunderstanding.

The extent of these skeptical worries must be settled by empirical evidence. The nature of these various conditions, the kinds of misunderstanding they give rise to, the extent to which subjects of these conditions are in a position to tell that they have them, and the incidence of such conditions in the general population must all be examined in detail. We don't fully understand these matters right now, and yet, I believe, there is sufficient reason to think that a good deal of confidence in one's first-person judgments, whether on the basis of introspective evidence alone, or on the basis of perceptual evidence as well, is probably misplaced. We should be extremely circumspect in making judgments about ourselves.

VI

Let me close with one final remark about an important difference between the kind of skepticism I have urged about the powers of introspection, on the one hand, and skepticism about our perceptual and inferential abilities, which I do not endorse, on the other. Some have attempted to defend a fairly general skepticism about our inferential abilities on the basis of a large body of psychological evidence which documents human foibles.[15] I find such arguments prima facie implausible.[16] Such arguments are implausible, I believe, because the whole of science is dependent upon human inference, and the successful conduct of science is made to appear a miracle if human inference is so hopelessly irrational as some make it out to be. My suggestion, however, that introspection may be unreliable suffers from no comparable prima facie difficulties, for there has been no successful science built on introspective evidence, and the attempt to construct a scientific psychology on the basis of such evidence, at the turn of the last century, was a manifest failure. Indeed, perhaps this should make us think that introspective evidence is of little value.

Let me return to my title question: What is it like to be me? A few years ago, I would have given a confident answer to this question. Right now, however, I am not so sure. Those who believe they know the answer to the analogous question about themselves may be quite confident, but it is simply unclear that such confidence is justified.[17]

---

[15] See the papers by Tversky and Kahneman collected in *Judgment under Uncertainty: Heuristics and Biases*, Daniel Kahneman, Paul Slovic, and Amos Tversky, eds., Cambridge University Press, 1981; and Stephen Stich, "Could Man Be an Irrational Animal?," *Synthese* 64(1985), 115–135.

[16] Although, at the same time, I believe they require detailed response. I have attempted to provide the beginnings of such a response in *Inductive Inference and Its Natural Ground*, MIT Press, 1993.

[17] I have received helpful comments on a draft of this essay from David Christensen, Stephen Jacobson, Mark Kaplan, Bill Lycan, Derk Pereboom, William J. Talbott, Rob Wilson, and anonymous referees. Versions of the essay were also presented at the University of Ottawa and the University of Connecticut, and useful discussion on these occasions prompted many changes.

3
Distrusting Reason

The activity of reason-giving is an important part of our intellectual lives. At times, we offer reasons to justify our actions or our beliefs, both to others and to ourselves. Moreover, most of us take reason-giving to have normative force: if we are presented with good reasons in favor of a belief or a course of action, we take this to provide us with a presumption in favor of forming that belief or performing that action. This is, after all, why reason is so important: it serves, and rightly so, as a guide to both belief and action.

But there are some who are distrustful of reason, who do not take the activity of reason-giving at face value. Reason-giving may be viewed with suspicion as yet one more instrument for wielding power over the oppressed. Views of this sort have been articulated and defended by some feminists, Freudians, Marxists, and deconstructionists, and some such inchoate view may be behind a certain climate of anti-intellectualism that is currently a potent force in public debate on many issues of real import.[1]

This distrust of reason needs to be taken more seriously than it has, to my mind, not only as a political force, but as an intellectual position. In this essay, I try to show that a certain skepticism about reason-giving deserves a hearing. In coming to understand why someone might rationally be suspicious of the practice of reason-giving, those of us who place our trust in this practice may come to understand better what its presuppositions are and what it would take to ground that trust. This essay thus attempts to make a contribution to the field of social epistemology: it

---

[1] A different, though complementary, source of distrust in reason comes from some evolutionary psychologists, who suggest that the kinds of circumstances with which our reasoning faculties are designed to deal are far narrower than the ones to which they are currently applied. For a particularly interesting application of such a view, see Colin McGinn, *Problems in Philosophy: The Limits of Inquiry*, Blackwell, 1993.

attempts to spell out some of the social prerequisites for the proper function of the activity of reason-giving.[2]

I

Let us begin by examining a case of rationalization. Andrew has beliefs about the effectiveness of the death penalty in reducing the murder rate which are, at bottom, a product of wishful thinking. Andrew has certain views about the morality of the death penalty, views which he holds on grounds independent of his views about its deterrent effect. His views about the effectiveness of the death penalty as a deterrent are not a product of his understanding of the relevant data. Instead, it is his view about the morality of the death penalty that is driving his view about its effects. Conveniently, he has come to believe that the policy he judges to be morally correct also happens to have the best consequences. Andrew's reason for his belief about the deterrent effect of the death penalty is not a good reason. It would not withstand public, or even private, scrutiny. But Andrew is unaware that this is why he believes as he does. He sincerely believes that his reasons for belief are quite different.

---

[2] I approach the practice of reason-giving as one contingent social practice among many that, like any other, may be called into question. In this, I contrast with those who see reason-giving as different, somehow constitutive of rationality. Thus, for example, Thomas Nagel claims that the practice of reason-giving is not "merely another socially conditioned practice" ("Kolakowski: Modernity and the Devil," in his *Other Minds: Critical Essays 1969–1994*, Oxford University Press, 1995, 212). And he goes on:

> A defender of the Kantian method must claim that it is legitimate to ask for justifying reasons for a contingent social practice in a way in which it is not legitimate to turn the tables and call reason itself into question by appealing to such a practice. The asymmetry arises because any claim to the rightness of what one is doing is automatically an appeal to its justifiability, and therefore subject to rational criticism. All roads lead to the same court of appeal, a court to which all of us are assumed to have access. Reason is universal because no attempted challenge to its results can avoid appealing to reason in the end – by claiming, for example, that what was presented as an argument is really a rationalization. This can undermine our confidence in the original method or practice only by giving us reasons to believe something else, so that finally we have to think about the arguments to make up our minds. (Ibid., 212–213. A large part of this passage is quoted, with hearty approval, by Daniel Dennett in his review of *Other Minds* in *Journal of Philosophy*, 93(1996), 428.)

I will not respond to this argument point by point. Instead, this essay may be viewed as presenting an alternative to Nagel's Kantian defense of reason-giving, a position that Nagel has further developed in *The Last Word*, Oxford University Press, 1997. As will become clear presently, I believe that the point about rationalization that Nagel mentions in passing has a much deeper significance than he attaches to it and that it may be used to challenge the entire practice of reason-giving. By the same token, if this challenge can be adequately responded to, as I believe it can, then we are presented with a substantive, rather than a transcendental, defense of the practice of reason-giving. For those who are suspicious of transcendental arguments, this is an important result.

Andrew is not entirely uninformed about the various empirical studies that have been done on the deterrent effect of the death penalty. Indeed, when such studies are reported in the newspapers, Andrew is extremely attentive to the details of the news story. The studies that Andrew has seen reported are mixed: some present prima facie evidence of the effectiveness of the death penalty in reducing the murder rate, whereas others present prima facie evidence of its ineffectiveness. Andrew has latched on to the stories that fit with his antecedent view. He remembers them better than the others, and when asked about the death penalty, he is often able to cite relevant statistics from them. He has less vivid memories of the other studies, those that run counter to his belief about the death penalty's effectiveness, and when he reads about these studies he is typically able to mount some perfectly plausible methodological challenge to them: some important variable was not controlled for, the number of cases involved is not statistically significant, and so on. Andrew is intelligent and articulate. He is very good at constructing reasons for his belief from the mixed evidence with which he is confronted, and he is very good at presenting these reasons to others in discussion about the issue. He believes that the reasons that he presents are the reasons for which he holds his belief. But he is wrong about this. The reasons for his belief are quite different. Thus, when Andrew offers reasons for his belief, he is offering a rationalization.[3]

Andrew's intelligence and articulateness are aids to the process of rationalization. Andrew's ability to construct and deploy arguments can be extremely convincing, both to others and to himself. Someone less sophisticated than Andrew would not be able to construct such convincing rationalizations, and opinions of such a person that were the product of wishful thinking would be more easily exposed, both to others and to the person himself. When Andrew offers rationalizations for his badly grounded opinions, his intelligence works against him.

Ordinarily, when we reflect on our reasons for one of our beliefs, we are motivated by a desire to have our beliefs conform to the truth. By scrutinizing our reasons, we hope to be able to recognize cases where our beliefs have outstripped our reasons and, thus, where we should not be confident that our beliefs do indeed conform to the truth. When we consider what to believe in prospect, we reflect on our evidence, and this

---

[3] Andrew's resourcefulness in handling data and the convenient asymmetries in his forgetfulness are not unusual. Indeed, this example is simply adapted from the results of a study on the effects of mixed data on prior opinion: C. Lord, L. Ross, and M. R. Lepper, "Biased Assimilation and Attitude Polarization: The Effects of Prior Theories on Subsequently Considered Evidence," *Journal of Personality and Social Psychology* 37(1979), 2098–2110.

process of reflection is designed to guide belief fixation so as to make it likely that the beliefs we come to have also conform to the truth. Both in the case of reflection on already existing beliefs and in the case of reflection on beliefs we might come to have, our motivation for thinking about reasons is to get at the truth.

Now in the case of rationalization, our motivation for reflecting on reasons is different. Our motivation in these cases may be to make ourselves feel better, to avoid cognitive dissonance, or the like. But if our motivations in these cases are different from those in the typical case, such motivations are not transparent to us. When we rationalize, at least when we do it sincerely, we are not aware of doing so; we are not aware of being motivated by anything other than a desire to get at the truth. And it is precisely because of this that the process of scrutinizing our reasons for belief may, at times, be terribly counterproductive from an epistemological point of view. Scrutinizing our reasons, when we are engaged in sincere rationalizing, will get in the way of the goal of believing truths.

Let us return to Andrew. When Andrew reflects on his reasons for believing as he does about the effects of the death penalty, he is able to devise reasons for his belief that give the appearance of supporting it. Indeed, the reasons he is able to offer are prima facie good reasons for believing as he does. Thus, when Andrew offers these reasons to others, if they are not independently well informed on this matter, they may come, quite reasonably, to believe as Andrew does; and when others do this, their believings, unlike Andrew's, may be motivated by nothing more than a desire to believe the truth. They, unlike Andrew, are being fully responsive to the evidence, it seems. The only problem for Andrew's interlocutors is that Andrew has selectively presented the evidence; but this, of course, is not something that they are in a position to know or even have any reason to suspect. The reasons Andrew presents are, on their face, good reasons. Rational interlocutors who lack independent evidence on the questions about which Andrew speaks should come to believe as he does.

This fact about the interpersonal case of reason-giving is particularly important because it helps to explain why it is that the process of rationalization is so easy to engage in. When we scrutinize our own reasons for belief, we, like Andrew's interlocutors, take the evidence that is available to us at face value.[4] Because the biasing processes that selectively filter our evidence take place behind the scenes, as it were, unavailable to

---

[4] See the discussion of the availability heuristic in Richard Nisbett and Lee Ross, *Inductive Inference: Strategies and Shortcomings of Social Judgment*, Prentice-Hall, 1980.

introspection, we are able to produce perfectly good reasons for belief, reasons that not only survive our private scrutiny, but would survive public scrutiny as well. The process of scrutinizing our reasons, in the case of sincere rationalization, gives the illusion of being responsive to available evidence. And the more intelligent one is and the better one is at the skills of presenting and defending arguments, the more powerful the illusion will be, if one engages in rationalizing, that one is forming beliefs in ways that are appropriately responsive to evidence.

These facts about rationalization, I believe, go some distance toward making sense of the phenomenon of distrusting reason. There are certain people who have a deep skepticism about the significance of rational argument. These people are often unmoved by rational argument, and, indeed, seem to find the activity of reason-giving less persuasive the more careful and detailed the argument given. Such people often say things like this: "I know that's a perfectly good argument for p, but I don't know whether I should believe p"; and this, on its face, seems deeply irrational. What should determine whether one should believe p, after all, if not the arguments available for and against it?[5]

But I don't think that this attitude need be irrational at all. First, the ability to form one's beliefs in a way that is responsive to evidence is not at all the same as the ability to present reasons for one's beliefs, either to others or to oneself. Reason-giving requires a wide range of skills that need not be present in the reasons-responsive person. One thing the skeptic about reason-giving may be responding to is the recognition that some people are terrifically adept at providing prima facie reasonable arguments for their beliefs, quite apart from whether those beliefs are correct. Just as a reasonable person might willfully ignore the appeals of a gifted speaker in order to avoid being misled, an intelligent person who recognizes his own weakness in distinguishing apparently good but mistaken reasoning from the genuine item might also willfully ignore detailed and subtle appeals to reason.[6]

---

[5] Consider, for example, these comments of Jerry Fodor and Ernest Lepore: "It seems to us that what there is no argument for, there is no reason to believe. And what there *is* no reason to believe, one *has* no reason to believe." *Holism: A Shopper's Guide*, Blackwell, 1992, xiii.

[6] By the same token, a person who is particularly good at presenting arguments and recognizes the high regard in which such detailed reason-giving is typically held may use his ability to present detailed arguments in a coercive or oppressive manner. In such cases, it is not the logical features of the argument that are at fault, nor is it irrational that many should fail to attend to such logical features and simply dismiss arguments of this sort out of hand. This kind of concern has been raised in some of the feminist literature.

But the second reason for thinking that skepticism about reason-giving may often be quite reasonable ties in directly with the points we have made about rationalization.[7] People who are especially intelligent and articulate and who are adept at providing reasons for their beliefs are also, in virtue of that very fact, especially well equipped at providing rationalizations for their beliefs, rationalizations that possess all of the hallmarks of good reasoning. It is not that devising a convincing rationalization for a belief is easy, even for those gifted at argument. But rationalization is often the product of very powerful motivating forces, and thus a great deal of intellectual energy may be brought to the task; the result of this is often a subtle and prima facie rational argument. This provides fuel for skepticism about rational argument, and it is precisely for this reason that the skeptic is especially wary of detailed and elaborate argument. Intricacy of argument, on this view, raises a red flag, for it raises the possibility of rationalization as the underlying source of the argument given rather than truth-responsive reason-giving. Inspection of the details of the argument would be pointless in trying to distinguish these two, for the subtle rationalizer is in a fine position to offer arguments that, on their face, are impeccable. The difference between truth-responsive reason-giving and subtle rationalization does not lie in features intrinsic to the arguments given. A reasonable person who is worried about the possibility of rationalization as a source of a particular act of reason-giving will thus not allow herself to be pulled into the intellectual task of examining the quality of reasoning offered, for this is the wrong place to look to see whether the conclusion is to be trusted. What needs to be examined is the source of the argument – its motivation – rather than its logical credentials. One needs to know whether the person offering the argument is motivated by a desire to believe truths or by something else instead.

One might object at this point that the motivation of the person offering the argument is simply irrelevant when we are trying to figure out what to believe. If the argument offered is a good one, then it doesn't matter whether it reflects the reasons for which the person offering it believes the conclusion.

---

[7] This concern as well has been a focus of some feminist discussions of reason-giving and the objection to what some have called "logocentrism." Although I am quite unsympathetic with most of what has been said under this label, the skeptic about reason-giving of this essay may be seen as my own reconstruction of what I take to be the most reasonable objection to so-called logocentrism. But I would not attribute the details of the position developed here to any particular feminist philosopher. For feminist philosophers who have developed such views, see, e.g., Lorraine Code, *Rhetorical Spaces: Essays on Gendered Locations*, Routledge, 1995, and Andrea Nye, *Words of Power: A Feminist Reading of the History of Logic*, Routledge, 1990.

We shouldn't care whether the argument offered is a reflection of the arguer's reasons for belief; all we should care about is whether the argument offered is a reflection of good reasons for us to believe.

There is something right about this objection. The mere fact that an argument offered does not reflect the reasons for which the arguer believes a conclusion does not by itself undermine the value of the reasons offered. Nevertheless, as a matter of empirical fact, the phenomenon of rationalization is typically accompanied by a number of factors that do tend to undermine the value of the reasons offered by the rationalizer. As the case of Andrew illustrates, there is a tremendous selectivity in the way in which rationalizers deal with evidence: they do not present the evidence fairly, either to themselves, in memory, or to others. This point, by itself, is sufficient to show that we must be on the lookout for rationalization.

In addition, many arguments involve subtle appeals to plausibility. There can be little doubt that the rationalizer's sense of plausibility is affected in important ways by the motivation he has for rationalizing, and this does not aid in the project of coming to believe truths. Thus, if an agent suspects that he himself is rationalizing, he has reason to worry about his overall evaluations of plausibility. That an argument is born of rationalization is importantly relevant in determining what one should believe.

More than this, the extent to which inchoate judgments of plausibility come into play in evaluating arguments should be a source of concern even apart from concerns about rationalization. Our sense of plausibility is a fragile reed. There can be little doubt that it is socially conditioned. Being surrounded by people who take a particular view seriously, or, alternatively, simply dismiss a view as unworthy of serious consideration, is likely to have some effect on one's own assessments of plausibility. If those around one are well attuned to the truth, this may be a fine thing. But in less optimal circumstances, where one's epistemic community is badly misguided, one's own sense of plausibility may be distorted as a result. What passes for good reasoning in such communities may have very little connection to the truth.

In the end, the difference between the person who places his full confidence in rational argument and the person who is skeptical of it may come down, in part, to a disagreement about the frequency with which rationalization occurs and the extent to which our sense of plausibility can be distorted. If one believes that rationalization is extremely widespread and that plausibility judgments are extremely malleable, then one may be well advised to be skeptical of rational argument. Under these conditions, attending to the logical niceties of argument would be no more useful in attaining one's epistemic goals than attending to the eye color of the person offering the argument. If, on the other hand, rationalization is rare, and plausibility judgments are firmly fixed in ways that track the truth, then focusing on the logical features of reason-giving may serve as an effective guide to true belief. What divides these two views, to the extent that each is rationally held, is a disagreement about human psychology.

Let me spell out this disagreement in greater detail. The skeptic about reason-giving may view the very activity of giving reasons as far more disconnected from the truth, and indeed, in some cases, from the activity of belief fixation, than we are ordinarily accustomed to thinking. I take the traditional view to be as follows. Human beings often form their beliefs as a result of self-consciously considering reasons. When they do this, they are typically led to beliefs that are likely to be true, at least relative to the evidence available to them. Even when self-conscious consideration of reasons does not occur prior to forming a belief, we often scrutinize our reasons for belief after the fact. When we do this, we begin by determining what our reasons for holding a belief come to, and we then consider the logical credentials of our reasons. When they are good reasons, we continue to hold the belief, and when they are not good reasons, we come to give up the belief. Our reasons are, for the most part, easily available to introspection, and the activity of considering our reasons is thus deeply implicated in the fixation of belief in a way that guides it toward the truth.

But the skeptic about reason-giving may have a very different picture about the relationship among the giving of reasons, belief fixation, and the truth. On this view, belief fixation often occurs independent of self-conscious consideration of reasons. This need not make belief fixation irrational or unrelated to the truth, for we may in many cases be responsive to good reasons even without self-consciously considering them. When we do turn to self-conscious consideration of reasons, on the skeptic's view, the activity of reason-giving may often have little effect on belief fixation. Far from reasons determining which beliefs are formed, as on the traditional view, it is the beliefs we antecedently hold that largely determine the reasons we will come to find. Reason-giving, on this view, is often a matter of rationalization. From the point of view of belief fixation, reason-giving is frequently epiphenomenal.[8]

Even when reason-giving is not epiphenomenal, on the skeptic's view, it may have little connection with the truth. Since our sense of plausibility is so easily affected by the standards of our community, a community whose

---

[8] I defend a qualified version of this view in my "Introspection and Misdirection," Chapter 1.

standards have been distorted by external factors will come to taint even the judgments of those otherwise unaffected by those distorting factors prevalent elsewhere in the community. When what passes for good reason really does play a role in belief fixation, then, it does not guide the self-conscious believer toward the truth, but instead serves only to further distort that person's judgment.

The issue between the skeptic about reason-giving and the person who places his trust in it is, I believe, an important one, and I would like to examine it in more detail. But before we try to figure out who is in the right here, we need to consider an objection to the skeptic's position, an objection that challenges its internal coherence. The skeptic's position is worthy of serious consideration only if it can avoid this particular challenge.

II

The challenge I have in mind is that the skeptic's view is self-undermining, for the skeptic, on the one hand, proclaims that the activity of reason-giving is not connected to the truth and that we should therefore be unmoved by it, and yet, on the other hand, in order to convince us of this particular view, the skeptic offers us reasons. If the skeptic is right about the activity of reason-giving, then her argument would not, and should not, convince us. According to the challenger, skepticism about reason-giving is thus self-undermining.[9]

This challenge fails, I believe, and it fails in two different ways. First, the skeptic's argument may be seen as a simple *reductio*.[10] The skeptic about reason-giving need not be seen as endorsing the argument she gives; instead, she may be seen as merely showing that the position of the person who puts his trust in reason-giving is internally inconsistent; that is, it fails to meet that person's own standards. The skeptic, on this view, demonstrates an internal tension in the view of the person who places his trust in

---

[9] The objection is similar to an objection frequently presented to total skepticism: that the total skeptic undermines his own position in arguing for it because the presentation of any such argument implicitly commits the skeptic to the existence of some sort of knowledge whose existence he explicitly denies.

[10] This follows the standard response to the claim that total skepticism is self-defeating. See, e.g., Robert Fogelin, *Pyrrhonian Reflections on Knowledge and Justification*, Oxford University Press, 1994; Michael Frede, "The Skeptic's Two Kinds of Assent and the Question of the Possibility of Knowledge," in *Essays in Ancient Philosophy*, University of Minnesota Press, 1987; and Michael Williams, "Skepticism without Theory," *Review of Metaphysics* 41(1988), 547–588.

rational argument, a tension which that person is in no position to resolve. This is sufficient to undermine the trust in rational argument.

Although this particular way of construing the skeptic's argument absolves her of the charge of undermining her own position, I think that there is a better way to represent what the skeptic is up to. I thus turn to a second response to our challenger.

As I see it, the skeptic does not mean merely to offer a *reductio* in the manner just explained. Instead, the skeptic wishes to endorse the position that reason-giving is so frequently a matter of mere rationalization, and our plausibility judgments so frequently off the mark, that reason should not be taken at face value. Indeed, this particular view of reason-giving is offered as the best available explanation of the social phenomenon of inquiring about and presenting reasons for belief. On this account of the skeptic's position, the charge of internal inconsistency, of self-defeat, is more acute. For on this account, the skeptic is presenting a rational argument *that she endorses* for the view that rational arguments should not produce conviction. How could such a position fail to be self-defeating?

The answer to this question lies in the recognition that our skeptic about reason-giving is not a *total* skeptic; indeed, she is very far from it. She is not a skeptic about the possibility of rational belief. She merely denies that a certain activity, an activity that many see as paradigmatically rational, is, indeed, genuinely rational, at least in the typical case. On the skeptic's view, rational belief is not only possible, it is often actual. Beliefs that are not self-consciously arrived at are frequently responsive to reason. Moreover, although the skeptic does not accept the practice of reason-giving at face value, this does not mean that the skeptic is forced to reject every case of reason-giving as bogus. Rather, her view about the frequency of reason-giving as reason-responsive, and reason-giving as mere rationalization, is just the reverse of the person who places his trust in the practice of giving reasons.

Consider the attitude of a rational and cautious person when buying a used car. Such a person will be faced with a good deal of reason-giving on the part of the used car salesman, and it may well be that, if taken at face value, the reasons offered for various purchases are wholly convincing. From the point of view of logic alone, the used car salesman's reasoning is impeccable. But the rational and cautious person does not take the used car salesman's arguments at face value.[11] Rather, in this situation, although

---

[11] When I speak of taking an argument at face value, I do not mean to exclude all critical evaluation; taking an argument at face value is not to be identified with gullibility. There is, however, an important difference between focusing on the subject matter of the argument given, however

one does not simply ignore everything which is said, one does not simply evaluate the logical cogency of the arguments offered either. One may certainly approach argument in this way at the used car lot, while forming beliefs on the basis of argument on other occasions.

Now the skeptic about reason-giving sees the practice of reason-giving generally in much the way that we all regard the arguments of the used car salesman. The skeptic is not concerned about dishonesty or insincerity; rather, she is concerned about sincere rationalization and a distorted sense of plausibility. But just as we all regard the used car salesman's utterances and arguments with a great deal of suspicion, the skeptic sees the default situation almost everywhere as one in which rational argument should not be taken at face value. By the same token, there are situations in which we will come to believe at least some of what the used car salesman tells us because we have independent grounds for overcoming our prima facie distrust. Similarly, the skeptic will insist that the prima facie concern about rationalization and distorted judgment is one that is not only in principle but in practice surmountable, and that when these concerns are properly defeated, we should follow the arguments where they lead. Reason-giving is not automatically irrelevant epistemically, on the skeptic's view; it should simply be regarded as irrelevant until proven otherwise.

Now it is important to recognize that the skeptic does not simply apply this approach to others, assuming that she herself is immune to rationalization or distorted judgment. Rather, she approaches her own explicit reasoning with the same degree of suspicion with which she approaches that of others. After all, her reason for concern about others has to do with rationalization and misguided judgment, not lack of sincerity, and the person who offers sincere rationalizations or whose judgment is somehow misguided is not only a purveyor of misleading arguments but a consumer of them as well. Thus, on the skeptic's view, we should approach all argument, even our own, with the default understanding that it reflects rationalization or misguided judgment, a mere cover for reasons that could not pass rational scrutiny if fully exposed. If an argument is to be taken at face value, then, there must be reason for supposing that the default condition does not apply.

There is no question that it is more difficult to do this in the first-person case than it is in the third-person case. If I can take my own reasoning at face value, then when I consider the reasoning of others of whom I have

critically, and turning one's attention to the motivations of the person giving it. I see the first as taking the argument at face value, whereas the second is what the skeptic has in mind instead.

reason to be suspicious, I have considerable resources on which to draw. In particular, I may reason self-consciously and explicitly about their motivations, their interests, and so on, in order to try to figure out when they are most likely to offer mere rationalizations and when it is that their reasoning can be accepted on its face. But if I cannot yet trust myself, or at least cannot yet trust my own explicit reasoning, then my resources are considerably thinner. Nevertheless, I believe that we can make perfectly good sense of the project to which the skeptic is committed.

After all, even those who are not skeptics about reason-giving in general will, on occasion, have reason to treat their own reason-giving with a certain measure of skepticism. We are all familiar with factors that may frequently interfere with the operation of good reasoning, and in ways that are typically invisible to the agent who is subject to them. We not only worry that judges who have a financial stake in the outcome of a certain decision might be biased by recognition of that fact; we worry that we ourselves might also be biased when put in such a situation. Now it just won't do in such a case to introspect and ask oneself whether one is subject to any untoward influence, and then, if one passes the test, go ahead and offer a decision. This won't do simply because we know that such biases work in ways that are not typically available to introspection. No doubt the best thing to do in this kind of case is simply to opt out; one should insist that one is not in a position to make the decision. But this is not to say that the only two options here are either to opt out or to follow the casual deliverances of introspection. And if opting out is not a possibility, then one may attempt systematically to eliminate, to the best of one's ability, the various factors that might serve as a source of bias.

Any such attempt will leave open the possibility of failure. One may, in spite of sincere and responsible attempts to eliminate all possible bias, nevertheless fall victim to it. But to say that there are no guarantees of getting things right here is not to distinguish this situation, epistemically, from any other. Evidence may be gathered here that is relevant to the question of one's own bias, and one may, in some cases, gain sufficient reason to believe that one is not biased in the particular case. At least I see no reason in principle or in practice why this should not be so.[12] But if in

---

[12] This is not to deny that individual cases may arrive in which one is not in a position to resolve the question of one's own bias. Cases must, however, be dealt with individually. There is no all-purpose argument to show either that one cannot have good evidence that one is bias-free or that one must always be able to determine whether one is influenced by bias.

this sort of case one may reasonably eliminate the hypothesis that one is moved by rationalization, then the skeptic may do the same. And once the skeptic can eliminate the likelihood of her own bias, in some particular case, then she may approach others in the way we all approach used car dealers. The task of evaluating reasoning for the skeptic is thus much more elaborate than it is for the person who takes reason-giving at face value, but it is not in principle impossible.[13]

In addition, it is important to point out that the skeptic about reason-giving is likely to be, as I mentioned briefly above, suspicious about pieces of reasoning in direct proportion to their logical perspicuity: the more detailed and carefully crafted the argument, the greater the suspicion that rationalization is at work.[14] Reason-giving of a more discursive sort will thus evoke little suspicion. The late Supreme Court Justice William Brennan Jr. described his own style of judicial decision-making, very much in this spirit, as seeking a "range of emotional and intuitive responses" rather than "lumbering syllogisms of reason."[15] The skeptic about reason-giving will thus have substantial resources with which to address and resolve, in many cases, her concerns about rationalization. Where she cannot turn back these concerns, she will simply ignore the arguments given.

The skeptic's view is not self-undermining. More than this, I believe, it is a view that needs to be taken quite seriously. So let us do that.

---

[13] I do not believe that this is the only way in which one might extricate oneself from the concern about rationalization. In particular, I believe that there may well be cases in which one might rationally eliminate concern about rationalization in particular others while still harboring reasonable concern about one's own propensity to rationalize. But I need not insist on this in order to extricate the skeptic about rational argument from the charge of undermining herself.

[14] Even as great a champion of rational argument as W. V. Quine has expressed a sentiment that is similar in important ways to that of the skeptic. Consider Quine's account of attending the American Philosophical Association convention with Carnap:

> We moved with Carnap as henchmen through the metaphysicians' camp. We beamed with partisan pride when he countered a diatribe of Arthur Lovejoy's in his characteristically reasonable way, explaining that if Lovejoy means A then p, and if he means B then q. I had yet to learn how unsatisfying this way of Carnap's could sometimes be. ("Homage to Carnap," in *The Ways of Paradox and Other Essays*, revised and enlarged ed., Harvard University Press, 1976, 42)

See also Robert Nozick's remarks about what he calls "coercive philosophy" in *Philosophical Explanations*, Harvard University Press, 1981, 4–8, in which he rejects the method of doing philosophy by way of "knock-down arguments" in favor of the more discursive "philosophical explanations."

[15] Quoted by Alex Kozinski in "The Great Dissenter," *New York Times Book Review*, July 6, 1997, 15.

III

The skeptic's view may at first sound like the mirror image of some well-known epistemic principles, principles that, though controversial, have a long history. I have in mind, for example, Thomas Reid's Principle of Credulity,[16] the idea that one should take other people's utterances to be true unless one has specific reason to believe otherwise, and Roderick Chisholm's various principles of evidence,[17] which involve accepting the "testimony of the senses" at face value, unless one has specific counterevidence. These principles are often explained by way of an analogy with the legal doctrine that one should assume a defendant innocent until proven guilty. In the case of Reid and of Chisholm, various sources of evidence are taken at face value unless there is some reason on the other side. Special reason is required to dismiss these sources of evidence; none is required if we are to follow where they seem to lead. The skeptic seems to have exactly the opposite presumption: reason-giving is to be distrusted until there is special reason to believe otherwise.

Chisholm defends his principles of evidence, however, as justified a priori, and it is important to recognize that the skeptic about reason-giving does not see her approach to reason-giving as having any such status. Rather, her presumption about reasoning is seen as an empirical hypothesis that, on her view, is well supported by available evidence. We may understand the skeptic's position only if we see it in that light.

We all recognize that sincere rationalization sometimes occurs, and that on such occasions, we would do well not to take the rationalizer's arguments, however logically impeccable, at face value. What the skeptic believes is that there is a fairly strong correlation between the logical perspicuity with which arguments tend to be offered and the amount of rationalization that underlies them. There is nothing intrinsically wrong with logic or good reasoning itself on this view; any such view would be absurd. Rather, as a matter of empirical fact, it is argued, those who tend to present their arguments with the greatest logical perspicuity are also, on those occasions, most frequently offering rationalizations, or at least so frequently offering rationalizations as to make the best epistemic policy the one of adopting the skeptic's presumption.

Consider the contemporary practice of philosophy, in which a very high premium is attached to giving detailed and logically perspicuous

---

[16] *Essays on the Intellectual Powers of Man*, MIT Press, 1969.
[17] *Theory of Knowledge*, 3rd ed., Prentice-Hall, 1989.

arguments. Surely philosophy is one of the natural homes of logical perspicuity. Is there reason to think that philosophers ought to be especially concerned about the possibility of rationalization? I think that there is. In ethics, for example, there is more than a little reason to think that a philosopher's views about right and wrong may often derive from features of that philosopher's upbringing that would do nothing at all to confer any justification on the views that result. For example, in many cases, a person's views about right and wrong are deeply influenced by that person's religious upbringing, even when that person would not appeal to any religious doctrine in support of those views. Now I do not mean to suggest that a religious origin for a view is automatically a source of distortion; but we all believe that some religious origins of moral views are an important source of distortion. When a person's view is due to some such distorting influence, and that person is able to offer detailed and logically perspicuous arguments that somehow sidestep the real source of the person's view, the worry about rationalization and its influence is particularly acute.

Nor is this peculiar to ethics. In social and political philosophy, there is also special reason to worry about the influence of distorting factors. We each have financial and personal interests that are at stake in any social and political arrangement. The idea that we might be subject to rationalization when considering which arrangements are most just is hardly a paranoid fantasy. It would, indeed, be quite remarkable if such factors rarely came to influence our views about justice, equality, and the like.

Nor do I think that this concern is rightly limited to moral philosophy broadly construed. Although the potential sources of distortion and subsequent rationalization are, I think, both most obvious and most pressing in the moral sphere, I would not wholly exempt other areas of philosophy from these concerns. Moreover, when we consider the extent to which our philosophical views are ripe for biasing influences and subsequent rationalization, it seems that, at a minimum, the responsible philosopher ought to be especially concerned about the possibility of rationalization's playing a large role in the adoption and defense of philosophical views. Here, as elsewhere, merely introspecting to see whether one's own views might have such a source is not a responsible reaction to the problem. Something much more nearly akin to the difficult project the skeptic about reason-giving is forced into may be forced on responsible philosophers as well.

Many will find this suggestion distasteful and, more to the point, epistemically counterproductive. It seems distasteful because in place of the rational discussion of substantive issues in ethics, for example, the skeptic seems to be endorsing the suggestion that when someone offers an argument for some moral view, the first thing we should think about, rather than the issue in moral philosophy that our interlocutor has attempted to raise, is the psychology of our discussant. Only by first analyzing our interlocutor's motivations may we determine whether the argument offered, and indeed, the person offering it, are to be taken seriously. It is surely distasteful to entertain such a suggestion, and it would surely be rude to behave in such a way. A person's motivations for offering an argument do sometimes need to be considered, but surely we entertain such thoughts only when the arguments offered fall very far short of logical standards. Entertaining questions about a person's motivations in offering an argument should be a last resort, not the first.

Leaving issues of etiquette aside, this strategy will also surely strike many as epistemically counterproductive, and for more than one reason. First, it will erode the quality of debate by distracting people from the issues we care most about – the moral issues, say – and focusing discussion on issues that are irrelevant to our real concerns: our interlocutors' motivations. In addition, raising these kinds of issues about people is not likely to be met with equanimity. Raising such personal issues as a subject's motivation in offering an argument, and, in effect, challenging that person's intellectual integrity, are not likely to allow for any issues at all to be discussed in ways that will allow for their resolution. But finally, and most importantly, the issue of a person's motivation in offering arguments is likely to be far more difficult to resolve than the substantive issue under investigation in, say, ethics. We have little access to the information we would need to understand fully a person's motivations, at least unless we know the individual extremely well. Moreover, there is more reason to be concerned about the possibility of rationalization in discussion of these personal issues of character than there is in most any of the issues that might be under discussion in the first place. Someone who is genuinely worried about the effects of rationalization in others and in himself should recognize that even so much as entertaining the issue of a person's motivation in offering an argument dramatically increases the likelihood that rationalization will come into play. Focusing on arguments themselves does not assure that rationalization will not play a role, but it is a better strategy than our skeptic is offering, the strategy of examining people's motivations directly.

There is, I believe, a great deal of good sense in this response to the skeptic's suggestions, but before I reply on behalf of the skeptic, I wish to point out how much of the skeptic's position is already granted in this response. This response grants that the concern about rationalization and misguided judgment is a legitimate one and, indeed, does not even insist that the skeptic's assessment of the situation is terribly wide of the mark. There is a need to get around the problem with which a tendency to rationalization and bad judgment presents us, and whereas the skeptic proposes one solution to that – involving an assessment of people's motivations – our respondent has in mind a different solution: simply focusing on argument unless, in the final resort, the arguments themselves are so bad that some view about a person's motivations is rationally forced on us. Focusing on the quality of argument here is seen as a pragmatic strategy for dealing with the very problem the skeptic raises, and the skeptic's strategy, it is argued, merely exacerbates the very real problem about which she is herself concerned.

In considering this response to the skeptic, we may therefore, at least temporarily, accept the skeptic's account of the problem – that apparently rational argument is often deeply infected by rationalization – and focus on the merits of the two solutions being offered. What I wish to suggest is that neither of these two solutions is correct across the board; any reasonable response to the problem will, I believe, require a mixture of these two strategies. How much of each strategy should be used will depend, to a very large extent, on one's assessment of the ultimate source of the problem about rationalization.

Consider our respondent's suggestion that issues about a person's motivation in offering an argument are more difficult, epistemically, than the issues addressed by the argument itself; better then to focus on the issue at hand than to try to clear up questions about the person's motivation before turning to the issue he attempted to raise. This is simply not true in all cases. There are, without a doubt, cases in which a person's motivation in offering an argument is entirely transparent, and what is transparent is that the person is offering a rationalization for something believed on other grounds. Moreover, in some cases of this sort, we are in no position to address the issue that the rationalizer attempted to raise; we simply do not know enough about the issue to enter into discussion with him. In such cases, we should not take the arguments offered by the rationalizer at face value. We should adopt the skeptic's strategy and opt out of the discussion. So we do not want to adopt the respondent's strategy across the board.

But how often do situations like this occur? How often are we in a position to attribute a rationalization to someone, or at least have a strong prima facie concern about it? How often is the question about an interlocutor's motivation more easily resolved than the question the interlocutor wishes to raise? This is where, I believe, a particularly interesting difference between the skeptic and her respondent comes out.

Here is one possibility. Rationalization may well occur quite frequently, but the sources of rationalization may be many and idiosyncratic. Thus, when I offer arguments, they are distorted by my peculiar concerns and irrationalities; when others offer arguments, concerns and irrationalities peculiar to them go to work. If this is the case, then figuring out the kind of rationalization that is operative in a particular argument, or whether rationalization is operative, will require a great deal of knowledge of the particular individual involved. We will rarely have such knowledge, and thus the epistemic task of determining the extent and kind of rationalizations involved in particular arguments will typically be quite difficult. This will make the skeptic's project of examining the motivations behind individual arguments practically infeasible. At the same time, it may also make the skeptic's project unnecessary. For if the sources of distortion vary a great deal, then merely focusing on the arguments themselves may be a very good strategy. My biased recall of relevant information may be salient to others who lack my particular bias, and they will bring this into the open, not by attending to the possible sources of my bias, but simply by focusing on the issue under discussion. The public discussion of reasons here, although it brackets discussion of sources of distortion, will thereby help to overcome the problem that the distorting influences present. This, of course, is just what the respondent to the skeptic suggested.[18]

But there is another possibility, and this involves a very different picture of the sources of distortion and rationalization. Thus, suppose that instead of these sources' being varied and idiosyncratic, there are a very small number of sources of significant distortion and rationalization. Let us suppose, indeed, that there is a single major source of distortion and rationalization that is very widespread. Thus, for example, Marxists have suggested that class interests form just such a source of distortion and rationalization; some feminists have suggested that the interests of male

---

[18] This is just a special case of the point that by using different measuring instruments to detect a given phenomenon, we may dramatically decrease the likelihood that our results are mere artifacts of the instruments themselves. The person who places his trust in argument sees individuals as roughly reliable detectors; their individual biases are features of the detectors that lead to experimental artifacts; and these artifacts are revealed as such by using other individuals, that is, other roughly good detectors, who are likely to exhibit a different pattern of experimental artifacts. The extent to which this method works in practice depends on the extent to which the different detectors used are both roughly reliable and exhibit the presupposed difference in experimental artifacts.

domination play such a role.[19] If some such hypothesis is correct, then the situation is exactly the reverse of the one described above. First, we need not know much about the particular individual offering an argument to have some sense of the extent or source of rationalization likely to be playing a role; our epistemic task here, once we have come to understand the social factors at work in society at large, is easy. And second, the idea that merely focusing on argument will allow the sources of distortion to come out into the open would, on this view, be mistaken. Because the ideas that tend to be discussed, on this scenario, are all shaped by a common bias, the hope that idiosyncratic biases will cancel one another out misses the point.[20] On this view, the skeptic's strategy is not only epistemically feasible, it is the only strategy that is likely to address the problem of bias and rationalization adequately.

Note too that if the skeptic is right in thinking that public debate is largely shaped by a single source of bias, and that this bias is extremely likely to come into play and overwhelm discussion when certain members of the epistemic community are part of the debate, then a policy of isolation or exclusion will be appropriate. This is just the opposite of the policy of including as many members of the community as possible in discussion in the hope of having the various biases cancel one another out. The policy of isolation or exclusion comes with dangers of its own, of course. But which of these policies best gets at the truth is very much dependent on features of the epistemic community, and the skeptic about

---

[19] Notice that these are, in effect, socialized versions of the kinds of problems suggested in the "heuristics and biases" literature of Tversky and Kahneman and Nisbett and Ross. (See Daniel Kahneman, Paul Slovic, and Amos Tversky, eds., *Judgment under Uncertainty: Heuristics and Biases*, Cambridge University Press, 1982; and Nisbett and Ross, op. cit.) The social fixation of the reasoning strategies that concern the skeptic is of special concern because such a process works far faster than Darwinian methods for fixing inferential strategies. Social fixation of reasoning strategies is Lamarckian.

[20] Note that Nagel's assumption in the passage quoted in Note 2 that there is "equal access to the court of reason" is thus denied by many Marxists and certain feminists. Consider also Frank Sulloway's claim (*Born to Rebel: Birth Order, Family Dynamics, and Creative Lives*, Pantheon Books, 1996) that firstborns are strongly disposed to resist conceptually innovative ideas and that later-borns are strongly disposed to accept them. Add to this Sulloway's contention that firstborns tend to be disproportionately successful in their careers. Sulloway notes:

> [This] has practical implications for the selection of scientific commissions and the evaluation of their conclusions. Because commission[s] tend to be packed with eminent individuals (and hence firstborns), their votes should perhaps be "weighted" to adjust for individual biases in attitudes toward innovation. (537 n. 43)

This suggestion of Sulloway's, which I take to be eminently sensible, is just an instance of the strategy recommended by the skeptic about reason-giving.

reason and the person confident about reason simply have differing views about the nature of that community.

Those who have placed their trust in reason and public discussion of argument are thus betting that the second of these possibilities governing the nature and distribution of bias – a small number of distorting influences affecting the entire tenor of debate – is not the case. The skeptic, on the other hand, suspects that it is precisely this problem that is responsible for our current situation. The skeptic's hypothesis, I believe, is one that we need to take seriously, and the bet that we make when we place our trust in the public discussion of reason is one of which we need to be aware. It is only by taking the skeptic's hypothesis seriously and, if possible, laying it to rest, that our trust in public reason may be fully rational. Moreover, insofar as the rational commitment to the public discussion of reasons presupposes a certain social structure – one in which the effects of bias and rationalization are canceled out – those who are committed to the public discussion of reason should also be committed to ensuring that such a social structure is more than just an ideal; we should be committed to making sure that it is realized and sustained.[21]

---

[21] I want to thank Louise Antony, David Christensen, Mark Kaplan, William Mann, Derk Pereboom, Joel Pust, Nishi Shah, Miriam Solomon, and William Talbott for especially helpful comments on drafts of this essay, often by way of vigorous disagreement. Versions of the essay were read at Middlebury College, Brigham Young University, Rutgers University, the University of Michigan, Universidad Nacional Autónoma de México, and Dalhousie University, where helpful discussions resulted in numerous changes.

4

The Impurity of Reason

Laurence BonJour's new book[1] on the a priori will force us all to rethink our commitments on this important topic. It is a wonderfully clear piece of work, both elegant in its prose style and forceful in its argument. BonJour takes on the empiricist orthodoxy and mounts a vigorous campaign in favor of a moderate rationalism. The arguments in this book are ones with which we will all need to come to terms and from which we will all learn. Perhaps what impresses me most about this book, and about BonJour's work generally, is its intellectual integrity: BonJour is not only a devastating critic of opposing views; he is utterly merciless in exposing what he takes to be weaknesses in his own position. Rather than gloss over difficulties or attempt to minimize them, BonJour is always at great pains to highlight not only the strengths of his position, but the problems it faces as well. This makes the book a model of how to write about philosophical issues, and indeed, a model of how to think about them as well.

Unqualified as my admiration is for this book, I remain unconvinced of its central theses. In what follows, I outline the substance of my main disagreements with it.

I A Case against the A Priori

Let me begin by briefly presenting a case against the a priori. There is nothing original in this presentation; it is surely nothing more than an argument to be found in Quine.[2] At the same time, it is worth pointing out that this version of the case against the a priori does not depend on any kind of skepticism about meaning, let alone on views about the alleged indeterminacy of translation or inscrutability of reference.

---

[1] *In Defense of Pure Reason: A Rationalist Account of A Priori Justification*, Cambridge University Press, 1998.
[2] See especially "Two Dogmas of Empiricism," in *From a Logical Point of View*, Harper, 1961.

There are many claims which we seem justified in believing and whose justification does not depend in any obvious way on anything empirical. The claims of mathematics and logic are among these, as are such claims as this: For any three events *a*, *b*, and *c*, if *a* occurs before *b*, and *b* occurs before *c*, then *a* occurs before *c* and not either simultaneous with it or after it. Claims of this sort present us with a strong intuitive case for the existence of a priori knowledge. The prima facie case for the a priori here is strong not only because these claims are clearly justified and yet have no obvious connection with any empirical evidence, but because, for many of these claims and for many of us, it is hard to imagine what could even count as empirical evidence for or against them. When thought about in this way, these claims present a prima facie case for a particularly strong version of the claim that there is such a thing as a priori knowledge, for these cases make it seem as if there is knowledge which is not only independent of any experience, but also immune to rational revision. This strong version of rationalism is, of course, stronger than the one BonJour wishes to defend, but it is very well represented historically. Indeed, the kind of moderate rationalism BonJour defends is a relative newcomer to the philosophical scene.

Now our inability to conceive of how a claim might be revised in the face of empirical evidence could be due to a number of different things. It could be due to direct and infallible rational insight. Or it could be due to some sort of fallible rational insight. Or it could be due to some sort of very indirect empirically conditioned theory construction. Or it could be due to a failure of imagination. But this much is clear: a number of the claims which seemed wholly transparent to reason, and which many very smart people literally could not imagine being false, turned out actually to be false. There are claims in mathematics and logic which led to a variety of paradoxes, and there are, for example, the implications of relativity theory which showed that the absolute notion of simultaneity was indeed mistaken, so that, under conditions of causal independence, when one event *a* precedes another event *c* in a given frame of reference, it will be simultaneous with it in a second frame of reference, and it will follow it in still a third. In short, events in time are not linearly ordered in a unique way. It is no exaggeration to say that the relativistic theory of time was one which pre-Einsteinian theorists could not conceive of, and our powers of conception were changed as a result of the progress of empirical theorizing.

The correct view of temporal order is clearly empirically justified, and, in retrospect, our inability to imagine that time should be anything but linearly ordered seems like nothing more than a failure of imagination.

While the view of time as uniquely linearly ordered nicely cohered with our other empirical beliefs prior to Einstein, the successive elaboration of physical theory showed that such a linear ordering was a genuine physical impossibility. An apparently a priori justified belief was thus overthrown by empirical evidence and rationally replaced with a (more nearly) correct belief which was straightforwardly justified empirically.

Just as the Einsteinian view of time is justified by way of its coherence with the rest of our current beliefs, the earlier view of time now seems to have been justified by way of its coherence with earlier beliefs. It did not seem, at the time, to be any sort of inductively based conclusion from our ubiquitous experience of temporal succession, but in retrospect, such an account does not seem implausible.

In addition, the way in which the pre-Einsteinian view of time was overthrown is of special import here. When I discover that the house I took to be red has in fact been repainted and is now blue, my beliefs are revised in light of empirical evidence, but my conceptual repertoire remains unchanged. In the move from a Newtonian to an Einsteinian view of temporal succession, however, belief revision takes place hand-in-hand with conceptual change. Our earlier concept of simultaneity was found to be inadequate to the facts, and as a result, it had to be replaced by a more empirically adequate concept. Empirical theory construction, and rational revision of empirical theories, includes not only simple replacement of one proposition by another – such as the replacement of the belief that the house is red by the belief that the house is blue – but successive accommodation of our concepts to the real structure of the world. An important part of empirical science, and an important part of mathematics, set theory, and logic, involves the development of theoretically adequate concepts. For this very reason, a fully adequate theory of rational belief revision would require an account of rational conceptual change. Justification of our beliefs and theoretical defense of the adequacy of our conceptual framework are two sides of the same coin.[3]

Now where do these considerations leave the notion of a priori justification? First, consider the radical rationalist, that is, the traditional rationalist view on which some a priori truths are appreciated by way of direct

---

[3] Here I disagree with BonJour, who comments that "while the issue of concept acquisition is important in its own right, it is not connected in any very close or essential way with the issue of justification; thus a concept of a priori justification that in effect conflates the two issues is less perspicuous than one that does not" (9–10). BonJour seems to recognize here that if one grants, as I argue we must, that justification of one's beliefs requires a defense of their constituent concepts, it will be very hard to defend the possibility of a priori justification.

and infallible rational insight. It is certainly open to the radical rationalist to insist that the particular claims which turned out to be false were not among the ones directly and infallibly appreciated by rational insight; indeed, they could not be since they turned out to be false. But this does not show, of course, that there are not others among the beliefs we cannot currently imagine being false, which are themselves the product of direct and infallible rational insight. There is nothing internally inconsistent about such a view, but it is a philosophical non-starter. The problems presented by the examples from the history of science, logic, and mathematics cannot be dealt with so simply. Claims like the simultaneity principle were indistinguishable in their epistemic credentials, prior to Einstein, from the claims which currently seem immune to empirical refutation. Infallible rational insight is capable of doing real epistemic work only if one is in a position to tell when one is actually making use of it, rather than simply seeming to make use of it. What the examples from the history of the sciences show is that we have no such capability.[4]

But to do away with the radical rationalist might seem to do no more than help to motivate BonJour's own brand of moderate rationalism. For BonJour makes no claims of infallibility or immunity from rational revision by empirical evidence. And even in the case of claims, such as the simultaneity principle, which turned out to be false, there is room for the view that fallible rational insight might have served as a source of justification which was subsequently undermined by empirical evidence. Other claims which currently are not undermined by such evidence might thus enjoy a wholly a priori justification.

Now I do not think that such a view is internally inconsistent and, as will become clear momentarily, I am not even committed to the view that nothing could possibly be justified a priori. But I do believe that a good deal more needs to be said if the appeal to a priori justification is to do any real epistemological work. The a priorist may well point out that we do not give up the claim that how things look is real evidence of how they actually are merely because appearances are sometimes deceiving;[5] and, by the same token, one should not give up the claim that the appearance of a priority is evidence of truth even if, on occasion, appearances of this kind have led to mistakes. At this point it may seem that the a priorist and I merely have a

---

[4] BonJour himself makes this point. Noting that philosophers who claimed that a priori insight is infallible then proceeded to disagree on which claims were actually a priori, BonJour comments, "to resolve this conflict by saying that the mistaken claims did not reflect *genuine* instances of rational insight threatens to trivialize the claim of infallibility" (110 n. 17).

[5] BonJour himself makes this point (142), crediting it to Tony Anderson.

disagreement about the frequency with which claims allegedly known a priori have, in the past, turned out to be false: I myself believe that the relative frequency here is quite high, while the a priorist must believe that the frequency is very low.

But the reason for real skepticism about the substance of appeals to a priori justification lies elsewhere. The force of the examples from the history of science, mathematics, and logic is that an agent's inability, at a given time, to conceive of things being otherwise has often given way, as a product of empirical theorizing, to the recognition that things are otherwise. Thus, many of the claims which we cannot currently imagine being false may well be ones which are indeed false, and which we will be able, with the progress of theory, to recognize as false at some suitable time in the future. In addition, it is likely as well that some of the claims which we currently cannot conceive to be false, and which are in fact true, are ones which we could rationally give up in the face of misleading evidence, for it would be surprising indeed if the only claims we could rationally come to give up, among the ones which we currently cannot imagine being false, are the ones which are in fact false. All of this suggests, I believe, that claims to be justified in a belief independent of any empirical evidence are highly suspect. Surely it would be unreasonable, given the extent to which we have been mistaken about such matters in the past, to turn our backs on questions about the extent to which apparently a priori claims fit with current empirical theories. Questions of this sort are always worth entertaining, even if, in the end, we should find that an apparently a priori claim continues to seem justified entirely independent of empirical information. So from the point of view of actually seeking to provide good reasons for believing a claim, its relation to empirical claims will always be relevant.

Now this is not to say that there could not be any claims which are genuinely justified independent of any empirical information, and which are such that they could not be rationally overturned by any empirical theorizing.[6] Perhaps there are such claims. But it would be rash to believe that one has identified such a claim, given the history of claims for empirical independence. And what this means is that the issue of a priority is unimportant from an epistemological point of view. Fit with empirical beliefs is always rationally at issue even if there should be cases of beliefs which somehow could not be given up in the face of empirical evidence. The appeal to a priority can do no epistemological work.

---

[6] This was pointed out to me by David Christensen.

Traditional rationalists, who held that rational insight is infallible, and, moreover, that one has direct and infallible access to the fact that one is making use of such insight, were in a position to defend the epistemological importance of the a priori. But once one allows, as BonJour does, and, as I believe, one must, that this radical position is untenable, the case for the epistemological importance of a priori knowledge is made far more difficult.

II BonJour's Prima Facie Case in Favor of the A Priori

Let me turn more directly to BonJour's arguments. While BonJour wishes to defend a moderate rationalism, a view which avoids the wholly unreasonable and Panglossian view of our intellectual faculties found in the traditional radical rationalists, it is important to stress that BonJour's defense of the a priori is in no way a timid one. BonJour wishes to defend the view that (i) "there is genuine *a priori* justification that is not limited in its scope to tautologies or matters of definition"; (ii) "it is arguably difficult or impossible to make good sense of most if not all claims of empirical knowledge, and indeed of reasoning generally, while eschewing any *a priori* appeal"; and (iii) "philosophy is *a priori* if it is anything (or at least if it is anything intellectually respectable); and ... the practice of even those who most explicitly reject the idea of substantive *a priori* justification inevitably involves the tacit appeal to insights and modes of reasoning that can only be understood as *a priori* in character, if they are justified at all" (ix).

BonJour begins by making a prima facie case for the importance of a priori justification. First, there are the examples of claims apparently justified a priori. BonJour recognizes that "the appeal to such examples can be resisted, at least initially, in ways that may seem to deprive it of much of its force" (2). Those who are skeptical about the epistemological importance of a priori justification will appeal here, as I did above, to the history of science. BonJour comments about this move that "such rejoinders vary widely in their intuitive plausibility, both in general and in relation to the various specific examples, but they are at least dialectically tenable so long as the present argument stands alone" (3). Now as I have indicated above, I believe that the appeal to the history of science is more than just a dialectically tenable move; I believe it places substantial pressure on the suggestion that the category of a priori knowledge can do any real epistemological work. But since BonJour grants that the examples by themselves cannot do all the work here, it is particularly important to see what it is which will bear the real weight of supporting the claim for the significance of the a priori.

Here, BonJour provides two additional arguments, one of which is a generalization of the other. BonJour argues that "justification of at least the vast preponderance of what we think of as empirical knowledge must involve an indispensable *a priori* component – so that the only alternative to the existence of *a priori* justification is skepticism of a most radical kind." This radical skepticism results from rejecting the a priori because, if we assume foundationalism, some sort of a priori principles are required in order to move beyond foundational knowledge. Generalizing this point, BonJour concludes that rejection of the a priori brings with it a total inability to ground inference of any sort. "Thus we see that the repudiation of all *a priori* justification is apparently tantamount to the repudiation of argument or reasoning generally, thus amounting in effect to intellectual suicide" (5).

Now what puzzles me about this argument is a question about to whom it is directed. The argument makes two explicit assumptions: first, it assumes internalism about justification; and second, it assumes foundationalism. Now I agree with BonJour entirely that internalist foundationalists will need to appeal to a priori justification, and that they will be unable to justify claims which go beyond the foundations of knowledge without such an appeal; rejecting the a priori would amount, on such a view, to the abandonment of reasoning generally. But internalist foundationalists have never rejected the a priori. The rejection of the a priori has come from philosophers who reject internalism or foundationalism or both. Certainly Quine is no foundationalist. The appeal to examples from the history of science, and the holism which they are meant to illustrate, is designed to motivate an alternative to foundationalism, at least as traditionally conceived. And contemporary externalists, whose views constitute another source of the rejection of the a priori, are not going to accept the premises of this argument either. So this argument seems to be addressed only to those who already accept its conclusion.

Now I recognize that BonJour is no fan of externalism – he regards versions of externalism as "ultimately uninteresting evasions of the central epistemological issues" (1) – and he has an earlier book[7] in which the rejection of externalism is argued for in detail. He has also given up his earlier commitment to coherentism. My point is simply that the argument presented here fails to take the real opponents of the a priori seriously. The prima facie case in favor of the a priori thus depends entirely on the

---

[7] *The Structure of Empirical Knowledge*, Harvard University Press, 1985.

putative examples of a priori justification, and these, BonJour acknowledges, cannot bear a great deal of argumentative weight.

I would like to make one further point about the prima facie case for the a priori. Putative examples of a priori knowledge aside, BonJour presents one with an argument which has the form of an epistemic offer one can't refuse: accept a priori justification or else be doomed to a radical skepticism, an "intellectual suicide." It is the threat of skepticism here which is used to buttress the admittedly weak support which the putative examples of a priority provide the rationalist. But what is needed here is not some sort of epistemic threat. Rather, what is needed is some insight into the nature of the justificatory support which an appeal to the a priori might provide, or, failing that, and aligning oneself with the radical empiricists, some insight into how apparently a priori claims might be empirically justified. BonJour has done a masterful job, I believe, of showing the utter emptiness of moderate empiricist appeals to a priori justification. But the worry which his prima facie case for a priority, or rational insight, presents us with is that the threat of skepticism is being offered as a substitute for epistemological insight into the justification of apparently a priori claims. BonJour's comment that "the capacity for rational insight, though fundamental and irreducible, is in no way puzzling or especially in need of further explanation" (16) merely exacerbates this concern.

I don't mean to suggest that BonJour is alone in this. Quite the opposite; I believe that this problem is characteristic of appeals to a priority.[8]

Indeed, the success of BonJour's unrelenting and thoroughly clear-headed dissection of moderate empiricism merely brings this problem to the fore. This is a problem to which I will return.

III BonJour on Quine

An essential part of any defense of the a priori is a discussion of Quine's radical empiricism, and BonJour devotes a good deal of attention to Quine's views. Quine's arguments against the a priori are notoriously elusive, and even those largely sympathetic with the tenor of Quine's discussion of this issue, as I am, frequently reject, as I do, many central

---

[8] Another example of the use of such an epistemic offer one can't refuse, I believe, is to be found in Tyler Burge, "Content Preservation," *Philosophical Review* 102(1993), 457–488; see especially 470. David Christensen and I critically discuss this paper in "Testimony, Memory and the Limits of the A Priori," *Philosophical Studies* 86(1997), 1–20. Roderick Chisholm's work makes this kind of move central as well.

Quinean claims. But the Quinean case against the a priori has many strands, and the strand I wish to focus on, as my remarks above suggest, is the metaphor of the web of belief and the appeal to the history of science. BonJour's discussion of this part of "Two Dogmas" constitutes an important part of his rejection of radical empiricism.

BonJour's reading of the web metaphor follows Alex Orenstein, who summarizes the argument as follows:

> We are forced to recognize that from the fact that sentences cannot be tested in isolation but only as parts of systems of sentences, it follows that every sentence at all logically relevant to a test risks the danger of experimental refutation ... No sentence can be singled out as being in principle incorrigible; for in the attempt to fit theory to observation, any one sentence may become a candidate for revision. Logic and mathematics, and all other purported a priori knowledge, are parts of our system of background assumptions and are in principle open to revision. If a priori knowledge is knowledge that is justified independently of experience, then Quine denies that there is any.[9]

BonJour's view of this argument is that it "is in fact utterly question-begging" (76), because this appeal assumes precisely what is at issue, namely "that *epistemic rationality is concerned solely with adjusting one's beliefs to experience*" (76), a view which the rationalist, of course, denies. But I don't believe that this is the right way to understand the Quinean move. First, the web metaphor is designed to show that there is available a way of looking at things which makes sense of a thoroughgoing rejection of the a priori. This is particularly important given the highly intuitive appeal of the familiar examples of putatively a priori knowledge. The web metaphor offers some real promise of epistemological insight into the empirical justification of apparently a priori claims, a promise which has been fulfilled, I believe, by historical studies of science and mathematics. At the same time, and an essential part of making sense of the radical empiricist position, the web metaphor shows how to avoid the kind of skeptical threat to which rejection of the a priori might seem to lead. Since BonJour himself lays heavy stress on the threat of skepticism, this is a particularly important point here. Finally, the use of historical examples is absolutely essential to the position for it makes clear that the rejection of the a priori is empirically justified. This allows the Quinean to respond to the many who have suggested that the position is somehow self-undermining since the argument against the a priori, being philosophical

---

[9] Orenstein, *Willard Van Orman Quine*, Twayne, 1977, 85–86, quoted at BonJour 76.

in nature, must itself be justified, if at all, independent of experience.[10] The Quinean argument is neither self-undermining nor question-begging. It not only shows the coherence of the radical empiricist position, but also makes a strong case for the view that the category of a priori justified belief is epistemologically idle.

BonJour does have other concerns about the import of the web metaphor. In service of his rejection of the a priori, Quine is at pains to argue that any sentence can be given up. But, BonJour points out, the claim that any sentence can be given up is utterly trivial. For, first, the opponent of the a priori needs, at a minimum, to show that any sentence can be *rationally* given up (75). And second, not just any way of rationally giving up a sentence is relevant here. Thus, BonJour comments,

> To take an extreme example, it would surely be possible for our linguistic conventions to be altered, perhaps by governmental decree, in such a way that the sentence "two plus two equals four" would come to have the meaning that the sentence "two plus two equals seven" currently has. In such a situation, the former sentence would no doubt be "given up," but this plainly has no bearing on the claim that this sentence with its *present* meaning expresses an *a priori* justifiable claim. Thus Quine must seemingly claim, not merely that any sentence may be given up, but that any sentence may be given up *without having changed its meaning*. (74)

Now BonJour recognizes, of course, that Quine is not about to appeal to a notion of meaning here, but the upshot of the argument is clear: "*Quine himself* apparently needs something very much like the notion of meaning, or at least change of meaning, if he is to avoid an interpretation of his main premise that renders it trivial ... I see no reason to think that the substitution of any alternative formulation that is adequate to avoid the trivialization of his thesis would alter anything of substance" (74).

---

[10] BonJour himself endorses a version of this argument on 81:

> there is a powerful general argument that seems to show that there could in principle be no adequate justification for Quine's claim that there is no *a priori* justification. After all, the justification of such a claim would have to itself be either *a priori* or *a posteriori* in character. For a Quinean, it obviously cannot be *a priori*, but there seems to be no plausible way to construe it as *a posteriori*. Quine himself, surprisingly enough, does not seem to even see this problem.

Essentially the same criticism is made by George Bealer, Mark Kaplan, and Harvey Siegel. See Bealer, "The Incoherence of Empiricism," in Steven Wagner and Richard Warner, eds., Naturalism: A Critical *Appraisal*, University of Notre Dame Press, 1993, 163–196; Kaplan, "Epistemology Denatured," *Midwest Studies* 19(1994), 350–365; Siegel, "Empirical Psychology, Naturalized Epistemology and First Philosophy," *Philosophy of Science* 51(1984), 667–676.

I do not believe that BonJour is right about this; indeed, I do not believe that he is right either about Quine himself or about what I take to be the very widely shared skepticism about the a priori which Quine has engendered even apart from his rejection of intentional notions such as belief and meaning, and, still later, reference as well. Since I myself do not share Quine's rejection of intentional notions, I want to respond to BonJour's criticism of the Quinean argument in a way that does not presuppose this particular Quinean view. But I do also want to say a word or two about Quine's position.

Let me return, yet again, to Quine's allusion to examples from the history of science. This is what motivates the Quinean view that any sentence at all may be given up. I take it that here there is simply no question that the sentences given up are *rationally* given up. Thus, when Einstein gives up the Newtonian simultaneity principle, Einstein's change in view is a rational one. I don't have a criterion of rationality ready to hand, but none is needed here. Any account of rationality which rejects key transitions in the history of science such as this one as irrational is, in virtue of that very fact, suspect. The examples that Quine alludes to are thus ones in which apparently a priori claims were, indeed, rationally given up.

Similar remarks apply to BonJour's point about meaning change. We may remain neutral on the question of whether the notion of meaning is to be resuscitated or repudiated. BonJour's point that there are trivial ways in which we may come to give up a sentence – such as governmental decree that the word 'four' is now to stand for seven – has nothing to do with the historical examples to which Quine alludes. For those who endorse the Quinean rejection of intentional notions, these examples illustrate why it is that there is no principled way to draw a distinction between change in meaning and change in belief. For those who do not reject intentional notions, the Newton–Einstein example is a clear case of empirical theorizing forcing a rational change in a belief which earlier had all the hallmarks of a priority. Either way, the force of the examples remains.

It is worth pointing out here that developments in the philosophy of language subsequent to "Two Dogmas" have, I believe, reinforced the significance of this point, although in ways Quine himself would not endorse. What I have in mind here is the causal or historical theory of reference. BonJour's trivialization of the Quinean point that any sentence can be given up is achieved by governmental decree changing, as BonJour puts it, the "meaning" of the sentence "two plus two equals four." BonJour says that he sees "no reason to think that the substitution of any alternative formulation," one which avoids talk of meaning, "is adequate to avoid the trivialization of [the Quinean] thesis" (74). But BonJour's example involves a change of *reference*. And work on the causal theory of reference surely supports the idea that reference may remain fixed even across very substantial changes in theory, such as in the Newton–Einstein case.[11] So the causal theory of reference may be brought in here to explain how it is that the changes effected by empirical theorizing were, indeed, substantive changes in belief rather than merely stipulative verbal changes. So there is, I believe, a reformulation of the Quinean point which explains why these changes are not trivial.

But we need not insist on the causal theory of reference, for these examples stand by themselves. There are trivial ways of giving up sentences, and there are irrational ways of giving up sentences, but the examples from the history of science are neither of these. The historical examples thus seem to make a case for the claim that any sentence can rationally be given up in non-trivial ways.

IV Does Radical Empiricism Lead to Skepticism?

BonJour presses hard on the Quinean picture, urging that it leads to a most radical skepticism. I want to examine BonJour's arguments in detail.

Quine frequently appeals to such notions as simplicity, conservatism, explanatory adequacy, and the like. BonJour asks,

> What reason can be offered for thinking that a system of beliefs which is simpler, more conservative, explanatorily more adequate, etc., is thereby more likely to be true, that following such standards is at least somewhat conducive to finding the truth? Someone who had not rejected the possibility of *a priori* justification might attempt to offer an *a priori* argument for the truth-conduciveness of at least some of these standards ... But Quine has ruled out such an appeal. Moreover, it is clear at once that any attempt at an empirical argument for this sort of conclusion would inevitably be question-begging. (91)

Now the Quinean view here is, I believe, straightforward enough. Quine begins with the view that science has given us an increasingly complete and adequate view of the world; those who do not accept this claim are simply not being addressed by Quine. Moreover, given the success of the scientific

---

[11] BonJour's discussion of theories of direct reference in section 6.5 is independent of this point, and his criticism of what he calls the symbolic view of thought does not, I believe, bear on this point either. But the issues here are quite complicated and there simply is not space here to go into them.

enterprise, whatever methods have been used in the development of scientific theorizing are ones which we should ourselves adopt if we wish to have more accurate beliefs. There is a straightforwardly empirical question about the methods which have actually been used in the development of scientific theorizing, and Quine suggests that the progress of theory has been achieved through the use of appeal to such standards as conservatism, simplicity, etc. That there are such standards which apply more or less universally across time and across different subject-matters is a highly controversial claim; but that it is an empirical claim, on which evidence from the history of science bears, is undeniable.

Moreover, having formulated certain hypotheses about the standards actually employed in the development of scientific theorizing, one can reasonably ask for an explanation of why – or even whether – such standards should in fact be truth-conducive. BonJour insists that this is "question-begging, since it would have to appeal to at least some of these very standards" (91), but in actual practice the attempt to show that certain standards actually used are indeed truth-conducive proves to be highly non-trivial. To take a favorite example of mine, the Tversky and Kahneman work on the actual practice of inductive inference makes it look as if the practice is not the least bit truth-conducive. The question of whether such practices are, first appearances notwithstanding, useful in arriving at the truth has led to a voluminous and constructive literature in cognitive science.[12] BonJour gives the impression that the only thing that could, in principle, result from such Quinean investigations is a wholly pointless pat on the back: we use our methods to investigate whether our methods are truth-conducive, conclude that they are, and then stop. But the Quinean project of investigating the methods which we actually use, and then attempting to explain how they might actually work, turns out to be a constructive project with tremendous potential for revision of our standards. There are no guarantees in principle that such self-examination will lead to self-satisfaction, and, in practice, it has not.[13]

Now this Quinean practice of self-examination, while it does constructively address doubts about the truth-conduciveness of our actual epistemic practice, does not address a certain sort of skepticism. A radical skeptic

---

[12] See in Daniel Kahneman, Paul Slovic, and Amos Tversky, eds., *Judgment under Uncertainty: Heuristics and Biases*, Cambridge University Press, 1982. I have discussed this issue in detail in *Inductive Inference and Its Natural Ground*, MIT Press, 1993.

[13] For a particularly useful discussion of this point, see Michael Friedman, "Truth and Confirmation," *Journal of Philosophy* 76(1979), 361–382.

about the entire practice of science is certainly ignored by this particular argument. But this hardly shows, what BonJour contends, that

> Quine's own strictures rule out the possibility of his having any reason for regarding his standards of non-observational justification as truth-conducive and hence of his having any reason for construing the justification that they yield as epistemic justification. (91)

BonJour argues that things are even worse for Quine than his last remark would suggest. Referring, once again, to the standards of simplicity, conservatism, and the like, BonJour comments,

> it is unclear why these standards impose any real constraint at all on possible revisions. After all, any such standard, since it cannot on Quinean grounds be justified or shown to be epistemically relevant independently of considerations of adjustment to experience, is itself merely one more strand (or node?) in the web, and thus equally open to revision. Thus in any situation in which one possible revision of one's system of beliefs might seem to be more justified than another by appeal to such epistemic standards, one need apparently only revise or abandon the standards themselves to make the alternative revision at least as acceptable. (92)

Now this is an odd claim for BonJour to be making, given his commitment to moderate, rather than radical, rationalism. As a moderate rationalist, BonJour is committed to the view that even a priori justified claims may be rationally revised in light of further evidence. The complaint in the passage just quoted is that, in denying that our most fundamental epistemic standards are a priori justified, Quine must always leave open the possibility of revising the standards themselves; but the moderate rationalist, like the radical empiricist, is committed to the rational revisability of even our most fundamental epistemic standards. So if Quine's view leads to total skepticism for this reason, BonJour's moderate rationalism does as well.[14]

---

[14] I am not certain how much this conclusion would bother BonJour. In his earlier book, BonJour argued for an epistemic standard of justification which leads to a radical skepticism, as he himself forthrightly acknowledged (BonJour 1985, 105). Although BonJour now rejects some of the central arguments of that book, the present book, if I am right in what I say in this paragraph, may be quite similar: that is, it may exhibit a defense of an epistemic standard of justification which leads to total skepticism. My own conclusion is that some of the premises common to the two books are at fault. In particular, I am especially concerned about BonJour's commitment to a particularly strong form of internalism. (But see my remarks about BonJour's commitment to internalism at the end of the section on "The Positive Case for the A Priori.") To discuss this issue, however, would take me too far afield from the subject of the present book. I have discussed BonJour's internalism on several occasions: see my "How Internal Can You Get?," *Synthèse* 74 (1988), 313–327; "The Unattainability of Coherence," in J. Bender, ed., *The Current State of the Coherence Theory*, Kluwer, 1989, 207–214; and my "Introspection and Misdirection," Chapter 1.

But we should not accept BonJour's implicit suggestion that only the rational unrevisability of our fundamental standards can protect us from skepticism. BonJour insists that,

> even apart from worries about their relevance to epistemic justification, the Quinean constraints on justified revision of one's system of beliefs comes to very little. At best, they make some total systems ... less justified than others. But for any less global issue, any question of common sense fact or scientific theory that does not include the specification of such principles, it will seemingly always be possible to find a revision of one's system of beliefs containing any answer one likes (together with appropriately adjusted epistemic and logical principles) that is as justified on Quinean grounds as any alternative revision. (93)

I don't understand why BonJour thinks that this should be so. It is difficult enough within science to come up with a single theoretical solution to a problem which meets Quinean standards of conservatism, simplicity, tolerable fit with observational data, and so on; the suggestion that "it will seemingly be possible to find a revision of one's system of beliefs containing any answer one likes" does not square with the actual conduct of science. The Quinean insistence that even one's deepest epistemic standards be held open to the possibility of revision in light of experience, and that they also be explanatorily unified within one's web of belief, does not make epistemic justification any easier. Quite the opposite is true: epistemic justification, on this view, is a highly non-trivial achievement.

BonJour concludes that "both Quinean epistemology and the Quinean case against the *a priori* come to nothing" (96). But I hope I have succeeded in showing that BonJour is very far from having made a successful case for this claim.

V The Positive Case for the A Priori

What is BonJour's positive case for the a priori? BonJour tells us that a priori claims are recognized by an act of rational intuition: "such an act is (a) direct or immediate, non-discursive, and yet also (b) intellectual or reason-governed, anything but arbitrary or brute in character" (102). But what reason is there to think that we are capable of such acts? BonJour tells us that "it once again seems abundantly clear at the intuitive level that one who understands the various ingredients of [many a priori justifiable] proposition[s] and the way in which they are structurally combined will be able to see or grasp or apprehend directly that the proposition[s] ha[ve] to be true" (104). Now in spite of my commitment to a thoroughgoing naturalism, I here confess that I have had experiences which seem to be of this sort. That is, I have had the experience of thinking about a certain claim and being convinced that it just had to be true; more than this, my recognition that the claim just had to be true seemed thoroughly direct and immediate. But I have not accepted these deliverances of introspection at face value. Yes, my beliefs on these occasions seemed to be a product of direct apprehension of the truth of a proposition. But introspection is notoriously unreliable in judging the origins of our beliefs.[15] Many of our beliefs which are deeply dependent upon other judgments we make are ones which, nevertheless, seem, introspectively, to be directly arrived at.[16] One of the most important morals of contemporary cognitive psychology seems to be that there is a great deal more to cognition than is available to introspection, and that introspection offers not only a terribly incomplete, but frequently an inaccurate, account of the origins of consciously available mental states. Since so many judgments which we now know to be heavily inferential have the introspective appearance of being directly arrived at, BonJour's reliance at this key stage of his argument on the deliverances of introspection seems a slender reed on which to base a defense of the a priori.

Note how important this point is. If the appearance of direct intuition really comes down to heavily inferential theory construction – as the Quinean picture would have it – then there simply is no a priori justification at all. Moreover, even if some of the appearances of direct rational insight turn out to be just that, the case for the epistemological importance of a priority is thoroughly compromised for the appearance of direct rational insight, by itself, counts for very little. The ways in which we would have to distinguish between genuine cases of rational insight and radically holistic theory construction would themselves require empirical theorizing about the nature of our mental processes. As BonJour himself acknowledges, "there is a sense in which the truth of the general rationalist thesis (assuming that it is true) can only be an empirical matter" (99 n. 2). But this very heavily attenuated rationalism is now very difficult to distinguish from the Quinean radical empiricism which simply denies the epistemological import of the a priori/a posteriori distinction.

The case for the directness of rational intuition is, I believe, a difficult one to support. BonJour comments,

---

[15] I have discussed this point at length in "Introspection and Misdirection," Chapter 1 above.
[16] Consider, for example, judgments of grammaticality and ungrammaticality, or judgments of depth.

> it is not as though I somehow just find myself thinking, willy-nilly, for no apparent reason, that nothing can be red all over and green all over at the same time, not as though this conviction were somehow a product of something analogous to revelation or oracular prophecy. On the contrary, I at least seem to myself to be able to see with perfect clarity just *why* this proposition holds and even to be able to articulate this insight to some extent though not in a way that lends itself to discursive reduction: it is in the nature of both redness and greenness to exclusively occupy the surface or area that instantiates them, so that once one of these qualities is in place, there is no room for the other; since there is no way for the two qualities to co-exist in the same part of a surface or area, a red item can become green only if the green replaces the red. (108)

BonJour's attempt here to distinguish rational insight from baseless belief seems to compromise the case for directness quite dramatically; indeed, he seems to be giving us an inferential justification for the allegedly directly acquired belief. This is, I believe, an important difficulty for BonJour's position, because the better his defense against the charge of baselessness, the weaker the case for the alleged directness of the cognitive act. Moreover, I do not believe that this particular case is at all unusual in this respect. It is not at all difficult to show deep inferential integration among even the beliefs which seem to be arrived at independent of inference. It is hard to believe that this inferential integration has nothing to do with the strength of the conviction that these particular beliefs could not be false. The claim that they are the product of direct apprehension of the truth, unmediated by inference, is thus severely compromised.

But this is only the beginning of the difficulties which BonJour's position faces. BonJour is a moderate rationalist because he recognizes that we are subject to mistakes in our claims for a priority; even the most carefully considered judgments of a priori truth turn out, at times, to be simply mistaken. More than this, BonJour acknowledges that an agent sincerely attempting to follow the dictates of good reason may be mistaken in thinking that a judgment is a priori justified.

> suppose that in a putative case of intuitive *a priori* justification, the person in question either believes mistakenly that he has reflected on the claim in question or else has a clearly mistaken understanding of the relevant concept of necessity. On the present account, such a person does not in fact genuinely possess *a priori* reason for thinking that the relevant claim is true (or that the relevant argument is deductively cogent), because the conditions for access to such a reason are not satisfied ... he fails to have even an apparent rational insight, his own subjective impression of the situation notwithstanding. (127)

There are, as BonJour recognizes, "a whole spectrum of possible cases here" (127), and these include cases in which,

> [t]hough ... a person seems to himself to be justified, his grasp of what is really going on is simply too defective to have any genuine epistemic force; in effect, he fails to pass what might be regarded as a condition of cognitive sanity. (128)

BonJour's recognition of this point forces him to acknowledge that his own account of a priori justification has

> an *externalist* dimension: it is possible to believe oneself to be justified *a priori* ... and still not be thus justified, where the reason for the failure of the justification is something that is, at least at the time in question and perhaps in extremely rare cases even permanently, outside one's subjective grasp. This is a stronger concession to externalism than I have heretofore been willing to make, but one that seems required by the facts of the situation. (128)

Now it is important here to reiterate BonJour's earlier characterization of versions of externalism as "merely wrong-headed and ultimately uninteresting evasions of the central epistemological issues" (1); BonJour also levels the familiar charge that externalism "seems to simply change the subject without really speaking to the issues that an adequate epistemology must address" (96). It is surprising, in the face of such dismissive characterizations of externalism, to find that BonJour's own position is, in the end, itself a version of externalism. Given the extent to which key arguments in this book depend on the explicit assumption of internalism, it is not at all clear that BonJour's considered position here is entirely coherent.[17]

---

[17] In a footnote, BonJour gives two reasons why the externalism he is committed to "is still not externalist in the strong sense that pertains to, e.g., recent versions of reliabilism. First, where the external undermining factor or condition is in fact not present, the person can still have an adequate internal grasp of the reason why the proposition in question is likely to be true ... Second, even though an apparent *a priori* reason may be undermined by a factor or condition of which the person is unaware, there is no general reason why he could not come to be aware of this factor or condition, even though it is possible that such an awareness may not in fact be achievable in a particular case. Neither of these things is true, *mutatis mutandis*, for standard versions of reliabilism" (128–129 n. 36).

But I do not believe that BonJour is correct about this. On the second point: it is no part of reliabilism to suggest that agents *cannot* become aware of the conditions that make them justified. Rather, reliabilism is committed only to the view that agents *need* not be aware of the facts in virtue of which they are justified in order to be justified. An agent who learns a good deal about the nature of the processes by which beliefs are produced, and who learns a good deal about the environments in which those processes operate, may well be fully aware of all of the relevant facts. So in this respect, BonJour's position and reliabilism are on a par. On the first point: BonJour speaks here of an "undermining factor or condition," as if the default setting, as it were, involved a faculty of

BonJour is driven to this difficult position by his recognition that "there is obviously a whole spectrum of possible cases" (127) in which agents form beliefs which they take to be a priori justified, and which seem, from the inside, to meet all the relevant standards for being a priori justified, and yet which, at one end of the spectrum, cannot be a priori justified on any reasonable construal of what a priority must be, while, on the other end, are paradigms of a priority. Surely this is precisely what opponents of the a priori have long been urging: one cannot distinguish in any principled and non-trivial way between full possession of relevant concepts which will allow for rational insight alone to generate justified belief, and partial or inadequate understanding of relevant concepts so that rational insight, or apparent rational insight, or what seems to the careful and serious cognitive agent to be apparent rational insight, does not generate justified beliefs. The defense of an epistemologically interesting notion of a priority just collapses.

BonJour's case for "pure reason" fails as soon as he retreats from the clearly unacceptable claims of radical rationalism[18] to the apparently more reasonable modest rationalism. For once the real possibility of error is recognized even for a priori claims, these too stand in need of justification by integration with one's other beliefs. The claims of reason no longer stand somehow outside the web, adjudicating once and for all what inferential moves are legitimate. Instead, they too are brought down to earth, forced to earn their epistemic worth just like any other claims, through integration with our total body of belief. Viewing reason itself as thus "impure" thereby taints it, as the rationalist sees things. BonJour comments, at one point, on the use of the term "intuition" to denote "judgments and convictions that, though considered and reflective, are not arrived at via an explicit discursive process and thus are (hopefully) uncontaminated by theoretical or dialectical considerations" (102). But where the rationalist sees contact with theoretical considerations as a

---

reasoning properly attuned to the truth. But surely a central concern of epistemology is the extent to which our cognitive faculties are indeed attuned to the truth, and this issue must be addressed head-on rather than settled by default. It is for this reason that the thoroughgoing empirical approach of naturalism is properly seen to address, rather than evade, the central epistemological concerns which BonJour and I share. I thus do not see how the form of externalism to which BonJour is, in the end, committed is weaker than that of reliabilism.

[18] This is not to disagree with BonJour's point (144) that radical rationalism cannot solve this problem either. I agree, of course, that the radical rationalist position does not work. But the extraordinary claims for our intellectual faculties which are characteristic of radical rationalism held out the hope of providing precisely this kind of internal certification of the faculty of a priori judgment. The moderate rationalist position, on the other hand, is obviously incapable from the very beginning of providing such a certification.

source of contamination, we should instead view such influence as potentially beneficial. Theory-mediated judgment is not automatically "contaminated"; under the right circumstances, and under the guidance of appropriate theory, it is instead a source of correction and illumination. We should not search for a realm of reason somehow insulated from and uninformed by our best available theories. Instead we should welcome the prospect of a conception of rational inference which is itself fully vetted by all available evidence.[19]

BonJour seeks to avoid these consequences by drawing a distinction between justification and meta-justification: rational insight is sufficient, by itself, on BonJour's view, to justify the judgments which result from it (section 5.5). A meta-justification of the reliability of rational insight would inevitably be empirical, BonJour acknowledges, but this does not in any way impugn the a priority of the original, first-order justification. Indeed, BonJour charges that the insistence that the epistemic authority of rational insight be secured with such a meta-justification is itself merely question-begging:

> The dialectical picture that such a demand in effect assumes is one in which apparent rational insight has no epistemic value in itself, but instead functions merely as a kind of earmark or symptom for picking out a class of believed propositions that the supposedly required metajustificatory premise then tells us are, on some independent ground, likely to be true ... But ... this is obviously the wrong picture and amounts simply and obviously to a refusal to take rational insight seriously as a basis for justification. (145)

But the demand for a meta-justification here does not come from some over-arching principle that there can be no justification without a corresponding and prior meta-justification. Such a principle would be entirely unacceptable. Rather, we have specific reasons for wondering whether the beliefs which appear to be a product of rational insight genuinely are ones which tend to be true and which, in addition, genuinely are a product of direct apprehension of the truth, as the rationalist claims. We are, as I've mentioned, familiar with a very large number of cases in which judgments of ours which appeared to be direct and unmediated by inference really turned out to be heavily inferential; we are familiar with ways in which background beliefs may influence our judgments in ways which are not introspectively available; and we are familiar with a non-trivial number of

---

[19] I have elaborated on such a conception of reason in my "Distrusting Reason," Chapter 3.

cases in which judgments which seemed to involve direct apprehension of truths turned out to involve theory-mediated false belief. Under the circumstances, the demand for a meta-justification before we accept the authority of apparent rational insight is hardly unreasonable. Note, in addition, that BonJour's charge that this move is question-begging is simply mistaken. If BonJour could provide a meta-justification here, even an empirical one, then there would be reason to believe that we do in fact possess the kind of faculty of rational insight which he claims for us, and I, as a good reliabilist, would be happy to sign on to the view that there are a priori justified beliefs. On this kind of view, a view which has been championed by Georges Rey,[20] human beings have a mental module[21] which is capable of generating true beliefs even without empirical input. This is itself an empirical hypothesis, and one which would need a good deal of support from an empirical psychology. But if BonJour could provide us with evidence that we have such a faculty, then I think we should all accept at least part[22] of what the modest rationalist says. Without any evidence whatsoever for such a hypothesis – other than the deliverances of introspection together with the putative examples of a priori knowledge – it is perfectly reasonable, I believe, to demur. This is not begging the question against the rationalist; it is simply making a request for some good reason to believe the thesis.

Having made the charge that the request for a meta-justification is question-begging, BonJour abandons the search for a meta-justification entirely. But I believe that this is a serious mistake on his part. The empirical question of whether we do in fact have the kind of rational faculty alluded to should be of paramount interest to rationalists. In an earlier day, the psychological questions raised here were addressed by introspective investigations. We now know that more subtle tools are

---

[20] As Rey emphasizes, however, this kind of view does not result in a defense of the a priority of philosophical claims, as BonJour wants. See Rey, "The Unavailability of What We Mean I: A Reply to Quine, Fodor and LePore," in J. Fodor and E. LePore, eds., *Holism: A Consumer Update. Grazer Philosophische Studien* 46(1993), 61–101, and "A Naturalistic A Priori," *Philosophical Studies* 92 (1998), 25–43.

[21] BonJour himself would reject this way of putting it; he says, "faculty psychology has long been discredited" (109). But surely this is just mistaken. Faculty psychology is one of the most influential organizing ideas in current cognitive science, especially, but not exclusively, since the appearance of Fodor's *Modularity of Mind*, MIT Press, 1983. More than just a matter of fashion, however, I believe that this is actually the most illuminating way of putting the point, and Rey's work, cited above, is especially valuable here.

[22] But see the qualifications in the following section on BonJour's justification of induction.

called for. But whatever the tools required, these are questions which the rationalist cannot ignore.[23]

VI BonJour's Justification of Induction

BonJour does not believe that it is just the truths of logic and mathematics, together with a few trivial truths about bachelors and the like, which are a priori justified. Indeed, BonJour claims, though he does not argue, that philosophy itself is a priori (ix), and it is claims such as this which make BonJour's position close in spirit to the great rationalists of the seventeenth and eighteenth centuries; his disagreement with them about the fallibility of a priori justification is, by comparison, a small point, I believe. It is for this reason that BonJour seeks to display an example of a philosophically important a priori claim in a final chapter, and the example he chooses concerns the justification of induction. BonJour's attempt at justification here illustrates some of the worries I have discussed above.

The problem of induction, as BonJour construes it, is roughly[24] this: If we have observed a large number of instances of A, and a certain fraction m/n of the observed As have also had an independent property B, what reason is there to believe that roughly m/n As are B? Or, in the limiting case, if all observed As have been B, what reason is there to believe that all As are B? BonJour's answer to this question is that the following claim is a priori justified:

> In a situation in which a standard inductive premise obtains, it is highly likely that there is some explanation (other than mere coincidence or chance) for the convergence and constancy of the observed proportion (and the more likely, the larger the number of cases in question). (208)

Indeed, BonJour insists that "once general prejudices about *a priori* knowledge have been defused, the *a priori* status of [the above claim] seems sufficiently obvious to require little discussion" (208).

Now BonJour notes that the a priori solution to the problem of induction has not been a popular one, and surely one reason for this is the deeply held conviction of many that "we cannot know *a priori* that the world is orderly rather than chaotic" (213). BonJour grants that this is the case. But,

---

[23] There is some interesting empirical work available here. First and foremost, I would suggest Lance Rips's book *The Psychology of Proof: Deductive Reasoning in Human Thinking*, MIT Press, 1994. But the kind of case the available empirical work suggests for a faculty of a priori reason, to my mind, supports a view much more like Rey's than BonJour's.

[24] I ignore complications here which are irrelevant to the issues I wish to discuss. There is no doubt that the problem of induction needs to be stated more carefully than this, and BonJour does precisely that.

> Where Reichenbach and the others erred was in thinking that the truth of this claim precluded any possibility of there being an *a priori* reason why the conclusion of a standard inductive argument is likely to be true *if* the empirical standard inductive premise is true.
>
> For the existence of such a reason does not require that an orderly world be *a priori* likely in the abstract, apart from any empirical evidence, only that the particular sort of order asserted by an inductive conclusion be *a priori* likely *relative* to the existence of standard inductive evidence. (213–214)

Let us take a concrete example. All the crows I've seen have been black. Should I believe that all crows are black, and, if so, why? BonJour grants that it is not a priori likely that the world is orderly rather than chaotic. And of course it is not a priori likely that all crows are black relative to no evidence at all. But relative to the evidence that all crows I've seen have been black, BonJour says that it *is* a priori likely that all crows are black. Now why should this be so? In particular, given that it is no more likely a priori that I live in an ordered world than that I live in a world without order, why should my observation of a bunch of black crows give me any sort of reason, by itself, to think that all crows are black? BonJour's answer is that we are justified in believing this a priori. I don't know whether I am idiosyncratic here, but I don't find this suggestion any more plausible than the suggestion which BonJour agrees is implausible, that it is a priori likely that the world is orderly rather than chaotic. I recognize that this doesn't count as an argument, but I'm at a loss as to what else I should say on this score.

More importantly, I believe that BonJour's answer to the problem of induction merely gives a vivid example of a worry I raised earlier: that simple appeals to a priority seem utterly empty; they offer no illumination of the epistemic problems they are designed to solve. BonJour insists, and rightly, to my mind, that when we ask whether we are justified in believing something, we are asking whether it is likely to be true. So the question about the justification of inductive inference, in the particular case above, is one about why it is likely to be true that all crows are black if one has observed nothing but black crows. How does appeal to rational insight give us any understanding of the answer to this question? I don't believe that it does.

Let me say something more about what I think it would take to solve the problem of induction. First, I think we need to have a more fine-grained understanding of what inductive inference is. Inductive inference, insofar as it is something worth worrying about, is a kind of inference which we use quite regularly to generate beliefs about generalizations.

Whether there is a single thing which answers to the name "inductive inference," on this construal, is a non-trivial question. Perhaps inductive inferences have a single logical form; perhaps, on the other hand, when we understand them better, we will see that there are many importantly different kinds of inductive inference. So to my mind, one thing we need to know right away is something about the inferences that people actually make which lead them to conclusions such as "All crows are black."

Once we are able to identify the character of these inferences, we need to know something about the environments in which people actually make them. The kind of inferences we make will tend to generate truths in some logically possible environments, and tend to generate falsehoods in many others. Indeed, more than this, these inferences will tend to generate truths in some actual environments, and tend to generate falsehoods in many others. Are we more likely to make these inferences in environments in which they tend to generate truths, and, if so, how is it that we are so attuned to these environments?

An approach widely taken nowadays, and one which I endorse, sees our origin in natural selection as relevant here. It is not that natural selection guarantees the reliability of the inferences which are native to us. It does not.[25] But any account of the inferences which are native to us must offer some explanation of how it is that creatures who are a product of natural selection might make inferences of that sort. This is compatible with a great deal of error. Indeed, arguably, it suggests that there are certain sorts of errors to which we should be peculiarly liable. But I will not worry about the details here. The account which we end up offering will show how our inductive inferences are truth-conducive – to the extent that they are – by giving us an account of the inferences we actually make, and an account of certain features of the world which are pervasive, and then go on to show how these inferences succeed in latching on to the relevant features of the world quite a bit more often than not.

Now if we could give an account such as this, and I believe that the outlines of such an account are available in the cognitive science literature,[26] then we would have a substantive explanation of why it is that inductive inference is justified: that is, as BonJour insists, why it is that such inference is likely to lead to truths. BonJour's rival suggestion,

---

[25] For a useful discussion of this point, see chapter 3 of Stephen Stich's *The Fragmentation of Reason*, MIT Press, 1990.
[26] I have tried to give an account of the main lines of such a view in *Inductive Inference and Its Natural Ground*.

that such inferences are simply justified a priori, seems to me to cut off discussion just where explanation is most needed. I do not see how the invocation of a priori insight offers a meaningful rival to the detailed empirical investigation which is required in order to explain the successes and failures of the inferences we make, an empirical inquiry which offers us both a meaningful justification of some of our inferential strategies, but also, at the same time, substantive epistemic advice as to how to revise our inferential strategies so as to make them more reliable. Nor do I see how the appeal to a priority offers intellectual illumination of some other sort.

The empiricists' doubts about the importance of a priority, in the end, come down to this: the important philosophical questions we wish to ask call for substantive and illuminating intellectual answers. The appeal to a priority seems to avoid, rather than address, the questions about which we care so deeply. If the appeal to a priority is to solve these questions, then a great deal more will need to be said about the kind of illumination which such appeals are meant to provide.[27]

---

[27] This essay was originally presented at an Author Meets Critics Session at the Pacific Division of the American Philosophical Association. I have received helpful comments on a draft of this essay from Laurence BonJour, David Christensen, and Michael Devitt.

5

*What Reflective Endorsement Cannot Do**

Human beings have beliefs and desires; we perform actions. In addition, we sometimes reflect on our beliefs, desires, and actions. We wonder: Is this what I should believe? Is this what I should want? Is this what I should do? When we reflect on our beliefs, desires, and actions, we sometimes endorse them. Call this reflective endorsement.

A number of philosophers have made reflective endorsement the centerpiece of their views on a surprisingly wide range of issues. Thus, for example, Ernest Sosa has argued that there are two importantly different kinds of knowledge: animal knowledge and reflective knowledge, the latter requiring that one reflectively endorse one's holding a particular belief. Only human beings are capable of reflective knowledge, Sosa tells us; it is a better kind of knowledge than mere animal knowledge: it is what we should aspire to.[1] Sydney Shoemaker tells us that there is an important difference between humans and other animals: only humans can rationally change their beliefs and desires. Only humans are capable of this, on Shoemaker's view, because only humans may reflectively endorse the various changes which their beliefs and desires undergo.[2]

---

* Versions of these ideas were presented at the University of Arkansas, the Canadian Society for Epistemology, the Johns Hopkins University, Mount Holyoke College, the Free University in Amsterdam, Colby College, the University of Alabama, and the Rutgers Epistemology Conference. Discussion after the talks was helpful in putting this essay together, as were comments from David Christensen and Derk Pereboom on a written draft. I have also benefited from discussions on related topics with José Bermudez, Laurence BonJour, Alvin Goldman, Ernest Sosa, Jonathan Vogel, and Michael Williams.

[1] "Knowledge and Intellectual Virtue," reprinted in Sosa's *Knowledge in Perspective: Selected Essays in Epistemology*, Cambridge University Press, 1991, 225–244; "Reflective Knowledge in the Best Circles," *Journal of Philosophy* 94(1997), 410–430; "Two False Dichotomies: Foundationalism/Coherentism and Internalism/Externalism," in W. Sinnott-Armstrong, ed., *Pyrrhonian Skepticism*, Oxford University Press, 2004, 146–160.

[2] "On Knowing One's Own Mind," reprinted in Shoemaker's *The First-Person Perspective and Other Essays*, Cambridge University Press, 1996, 25–49.

Harry Frankfurt has offered an account of freedom of the will on which one enjoys such freedom when one reflectively endorses the desire from which one's behavior flows, and endorses action on the basis of that desire. Only humans are capable of such freedom, according to Frankfurt, for non-human animals lack second-order volitions.³ And in the most ambitious use of reflective endorsement, Christine Korsgaard has argued that reflective endorsement is the source of normativity, thereby explaining, she argues, why humans are subject to certain normative requirements which non-human animals are not.⁴

The views of these philosophers are not at all idiosyncratic. Indeed, in each case, they are merely especially clear representatives of a family of views which assign special value to reflective endorsement. I believe they represent a trend in philosophy generally, and particularly in recent philosophy, which overvalues, and misunderstands, human reflection.

I argue that reflective endorsement cannot perform any of the tasks on which these philosophers propose to put it to work. Seeing these views side by side will allow us better to understand just what it is that reflective endorsement can and cannot do. In addition, a proper understanding of these issues will show that while there are real and important differences between humans and other animals, the differences are not nearly as large as any of these philosophers would suggest.

I

Ernest Sosa draws a distinction between animal knowledge and reflective knowledge:

> One has animal knowledge about one's environment, one's past, and one's own experience if one's judgments and beliefs about these are direct responses to their impact – e.g., through perception or memory – with little or no benefit of reflection or understanding.
>
> One has reflective knowledge if one's judgment or belief manifests not only such direct response to the fact known but also understanding of its place in a wider whole that includes one's belief and knowledge of it and how these come about.⁵

---

³ "Freedom of the Will and the Concept of a Person," reprinted in Frankfurt's *The Importance of What We Care About: Philosophical Essays*, Cambridge University Press, 1988, 11–25.
⁴ *The Sources of Normativity*, Cambridge University Press, 1996.
⁵ "Knowledge and Intellectual Virtue," 240.

If one assumes, as current evidence seems to suggest,[6] that non-human animals do not have second-order beliefs, then non-human animals have nothing but animal knowledge. Humans, however, who are capable of reflection on their first-order mental states, sometimes have reflective knowledge, and sometimes have nothing but animal knowledge. This seems to follow from Sosa's definition of "reflective knowledge" together with the fact that, quite often, human beings fail to reflect on their first-order beliefs. But Sosa suggests otherwise. Immediately after drawing this distinction, Sosa claims that human beings never have mere animal knowledge:

> Note that no human blessed with reason has merely animal knowledge of the sort attainable by beasts. For even when perceptual belief derives as directly as it ever does from sensory stimuli, it is still relevant that one has not perceived the signs of contrary testimony. A reason-endowed being automatically monitors his background information and his sensory input for contrary evidence and automatically opts for the most coherent hypothesis even when he responds most directly to sensory stimuli. For even when response to stimuli is most direct, if one were also to hear or see the signs of credible contrary testimony that would change one's response. The beliefs of a rational animal hence would seem never to issue from unaided introspection, memory, or perception. For reason is always at least a silent partner on the watch for other relevant data, a silent partner whose very silence is a contributing cause of the belief outcome.[7]

While Sosa's definition of "reflective knowledge" explicitly requires that a first-order belief be accompanied by "understanding of its place in a wider whole that includes one's belief and knowledge of it and how these come about," Sosa here abandons that requirement, suggesting instead a certain counterfactual test: "if one were also to hear or see the signs of credible contrary testimony[8] that would change one's response." The counterfactual test, however, abandons the requirement of reflection of any sort, and introduces instead a standard which non-human animals regularly meet: they too are responsive to new evidence; their beliefs change when they are presented with new information. Thus, if one follows Sosa's initial definition, humans sometimes have mere animal knowledge and sometimes have

---

[6] See, e.g., Dorothy Cheny and Robert Seyfarth, *How Monkeys See the World: Inside the Mind of Another Species*, University of Chicago Press, 1990; Marc Hauser, *The Evolution of Communication*, MIT Press, 1996; Daniel Povinelli, *Folk Physics for Apes: The Chimpanzee's Theory of How the World Works*, Oxford University Press, 2000.

[7] "Knowledge and Intellectual Virtue," 240.

[8] In this context, Sosa is not, I believe, referring to human speech; rather, "testimony" here is meant quite broadly, so as to include, for example, the "testimony" of the senses.

reflective knowledge. If one substitutes the counterfactual requirement for reflective knowledge, humans have nothing but reflective knowledge, but animals, it turns out, have reflective knowledge as well. This latter point should not be surprising because the counterfactual test for reflective knowledge abandons the very requirement which gives reflective knowledge its name: no reflection is called for, only sensitivity to counter-evidence. Neither way of drawing the distinction, however, gets Sosa the result he claims, that humans have nothing but reflective knowledge and non-human animals have nothing but animal knowledge.

Sosa wishes to argue that reflective knowledge, of the sort required by his definition, is better than mere animal knowledge. Why should we think that reflective knowledge is superior to mere animal knowledge?

> Since a direct response supplemented by such understanding would in general have a better chance of being right, reflective knowledge is better justified than corresponding animal knowledge.[9]

But the relationship between reflection and reliability – the chances of being right – is not so simple as this would suggest. First-order mechanisms of belief acquisition – those which operate prior to and independently of reflection – vary dramatically in their reliability: many are extremely reliable, but some are only modestly reliable, and some are extremely unreliable. The same, of course, is true of the various mechanisms involved in reflection. At times, we reflect on our beliefs in ways which improve our overall reliability. But there are mechanisms involved in reflection which sometimes act as sub-personal cognitive yes-men, endorsing whatever beliefs the first-order mechanisms produce. These mechanisms do not improve our reliability, but merely further entrench our first-order beliefs, however reliable or unreliable they may be. In addition, of course, there are mechanisms of reflection which interfere with the smooth working of reliable first-order processes of belief acquisition: they lower the reliability of the overall belief-acquisition process. So the suggestion that first-order belief supplemented by reflection is more reliable than first-order belief alone is simply mistaken. If what one cares about is the reliability of one's process of belief acquisition, then reflecting on one's beliefs is a mixed bag: sometimes better, sometimes worse, and sometimes just the same as belief uninfluenced by subsequent reflection.

It is worth amplifying on these points, if only briefly. The phenomenology of reflection notwithstanding, the processes of reflection do not put

---

[9] "Knowledge and Intellectual Virtue," 240.

us in direct contact with the first-order processes by which our pre-reflective beliefs are formed. The reflective processes typically involve a substantial amount of reconstruction, that is, inference to an explanation about the likely sources of our beliefs; the fact that our reflective judgments are inferentially mediated, however, is unavailable to introspection. When we stop to reflect on the question of whether our pre-reflective beliefs are justified, a host of different biases go to work. We better remember evidence which supports the beliefs we hold than evidence we encountered which runs contrary to them. We better remember occasions on which we have been correct than those on which we have erred. We have a tendency to judge arguments which support our beliefs quite favorably, while arguments which run contrary to our beliefs are held to a very high standard. When we form judgments about the processes by which our pre-reflective beliefs were formed, we seem to employ as a minor premise the belief that we are, all things considered, quite reliable in our judgments, and we thus have a strong tendency to see our beliefs as based on evidence which we ourselves take to be highly probative, whether the beliefs were in fact formed on such a basis or not. As a result, far more often than not, the result of reflection turns out to be little more than a ratification of the beliefs held prior to reflective evaluation. Rather than serving as a source of correction for first-order processes of dubious reliability, reflection tends to act in ways which further cement our pre-reflective beliefs into place within the larger web of our convictions. Many reflective processes thus act not to correct our pre-reflective beliefs, but only to increase our confidence in them; we thus become more self-satisfied, even if no more accurate, epistemic agents.[10]

Sosa sometimes suggests that there are other epistemic benefits to be had from reflection.

> This is not to deny that there is a kind of "animal knowledge" untouched by broad coherence. It is rather only to affirm that beyond "animal knowledge" there is a better knowledge. This reflective knowledge does require broad coherence, including one's ability to place one's first-level knowledge in epistemic perspective. But why aspire to any such thing? What is so desirable, epistemically, about broad coherence? Broad coherence is desirable because it yields integrated understanding, and also

---

[10] I have discussed these issues in some detail in *Knowledge and Its Place in Nature*, Oxford University Press, 2002, 111–122. For a nice overview of the empirical literature here, see Timothy Wilson, *Strangers to Ourselves: Discovering the Adaptive Unconscious*, Harvard University Press, 2002.

because it is truth conducive, even if in a demon world broad coherence fails this test and is not truth conducive.[11]

The problem about truth-conduciveness, as we have seen, is broader than Sosa recognizes: it is a mistake to see reflection as truth-conducive across the board even in this world. But the suggestion that reflection produces integrated understanding offers another account of why we should aspire to it. Reflection is a good thing, on this view, because it produces coherence in our beliefs, and this is a good thing because it produces integrated understanding. Unfortunately, talk of coherence and talk of integrated understanding are so close as to lend no illumination at all. Reflection certainly provides one with additional beliefs which one would not have had without it, and these additional beliefs may, at times, constitute additional knowledge. What this doesn't tell us, however, is why an agent's first-order belief that p somehow constitutes better knowledge that p when it is accompanied by additional knowledge about other matters.

Sosa introduces the distinction between animal knowledge and reflective knowledge because he wishes to motivate a position on some middle ground between thoroughgoing externalist accounts of knowledge, which identify knowledge with the kind of responsiveness to the environment Sosa calls "animal knowledge," and uncompromising internalist accounts of knowledge, which require true belief together with some sort of reflective justification. On Sosa's virtue-reliabilist account, human knowledge, which is better than mere animal knowledge, is identified with what is here called "reflective knowledge": it requires both the externalist's responsiveness to the environment and the internalist's reflection on the relations among one's beliefs. Sosa's attempts to say what is better about reflective knowledge, however, fail.[12]

---

[11] "Reflective Knowledge in the Best Circles," 422.
[12] Sosa does suggest, very briefly, some other considerations. In "Replies" (in *Ernest Sosa and His Critics*, John Greco, ed., Blackwell, 2004, 275–325), he mentions that

> reflection aids agency, control of conduct by the whole person, not just peripheral modules. When reasons are in conflict, as they so often are, not only in deliberation but in theorizing, and not only in the higher reaches of theoretical science but in the most ordinary reasoning about matters of fact, we need a way holistically to strike a balance, which would seem to import an assessment of the respective weights of pros and cons, all of which evidently is played out through perspective on one's attitudes and the bearing of those various reasons. (292)

This suggests a position not unlike Sydney Shoemaker's, which is discussed in Section II below. Sosa also mentions the role reflection plays in "our intellectual autonomy" (291). A position which ties agency and autonomy to reflection is considered below in Section III. Finally, Sosa mentions the role of reflection in responding to skepticism.

More than this, the entire distinction between animal knowledge and reflective knowledge is unmotivated. Reflection seems to be a process of belief acquisition which human beings have and other animals do not. This means that humans have available to them certain means of forming beliefs, and modifying their beliefs, which are unavailable to other animals. But, by the same token, there are animals who have various processes of belief acquisition available to them which humans do not have. Thus, for example, bats are able to recognize objects at a distance by means of echolocation in a way of which humans are incapable. The fact that bats have a process of belief acquisition available to them which we do not should not make us think that there are two different sorts of knowledge here: ones which make use of echolocation and ones which do not. We should not think that, for each different process of belief-acquisition we discover, a new sort of knowledge results. Rather, knowledge is true belief which is produced by reliable mechanisms, and different animals have different mechanisms for achieving reliably produced belief. The sophistication of these mechanisms will, no doubt, have an effect on what it is that these animals can know. What reflection adds is not an additional sort of knowledge, but an additional means of knowledge acquisition. Reflection is just one process among many for acquiring and revising one's beliefs.[13]

II

Sydney Shoemaker argues that rational change of belief, and rational change of desire, require reflective endorsement of those changes.

> I agree that we don't need any self-awareness in order to explain why beliefs and desires jointly produce effects which they rationalize – i.e., actions which it is rational for the subject of such a set of desires to perform. Given that the agent is rational, the mere existence of such beliefs and desires is sufficient to explain their having the appropriate effects. But if the beliefs and desires are all first-order beliefs and desires, i.e., beliefs and desires that are not themselves about the agent's beliefs and desires, then one thing they do not rationalize is changes in themselves. For such changes to be rationalized, the beliefs and desires would have to include second-order beliefs and desires – desires to promote consistency and coherence in the system of beliefs and desires, and beliefs about what changes in the beliefs and desires would be needed in order to satisfy the second-order desires, which in turn would require beliefs about what the current beliefs and desires are.[14]

---

[13] I have discussed Sosa's views on this topic at greater length in "Sosa on Human and Animal Knowledge," in John Greco, ed., *Ernest Sosa and His Critics*, Blackwell, 2004, 126–134.
[14] "On Knowing One's Own Mind," 32–33.

So on Shoemaker's view, a person cannot rationally change his beliefs or desires without first knowing what they are, desiring to promote consistency and coherence in his beliefs or desires, and then changing them on the basis of that very desire. First-order beliefs and desires alone will not do; reflective endorsement involving second-order mental states is needed for rational belief change.[15]

Now someone might hold that rational action is not possible without a similar sort of second-order endorsement: one cannot act rationally, on such a view, without recognizing that one has a certain belief and a certain desire, and also wanting to act in a way which satisfies one's desires given the way one takes the world to be. But Shoemaker does not hold any such view. He recognizes that this would over-intellectualize rational action. Jack acts rationally when he, without reflecting on his beliefs or desires at all, makes a complicated series of turns in the course of his drive home at the end of the workday. Jack has done this often enough that he need not think about the route home; he certainly doesn't need to think about what he wants – to get home – or his beliefs about how to get there, or whether acting on the basis of his desire to get home, given how he takes the world to be, is most likely to satisfy his desire. Jack, like most of us at the end of a long day, just gets in the car and drives. But his action is no less rational for that. And Shoemaker would not have it any other way.

So why does Shoemaker think that things are any different when it comes to rational change of belief? Jack believed, when he first got into the car, that he could get home by turning left on Main Street. When he got to Main Street, however, he found that there was construction blocking the route. Seeing the construction had the effect of changing his belief about how he might get home: he no longer believed that turning left on Main would do the trick. Is Jack's change in belief rational only if he also, first, thinks about what he believes, and second, thinks about his desire for consistent and coherent belief, and finally, in light of all of this, changes his

---

[15] The view that second-order judgments of this sort are required for rational belief change is also defended by Robert Brandom, Donald Davidson, John Haugeland, and Michael Williams. See Brandom, *Making It Explicit: Reasoning, Representing and Discursive Commitment*, Harvard University Press, 1994, and *Articulating Reasons: An Introduction to Inferentialism*, Harvard University Press, 2000; Davidson, especially "Thought and Talk," in *Inquiries into Truth and Interpretation*, Oxford University Press, 1984, 155–170, and "Rational Animals," in *Subjective, Intersubjective, Objective*, Oxford University Press, 2001, 95–105; Haugeland, *Having Thought: Essays in the Metaphysics of Mind*, Harvard University Press, 1998; and Williams, "Is Knowledge a Natural Phenomenon?," in R. Schantz, ed., *The Externalist Challenge*, de Gruyter, 2004, 193–210. I have discussed these views, which differ in important ways from Shoemaker's, in chapter 3 of *Knowledge and Its Place in Nature*, and also in "The Metaphysical Status of Knowledge," *Philosophical Issues* 17(2007), 145–164.

beliefs in light of the previous reflections? If this is what rational belief change requires, it seems that most of our belief changes are not rational for we rarely go through such an elaborate and explicit process of reasoning. Rather, our beliefs often change in response to reasons without the intervention of second-order mental states. But there seems no more reason to insist on the intervention of second-order beliefs and desires here than there is in the case of rational actions of other sorts.

Shoemaker is aware of this sort of problem. In response, he argues, first, that rational individuals behave as if they have the relevant second-order beliefs and desires:

> In a rational being, there are two sorts of causal efficacy exerted by the first-order beliefs and desires. They jointly produce such effects as their contents make it rational for them to produce. And they jointly produce such effects as are needed in order to preserve or promote consistency and coherence in the belief-desire system. The latter may require the initiation of investigations aimed at discovering which of two inconsistent propositions is true, and of reasoning aimed at discovering which of two such propositions coheres best with certain other propositions, which are the contents of the beliefs that are part of the system. Now it seems to me that the least we can say of this case is that it is as if the system contained a desire to be a rational and coherent belief-desire system, and beliefs (true beliefs) about what beliefs and desires it contains.[16]

Let us grant, for the sake of argument then, that Jack behaves as if he desires to be rational and as if he knows what he wants and believes. Even so, one might still think that there will be cases in which such behavior is actually accompanied by second-order beliefs and desires of this sort, and there are cases, many of them, which are not so accompanied. Even the latter, it seems, involve rational change of belief.

But Shoemaker denies this.

> I am tempted to say that if everything is as if a creature has knowledge of its beliefs and desires, then it does have knowledge of them. There is no phenomenology of self-knowledge of such states that is in danger of being ignored if we say this – there is nothing it is like to believe something, and there need not be anything it is like to know or believe that one believes something. What I am inclined to say is that second-order belief, and the knowledge it typically embodies, is supervenient on first-order beliefs and desires – or rather, it is supervenient on these plus a certain degree of rationality, intelligence, and conceptual capacity. By this I mean that one

[16] "On Knowing One's Own Mind," 33.

has the former in having the latter – that having the former is nothing over and above having the latter.[17]

Notice that Shoemaker does not say that second-order belief is supervenient on first-order belief alone. This is important because there are many creatures, such as non-human animals and very young children, who have first-order beliefs but clearly do not have any second-order beliefs at all. Indeed, non-human animals and infants do not even have the concept of belief, and without any such concept, they cannot have beliefs about the beliefs they have. Thus, on Shoemaker's view, merely having a belief that p does not entail that one also have the belief that one has the belief that p. The second-order belief supervenes on the first-order belief "plus a certain degree of rationality, intelligence, and conceptual capacity." So infants and non-human animals, who lack the concept of belief, therefore do not have second-order beliefs. But why should the having of a first-order belief, together with these other capacities, automatically bring second-order belief in its train? We have many capacities which we do not exercise. Surely it is possible to have certain conceptual and intellectual capacities without bringing them to bear wherever they might apply. It may well be that if Jack were to focus his attention on the question of what it is that he believes, the fact that he does believe that p, together with his intellectual and conceptual capacities, would guarantee, or at least make it likely, that he come to recognize that he believes that p. This does not mean, however, that second-order belief supervenes on first-order belief plus these various capacities. If the capacities are not exercised, no second-order beliefs will result. So there is no reason to deny that Jack might change his beliefs even without having any sort of second-order endorsement of those changes. And there is no reason to deny that when that happens, the resulting changes are rational.

Indeed, once Shoemaker allows that second-order beliefs do not supervene on first-order beliefs alone, as he must, the claim that rational belief change requires reflective endorsement is undermined. Creatures who lack the concept of belief surely change their beliefs in response to evidence. Just as Jack stops believing that he can get home by turning left on Main Street even without having first to form beliefs about his beliefs, Jack's infant child will stop believing that Jack is in front of him as soon as Jack leaves the room even without forming any beliefs about what beliefs he has, let alone forming any sort of desire for coherent or consistent belief.

[17] Ibid., 34.

Jack's dog is much the same. Its beliefs too are responsive to changes in its environment. Once we allow, as Shoemaker does, that Jack may act rationally without any intervening second-order beliefs or desires, and that his infant child and his dog may do so as well, it is very hard to see why we should insist that these changes in belief without the benefit of second-order reflective endorsement are any less rational.

Rational belief change is nothing more than belief change which is responsive to reason. While such responsiveness may be achieved, at times, by way of reflection on one's beliefs and desires, it does not require any such reflection. If first-order beliefs, by themselves, were incapable of being responsive, in rational ways, to the presence of reasons, adding second-order beliefs surely wouldn't help. What special feature is it that second-order beliefs might have, and yet first-order beliefs must inevitably lack, that could allow second-order beliefs alone to be reasons-responsive? There is no mystical reason-adhering glue which is available only for second-order beliefs. If first-order beliefs by themselves cannot be responsive to reason, adding second-order beliefs won't help. But if first-order beliefs, by themselves, can be responsive to reason, as it surely seems they can, then second-order belief is not necessary for rational belief change.

III

Harry Frankfurt draws a distinction between freedom of action and freedom of the will.

> According to one familiar philosophical tradition, being free is fundamentally a matter of doing what one wants to do. Now the notion of an agent who does what he wants to do is by no means an altogether clear one: both the doing and the wanting, and the appropriate relation between them as well, require elucidation. But although its focus needs to be sharpened and its formulation refined, I believe that this notion does capture at least part of what is implicit in the idea of an agent who acts freely. It misses entirely, however, the peculiar content of the quite different idea of an agent whose will is free.[18]

Frankfurt's account of freedom of the will is best understood by way of a comparison between genuine persons and "wantons":

> The wanton addict cannot or does not care which of his conflicting first-order desires wins out. His lack of concern is not due to his inability to find

---

[18] "Freedom of the Will and the Concept of a Person," 19–20.

a convincing basis for a preference. It is due either to his lack of the capacity for reflection or to his mindless indifference to the enterprise of evaluating his own desires and motives. There is only one issue in the struggle to which his first-order conflict may lead: whether the one or the other of his conflicting desires is the stronger. Since he is moved by both desires, he will not be altogether satisfied by what he does no matter which of them is effective. But it makes no difference to him whether his craving or his aversion gets the upper hand. He has no stake in the conflict between them and so, unlike the unwilling addict, he can neither win nor lose the struggle in which he is engaged. When a person acts, the desire by which he is moved is either the will he wants or a will he wants to be without. When a wanton acts, it is neither.

It is only because a person has volitions of the second order that he is capable both of enjoying and of lacking freedom of the will. The concept of a person is not only, then, the concept of a type of entity that has both first-order desires and volitions of the second order. It can also be construed as the concept of a type of entity for whom the freedom of its will may be a problem. This concept excludes all wantons, both infrahuman and human, since they fail to satisfy an essential condition for the enjoyment of freedom of the will.[19]

Non-human animals, since they lack both second-order desires and second-order volitions, lack freedom of the will, although they may frequently do as they want, and, in that sense, act freely. Adult human beings, however, who at least typically have both kinds of second-order states, are capable of freedom of the will as well as free action.

Let us consider Frankfurt's wanton addict who has conflicting first-order desires. Let us suppose that our wanton has the desire for heroin, but also, since he is hungry, a desire for food. Unfortunately, he currently has neither food nor heroin, and he doesn't have enough money to buy them both. He thus has conflicting desires. Frankfurt says that since he faces such a conflict, "he will not be altogether satisfied by what he does no matter which of them is effective," and this is surely right. But this in no way distinguishes the wanton from a person who has conflicting first-order desires and resolutely acts on one of them. When one wants two things and can't have them both, one will, inevitably, find oneself not fully satisfied. Frankfurt says that in cases of conflict, the wanton "has no stake in the conflict" between his desires, and so "he can neither win nor lose the struggle in which he is engaged." This contrasts, Frankfurt tells us, with the person who has formed a higher-order preference to act on one or

---

[19] Ibid., 18–19.

another desire, or who forms a volition to act on one of his desires, for the person wins his struggle if and only if his action conforms to his higher-order volition. But the wanton does have a stake in the conflict. Suppose his desire for heroin is far stronger than his desire for food: he is only mildly hungry, but he has a very strong craving for heroin. His desires conflict, but the contest among his desires is easily resolved. Surely the wanton has a stake in this conflict. Should he find the heroin difficult to obtain and subsequently give in to his mild hunger by spending his money on a more easily available meal, he will be far less satisfied than had he resisted and satisfied his desire for the drug. He has no second-order desires or volitions, but the strength of his desires gives him a real stake in the outcome of the battle between them. And should food and heroin be equally available, he will, of course, go for the drug. The battle between his desires is, as we say, no contest. But the ease with which one desire wins out over the other does not show that the wanton had no stake in which side won. Quite the opposite: it reveals the strength of his preference for one thing over another. That is precisely what it is to have a stake in something.

Frankfurt's discussion of the wanton makes it sound as if such a creature is merely the arena for the battle between his various desires: he is pushed around by his desires, but has no stake in which of them wins out. But if this is one's picture of an individual's relationship to his desires and the actions which rationally flow from them, how would adding second-order mental states make things any different? The person with conflicting first-order desires, and second-order preferences about which of these desires he would like to act upon, is also an arena for the battle among his various desires; it is just that the arena has more contestants.[20] There are now first-order desires competing with one another, and higher-order desires and volitions as well.

Frankfurt focuses primarily on persons whose second-order desires are entirely unconflicted. But conflict may arise at the second order as well. Frankfurt's comments on this kind of case are revealing.

> People are generally far more complicated than my sketchy account of the structure of a person's will may suggest. There is as much opportunity for ambivalence, conflict, and self-deception with regard to desires of the second order, for example, as there is with regard to first-order desires. If there is an unresolved conflict among someone's second-order desires, then

---

[20] This point echoes Gary Watson, "Free Agency," *Journal of Philosophy* 72(1975), 205–220; see especially 218.

he is in danger of having no second-order volition; for unless this conflict is resolved, he has no preference concerning which of his first-order desires is to be his will. This condition, if it is so severe that it prevents him from identifying himself in a sufficiently decisive way with any of his conflicting first-order desires, destroys him as a person. For it either tends to paralyze his will and to keep him from acting at all, or it tends to remove him from his will so that his will operates without his participation. In both cases he becomes, like the unwilling addict though in a different way, a helpless bystander to the forces that move him.[21]

Notice how Frankfurt describes the person whose second-order desires conflict, and who fails to form a second-order volition to act on one or the other of these: Frankfurt describes this as a case of unresolved conflict. But just as with my wanton addict, these second-order desires may be quite different in strength. There may be a marked preference to act on one first-order desire rather than another, and, just as the wanton may act on his first-order desires without the intervention of an act of volition, the person with conflicting second-order desires may act on one of these without the mediation of a second-order volition. Indeed, the greater the difference in strength between the conflicting desires – the more it is really "no contest" – the more easily we may imagine that the desires give rise to action without the necessity of any intervening higher-order mediation. This would not be a case of unresolved conflict; the conflict is, in fact, easily resolved. Resolution does not require the intervention of higher-order states.[22]

Frankfurt speaks of such cases as ones where the agent is reduced to "a helpless bystander to the forces that move him." This description does not seem at all plausible for the person who is moved by one desire which is far stronger than another.[23] When Jill is pushed by Jack, she is a helpless bystander to the forces which move her; but when she is moved by her own strong desires, she is doing exactly what she wants. It is not obvious how the latter diminishes her agency. And if the relative strength of one's desires and their rational engagement with one another by way of one's

---

[21] "Freedom of the Will and the Concept of a Person," 21.
[22] Notice what "resolution" involves on Frankfurt's view: the forming of a higher-order volition which meets no opposition at all. But why is this not just a case of being "pushed around" by one's higher-order volition? If behavior resulting from a conflict between desires of different strengths amounts to being "pushed around" by one's desires, whatever the relative strength of those desires, then surely behavior resulting from a single desire which faces no conflict with others would equally amount to being pushed around. And if unopposed desire pushes one around, surely unopposed volition does the same.
[23] Nor is it any more plausible for cases in which the strength of the desires is more evenly matched. It will be sufficient, however, for bringing out the problems with Frankfurt's position, to focus on the case of unevenly matched desires.

beliefs is not sufficient for agency, how would adding more forces within the agent somehow change the dynamic? If we insist on describing individuals as bystanders to the forces acting within them, then it won't matter whether those forces include higher-order mental states or not. And if appropriate rational engagement among one's mental states does allow for agency, then all that higher-order mental states do is make for a more complicated agent.

First-order mental states form part of a complex causal network which brings about behavior. Higher-order mental states, whether they be desires or beliefs or volitions, do not stand outside that network of causal forces; they are just additional mental states providing additional causal vectors. If behavior caused by first-order mental states involves nothing more than being pushed around by a bunch of causal factors, then the same is true of behavior caused by higher-order mental states. And if the rational interaction among one's mental states makes room for agency, then it may surely operate, at times, within the realm of first-order states.

IV

Christine Korsgaard's use of reflective endorsement is by far the most ambitious. On her view, reason itself is grounded in reflective endorsement; reflective endorsement is the source of normativity.

> A lower animal's attention is fixed on the world. Its perceptions are its beliefs and its desires are its will. It is engaged in conscious activities, but it is not conscious of them. That is, they are not the objects of its attention. But we human animals turn our attention on to our perceptions and desires themselves, on to our own mental activities, and we are conscious of them. That is why we can think about them.
> And this sets us a problem no other animal has. It is the problem of the normative. For our capacity to turn our attention on to our own mental activity is also a capacity to distance ourselves from them, and to call them into question. I perceive, and I find myself with a powerful impulse to believe. But I back up and bring that impulse into view and then I have a certain distance. Now the impulse doesn't dominate me and now I have a problem. Shall I believe? Is this perception really a reason to believe? I desire and I find myself with a powerful impulse to act. But I back up and bring that impulse into view and then I have a certain distance. Now the impulse doesn't dominate me and now I have a problem. Shall I act? Is this desire really a reason to act? The reflective mind cannot settle for perception and desire, not just as such. It needs a reason. Otherwise, at least as long as it reflects, it cannot commit itself or go forward.

If the problem springs from reflection then the solution must do so as well. If the problem is that our perceptions and desires might not withstand reflective scrutiny, then the solution is that they might. We need reasons because our impulses must be able to withstand reflective scrutiny. We have reasons if they do. The normative word "reason" refers to a kind of reflective success.[24]

Let us begin with the case of belief which Korsgaard describes. I find myself with a strong inclination to believe a certain proposition, and I stop and reflect: I wonder whether I really ought to believe it. This, as Korsgaard rightly says, presents me with a problem. Now suppose I subject this belief to critical scrutiny and I find that it passes my standards; it meets with a certain reflective success. Does this mean that I ought to believe this particular proposition? Does it mean that I have reason to believe it?

It is not obvious that the answer to either of these questions is "yes." It may be that the standards I bring to bear when I reflect are not very good ones. As we saw in the discussion of Sosa, when individuals reflect on their beliefs, the process of reflection may do little more than serve to ratify whatever belief is being considered. The normative question about what I ought to believe, and what I have reason to believe, is not a question about whether the proposed belief passes my standards, whatever those standards may be. I might reasonably wonder whether the standards I have are good ones or reasonable ones; whether passing my standards gives me any reason at all to think that the proposed belief is true. The concern which the reflective agent has does not seem to be a concern about whether his or her belief would be reflectively endorsed, for we are all familiar with cases in which an agent stops to reflect on one of his beliefs, finds that it passes his own benighted standards, and goes on holding the belief in a far more self-confident, but no less misguided way. The reflective epistemic agent is concerned to have beliefs which are true, and what he is looking for is reasons to believe that the belief in question is true or is likely to be true. Passing reflective scrutiny may sometimes provide us with reasons, if the standards we reflectively apply are good ones; but passing reflective scrutiny cannot be identified with having a reason regardless of the standards applied.

Just as first-order beliefs are not automatically rational, second-order beliefs about what one ought to believe are not automatically rational.

---

[24] *The Sources of Normativity*, 92–93.

And this just means that when one reflectively endorses a particular belief, one may still have no reason at all to believe it.[25]

Now no one believes that having a reason is to be identified with reflective endorsement regardless of how that endorsement is achieved; certainly Korsgaard doesn't believe this. The process of reflective scrutiny may, for example, be broken off too soon. For example, in the case of moral reasons, Korsgaard comments:

> Kantian positions in general set a high value on reflection and are idealizing positions in the sense that moral concepts, as Kant defines them, are derived from the ideal of a fully reflective person. The fully reflective person is a corollary of Kant's idea of the unconditioned. We seek the unconditioned by imagining a person who reasons all the way back, who never gives up until there is a completely undeniable, satisfying, unconditional answer to the question. Obviously human beings often stop reflecting very far short of that.[26]

And clearly the same is true in the case of reasons for belief. But the problem is not solved simply by reasoning "all the way back" until the individual is completely satisfied. The suggestion that reflective endorsement is merely an idealization of ordinary, everyday processes of critical reflection presupposes a substantive view about the perfectability of human reason.

In his first inaugural address, President Bill Clinton offered an extremely optimistic view of the United States: "There is nothing wrong with America that can't be cured by what is right with America." A similar view about human reason seems to underlie Korsgaard's account of reflective endorsement. Human beings are susceptible to certain sorts of bad reasoning.[27] At the same time, we are able to discover that some of the

---

[25] Even the most ardent internalist should believe this. To believe otherwise is either to give second-order beliefs an epistemic free-ride which one denies to first-order beliefs, or to endorse an unreasonable form of conservatism which allows that the mere fact of believing something, however otherwise unreasonable that belief may be, provides one with a reason to go on believing it. For an important and, to my mind, completely persuasive argument against the latter, see David Christensen, "Conservatism in Epistemology," *Noûs* 28(1994), 69–89. Those who endorse conservatism should still reject Korsgaard's view, however, for the very weak reasons which conservatism provides, on such views, may easily be outweighed by other reasons.

[26] This passage occurs in an interview with Korsgaard: "Christine M. Korsgaard: Internalism and the Sources of Normativity," in Herlinde Pauer-Studer, *Constructions of Practical Reason*, Stanford University Press, 2003, 60.

[27] A particularly useful account is Richard Nisbett and Lee Ross, *Human Inference: Strategies and Shortcomings of Social Judgment*, Prentice-Hall, 1980. Two useful anthologies of related literature can be found in Daniel Kahneman, Paul Slovic, and Amos Tversky, eds., *Judgment under Uncertainty: Heuristics and Biases*, Cambridge University Press, 1982; and Thomas Gilovich, Dale

reasoning to which we are prone is bad, and we do this, at least in part, by reflecting on the character of our reasoning. So what is good in our reasoning seems to work to correct what is bad. If we were to continue this process, "all the way back," would we end up with proper reasoning? That is certainly one possibility. But it is an empirical bet, and a highly controversial one at that. Even if reason were perfectible in this way, it is one thing to suggest that we are fortunate enough to be natively endowed with basic processes of reasoning which are good enough so that turning them back on themselves will result in an understanding of proper principles of reasoning; it is quite another thing to identify good reasoning with the outcome of such a process. Even on the extremely optimistic view that human reason would fully correct itself, it would be a mistake simply to identify good reasoning a priori with whatever might be the outcome of the self-reflective process. But without any such additional assumption, the suggestion that even an idealized reflective endorsement serves to provide us with an account of reason, or the source of normativity, is entirely unmotivated.

Human beings are often reasons-responsive: our first-order beliefs are often, though not always, responsive to reasons, and our higher-order beliefs are often, though not always, responsive to reasons as well. We would like to be more responsive to reasons than we are. But appealing to higher-order beliefs, or reflective endorsement of our first-order beliefs, is no royal road to reasons-responsiveness; it need not even serve correctly to identify genuine reasons. If we wish to have more accurate beliefs about the world, one thing we can do is reflect further on the nature of the world itself. This frequently serves as a useful corrective to mistaken belief and conclusions hastily drawn. We can also think about our reasons themselves and thereby engage in second-order investigations. But going second-order provides us with no more guarantee of success than simple first-order researches. We should not think that we engage with reason for the first time when second-order investigations begin. Nor should we think that the problems we encounter in our first-order inquiries will automatically be resolved when we reflect on our reasons themselves. Our second-order beliefs are, after all, just more beliefs, and we will encounter all of the same problems at the second order that we faced when engaged in more mundane first-order concerns.

Griffin, and Daniel Kahneman, eds., *Heuristics and Biases: The Psychology of Human Judgment*, Cambridge University Press, 2002.

V

There is no second-order magic. Second-order mental states are not so very different from first-order mental states: both are firmly entwined in the same causal net; both are, at times, reasons-responsive, and, at times, disengaged from reason. The human capacity to have second-order mental states and engage in second-order investigations gives us abilities which other animals apparently do not enjoy, but the additional complexity which this lends to our mental lives and to our behavior does not make us nearly as different from other animals as any of the philosophers discussed here would have us believe.

6
*Belief in the Face of Controversy**

Disagreement is ubiquitous. One need not be especially opinionated, or especially well informed, to be aware that, whatever one's beliefs, there are a great many people who have beliefs that are contrary to one's own. As I write these words, the United States is about to head to the polls for another election, and many of the issues that voters will face are ones on which the electorate is deeply divided. The electorate is divided about moral and political issues, and it is divided, as well, about the likely effects of various policies; it is also divided about simple matters of historical fact. Anyone who has views on religious questions of any sort, including agnostics and atheists, is well aware that there are many others who see matters differently. Famously, there is deep division of opinion about evolution, especially in the United States, but, to a growing extent, in other industrialized countries as well. At times, it can seem that there is hardly any subject on which one might have opinions on which there are not many others who disagree. What is the epistemological significance of such disagreement? To what extent, if any, need one modify one's views in the face of disagreement?

Of course, not all disagreement presents even a prima facie epistemological challenge to one's own beliefs. I believe that the capital of Maine is Augusta. In fact, I know full well that the capital of Maine is Augusta. In order to make certain of this, I just checked it on a map. I also know that many people believe that the capital of Maine is Portland. This does not make me reconsider my opinion at all, nor should it. I have an explanation of why it is that so many people are mistaken: people often assume that the capital of a state with which they have little experience is its largest city. More than that, having checked my belief against a reliable source, I also

---

* I have received helpful comments from the audience at a presentation of this essay at the Free University, Amsterdam, and at MIT. I also wish to thank David Christensen, Adam Elga, and Tom Kelly for comments on a draft of the essay.

know that those who disagree with me would come to recognize their error, and change their belief, when confronted with the evidence I have. There is not some deep disagreement here about what constitutes good evidence for believing that a city is the capital of a given state. So, in this particular case, I have good reason to believe that I am in a superior epistemic position vis-à-vis the question of the capital of Maine, and the disagreement I have with others is epistemically unproblematic. I should go on believing as I do even in the face of this disagreement. In this case, at least, I know that I have better evidence on this question than do others who disagree with me.

There are other cases as well in which I may shrug off the disagreement of others, not because I have better evidence than they, but because I have better judgment. If, in trying to help a young child with his arithmetic homework, I explain that he has made a simple error of addition – five plus seven is twelve, I try to remind him, not thirteen – I should be completely unperturbed if he should insist that, no, he is right; five plus seven, he tells me, really is thirteen. My arithmetical skills are not, of course, infallible, but surely in this case it is perfectly reasonable for me to go on believing as I did before facing this disagreement. I know full well what the sum of five and seven is, and disagreement from an arithmetical neophyte should not cause me to reassess my views about arithmetic or about my mathematical abilities.

It is clear, however, that not all cases of disagreement are like either of these two cases, and so I cannot simply chalk up my disagreements with others to their inferior evidential situation or their inferior judgment. I certainly cannot insist that others' evidence or judgment must be inferior to my own simply in virtue of their disagreement with me. And it is for this reason that the fact of widespread disagreement raises troublesome epistemological questions. There is a very wide range of topics on which we knowingly disagree with others, and yet we seem to lack any reason to think that their evidence or their judgment is inferior to our own. What should we do in such cases? What is it reasonable to believe in the face of such disagreement?

Disagreements within philosophy constitute a particularly interesting case of this kind of disagreement. Consider the debate between internalists and externalists about epistemic justification. I am a committed externalist. I have argued for this position at length and on numerous occasions. My arguments for the position are not merely a pose. I have not presented arguments for externalism merely to serve as a gadfly, provoking discussion. I sincerely believe that the arguments I have presented are good arguments, and I sincerely believe their conclusions. At the same time, I recognize, of course, that there are many philosophers who are equally committed internalists about justification, and that the arguments they offer are ones not only to which they are committed, but which they believe are good ones, and whose conclusions they sincerely believe.

It would be reassuring to believe that I have better evidence on this question than those who disagree with me, that I have thought about this issue longer than internalists, or that I am simply smarter than they are, my judgment superior to theirs. It would be reassuring to believe these things, but I do not believe them; they are all manifestly untrue. So, on the question of whether externalism or internalism is correct, I find that I have an opinion, but there are others who disagree with me who are, to adopt a useful term,[1] my epistemic peers: they are just as smart as I, just as well informed, and have thought about the issue just as long as I and just as carefully. That my epistemic peers disagree with me on this question is surely relevant evidence that I ought to take into account. It is indirect evidence on the question of internalism versus externalism, but it is important evidence nonetheless. And it surely seems that the proper way to respond to evidence of this sort is to suspend judgment, to suspend belief about the proper resolution of the debate between internalists and externalists.

As Richard Feldman has pointed out,[2] this is precisely what it seems we ought to do, and what we in fact typically do, in perceptual cases. Thus, to take his example, if you and I are each looking out of a particular window, in exactly the same direction, and I see someone standing in the middle of the quad and you see no one there at all, then we have a puzzle. If you and I have equally good vision and we are both in our right minds, then we should each be surprised by the other's judgment. "What do you mean," I will say, "that you don't see anyone there?" "What do you mean," you will say, "that you really see someone out there in plain view?" Once we become convinced, however, that each of us is playing no joke, that we are looking in the same direction, and that we are, to all appearances, functioning normally, we should suspend belief about what there is in the middle of the quad. Someone here is making a bad mistake, and that person may well have some serious problem, and we will surely both agree

---

[1] This term was introduced by Gary Gutting in his *Religious Belief and Religious Skepticism*, University of Notre Dame Press, 1982.
[2] Richard Feldman, "Epistemological Puzzles about Disagreement," in Stephen Hetherington, ed., *Epistemology Futures*, Oxford University Press, 2006, 223.

that all of this is true. But it would be completely unreasonable for me to conclude, for this reason, that you are the one with the problem. I have no more reason to think that you are making a mistake than that I am, and, for that very reason, I should suspend judgment, as should you. When we give proper weight to the judgment of our epistemic peers in perceptual cases, it seems, suspension of belief is required.

As David Christensen has pointed out,[3] the same seems to be true in mathematical cases. To take his example, suppose that you and I go out to a restaurant with a number of friends. After a large meal, the check comes and we agree to split the bill evenly. You and I are each quite good at mental arithmetic. I take a look at the bill and figure out what each person owes, and I put my share in the middle of the table. You look at the bill and figure out what each person owes and put your share in the middle of the table, and then we notice that we have put in different amounts. We are each well aware of the other's mathematical abilities, and we are each convinced of the other's honesty. At least one of us has made a mistake. It would surely be unreasonable for me to conclude that, since one of us has made a mistake, it must be you. The reasonable thing to do in this situation, and surely what most people in fact do in this situation, is suspend belief. We each go back to the bill and try to recompute the proper share.

The dispute about the bill at the restaurant and the dispute about the person in the quad are importantly different from the philosophical dispute about internalism and externalism. In the restaurant case, our disagreement will, in actual practice, quickly be resolved. One of us has made a simple arithmetical error. We are each quite good at mental arithmetic, and we will quickly determine who has erred when we recalculate. We suspend judgment when we first note our disagreement, but our judgment is suspended only briefly. After quickly recalculating, we will figure out which of us was right about the bill, and we will comfortably agree about its proper division. In the perceptual case as well, we are often able to resolve our dispute in short order. We look more carefully; we call in a third person; we go out into the quad. The dispute is, often enough, only momentary, and our puzzlement is resolved. ("Oh, now I see," I say, "it was only a shadow.") While not all such disputes are resolved, of course, they leave few lingering doubts about perception or perceptual belief. The occasional disagreements that arise on such matters and that resist easy

---

[3] David Christensen, "Epistemology of Disagreement: The Good News," *Philosophical Review* 116 (2007), 187–217.

resolution do not leave us suspending belief about perceptual matters generally, nor should they.

But philosophical matters are importantly different. If you and I disagree about internalism and externalism, and we have each, as I have supposed, thought about this issue for many years, then a quick run-through of the arguments will not resolve the issue between us; this is, in no way, like the restaurant case. By the same token, we cannot profitably, as in the perceptual case, do anything analogous to looking more carefully (since we have already scrutinized the arguments with great care), call in a third party (since we know that there are many third parties on each side), or head out into the quad for a closer look. If we set aside our opinions about internalism and externalism as a result of our dispute, then we are likely to be suspending judgment on this issue for quite some time. When we disagree about our share of the bill at the restaurant, or about what is going on in the quad, we recognize that these are isolated disagreements against the background of extraordinarily broad agreement about arithmetic and perceptual matters generally, and, for this very reason, there is no threat of skepticism here about mathematics or the physical world. Even if our disagreement should prove to be unusually difficult to resolve, for whatever reason, it is an isolated disagreement, one that does not threaten to force us to suspend judgment very widely. But, if the right thing to do in the internalism and externalism case is to suspend judgment, then it seems that we will be suspending judgment on philosophical matters generally, and not just for a moment. And, since most of us have very deep philosophical commitments on a great many matters, this would involve substantial revisions in our corpus of beliefs, revisions most of us are not eager to undertake. A broad skepticism about philosophical matters threatens.

I will assume, for the purposes of this essay, that the proper resolution of the disagreements in the perceptual and mathematical cases is, in fact, as I have described: in the face of disagreement from epistemic peers, given no special reason to believe that either party is mistaken, one must, if one is to be epistemically rational, suspend belief. I believe the case for this has been well made by Feldman,[4] Christensen,[5] and Adam Elga,[6] and in related work by Roger White.[7] Supposing that this is correct about such

---

[4] Feldman, "Epistemological Puzzles about Disagreement."
[5] Christensen, "Epistemology of Disagreement."
[6] Adam Elga, "Reflection and Disagreement," *Noûs* 41(2007), 478–502.
[7] Roger White, "Epistemic Permissiveness," *Philosophical Perspectives* 19(2005), 445–449.

mundane matters, however, how should we respond in the case of philosophical opinion?

Are we to suspend judgment there as well? If so, does this force us to a broad skepticism about philosophical matters? And, if we are rationally forced to such a skepticism about philosophical matters, how broadly does this skepticism generalize? These are the questions I wish to address in this essay.

I

When I find that others disagree with me on a certain question, this gives me, *ceteris paribus*, reason to be less confident than I was that I am right. In the cases we have been looking at, disagreement from epistemic peers gives one reason to suspend judgment entirely on the disputed question. It is clear, moreover, that the mere possibility that someone might disagree with me does not have the same epistemic significance. Indeed, if it did, then, since there might always be people who disagree with one on any question at all, treating merely possible disagreement as on a par with actual disagreement would result in total skepticism. The worries generated by problems of disagreement, however, broad as they are, are not of this sort. So there seems to be an important asymmetry between actual disagreement and merely possible disagreement.

As Thomas Kelly urges,[8] however, one should not overstate the difference here. "Suppose," as Kelly suggests, "that there would be considerable disagreement with respect to some issue, but all of the would-be dissenters have been put to death by an evil and intolerable tyrant." In such a case, disagreements that do not in fact occur, disagreements that are not actual, are no less epistemically significant than actually occurring disagreements.

"The significance of actual disagreement," Kelly concludes, "need be no more intellectually threatening than certain kinds of merely possible disagreement." How then should we determine the role that actual and merely possible disagreement should play in determining what to believe? Kelly argues that considerations of disagreement, in the end, drop out of account.

> Whether we find the possibility of disagreement intellectually threatening, I suggest, will and should ultimately depend on our considered judgments about *how rational* the merely possible dissenters might be in so dissenting.

---

[8] Thomas Kelly, "The Epistemic Significance of Disagreement," *Oxford Studies in Epistemology* 1 (2005), 181.

And our assessment of whether rational dissent is possible with respect to some question (or our assessment of the extent to which such dissent might be rational) will depend in turn on our assessment of the strength of the evidence and arguments that might be put forward on behalf of such dissent. But if this is correct, then the extent to which merely possible dissent should be seen as intellectually threatening effectively reduces to questions about the strength of the reasons that might be put forward on behalf of such dissent. Now there might be cases in which we judge that the arguments and evidence that could be brought forth on behalf of a hypothetical dissent are truly formidable, and this might justifiably make us doubt our own beliefs. But in that case, the reasons that we have for skepticism are provided by the state of the evidence itself, and our own judgments about the probative force of that evidence. The role of disagreement, whether possible or actual, ultimately proves superfluous or inessential with respect to the case for such skepticism.[9]

Now Kelly clearly has in mind cases in which disagreements actually arise, and arguments are offered on behalf of competing views, or, alternatively, although no actual disagreement has arisen, arguments against a particular view are available. And, in these cases, Kelly urges that we simply look at the arguments for or against the views in question, and let the fact of disagreement, when there is one, drop out of consideration. Whether such a disagreement actually arises, or, instead, is merely possible, is of no epistemic weight at all, according to Kelly.

It is important to note, however, that in many cases where disagreements arise, arguments of the sort Kelly has in mind are not in play. Thus, remember Christensen's restaurant case, where you and I reach different conclusions about the fair division of the check. Neither of us offers reasons for our conclusion about how the bill should be split, and yet we are each faced with a significant challenge to our respective beliefs. When I suggest that a fair division requires one payment and you suggest, instead, that it requires another, the problem is already set. Given that we each are aware of the fact that we are both highly reliable in figuring out such answers, the problem is set precisely by the fact of disagreement, and, at this point in the conversation between us, we cannot explain the epistemic problem we each face without pointing to that disagreement itself.[10] So, at

---

[9] Kelly, "The Epistemic Significance of Disagreement," 181–182.
[10] There is, of course, an argument that each of us can give that explains our epistemic predicament, but any such argument makes essential reference to the fact of disagreement. These are not, of course, the kinds of arguments Kelly has in mind.

least in cases such as this, the role of the disagreement itself is anything but superfluous, contrary to Kelly. Perceptual cases are often much the same.

Kelly is right, of course, that my belief will not be threatened when you disagree with me if I know that your contrary opinion is unreasonable. This does not mean, however, that I must know the basis for your belief before it can threaten my own. As in the restaurant case, and in perceptual cases as well, I may know that your beliefs on this sort of matter are generally reliable, without knowing anything specific about the basis of your belief; I need not, in particular, know any of your reasons at all. In cases of this sort, the fact of disagreement, in light of my background knowledge of your reliability, is an ineliminable part of my reason for suspending belief.

What should we say, however, about the kinds of cases Kelly clearly has in mind, cases where each party to the disagreement has actually offered arguments for his or her view – at least when there is an actual disagreement – or, alternatively, when there is no actual disagreement, and yet arguments are available for each of two conflicting views? This is precisely the kind of case which arises in philosophy. In the internalism and externalism case, there are arguments that have been widely noted on both sides of the issue, and the participants to the debate, whatever position they may hold, are aware of these arguments. Similarly, as Kelly points out,[11] there are issues in philosophy where arguments are available on either side of an issue, and yet one side of the argument has no actually existing adherents. Kelly's view, in both sorts of case, is that the fact of disagreement, or the lack of disagreement, should drop out of rational consideration. We should consider the arguments, and let it go at that.

Now there is no question that this accords well with standard philosophical practice. We simply do not tend to see arguments of the following sort in the philosophical journals.

> Smith has offered an argument that p, and I must admit that the argument appears to be sound. But Smith has failed to take account of important evidence that p is false: I am one of Smith's epistemic peers, and although I grant that Smith's argument appears sound, I find that I am not convinced by it. As a matter of fact, I believe that not p. So there you have it: Smith believes that p; I believe that not p. It is a tie. Given this evidence, we should just both suspend belief.

[11] Kelly, "The Epistemic Significance of Disagreement," 184–185.

Nor does one see probabilistic variants of this kind of reasoning, in which the distribution of opinion within the field is offered as evidence for the degree of confidence that should be assigned to a disputed claim. Standard practice is to do as Kelly recommends: ignore the distribution of opinion and focus on the arguments.

Kelly's suggestion that we focus on arguments in such cases is not meant as merely pragmatic advice. He is not suggesting that focusing on arguments in these cases will advance the cause of inquiry, or that it is more likely to help get one's work published in respectable journals, or that it will be likely to advance one's professional standing. His point, of course, is that the arguments are where the relevant evidence is to be found. That there is an actual disagreement, or that the preponderance of opinion falls on one side or another of the disagreement, is, on Kelly's view, simply irrelevant to the question at issue.

So let us imagine following Kelly's prescription. I have offered arguments for externalism, and, when I examine them, I find them thoroughly convincing. You have offered arguments for internalism, and, when I examine them, I do not find them convincing. Now I know that the situation here is perfectly symmetrical: you are convinced by your arguments, and you are not convinced by mine, but these facts, Kelly tells us, are ones that I should not take into consideration in evaluating what to believe; they are simply irrelevant here. I should focus on the arguments and forget about who believes what.

But why should I do this? I know that you have thought about this issue as long as I have; that you are as familiar with the arguments on both sides of this issue as I am; and I know that you are just as smart as I am. We are epistemic peers. So, just as in the restaurant case, I have good reason to regard you as reliable, or, at a minimum, as reliable as I am. And, if this can serve as a reason for taking the fact that your opinion is different from mine as reason for doubt when I know nothing of your reasons, it is hard to see why it should be that it cannot equally serve as reason for doubt when I do know your reasons.

After all, once our reasons are on the table, the dispute between us comes down to our abilities to assess the cogency of complicated arguments.[12]

---

[12] Actually, I do not think this is entirely correct, but I will assume it for the sake of argument in the text, since it is most favorable to Kelly's position. In fact, I believe, the reasons we are able to articulate often fail fully to do justice to the reasons for which we believe. It is these latter reasons, rather than the ones we can verbalize, that determine the epistemic status of our beliefs. I have discussed this further in my "Distrusting Reason," Chapter 3, and *Knowledge and Its Place in Nature*, Oxford University Press, 2002, ch. 4.

And we agree that we are each quite good at that; we are epistemic peers. But we disagree about the cogency of the arguments at issue. So the disagreement about internalism and externalism has now been replaced by a different disagreement, a disagreement about the cogency of various arguments. How are we to resolve this dispute? On Kelly's view, we would have to give reasons here as well, and it is these reasons, presented in the form of arguments, on which the rational resolution of the dispute must turn.

Now no one, I think, will disagree with the suggestion that formulating such explicit arguments may be a useful thing, and it may serve to advance our inquiry. We should each do our best to formulate the arguments that we find most revealing, as well as the counterarguments that, we each believe, show the errors in our opponent's view. But these points are pragmatic ones, points about what we should do in order to advance inquiry. And Kelly's claim is not one about such pragmatic concerns, but one about what it is reasonable to believe right now in the face of disagreement.

So let us return to the disagreement you and I have about, as I have been supposing, internalism and externalism. You and I have opposing views, and we are each aware of the other's view; we are also each aware of the other's arguments. And the question at issue is not what we should do now to advance our inquiry; looking at arguments is, no doubt, a good strategy to pursue for that purpose. The question at issue is what, at this very moment, each of us is justified in believing in the face of all of the evidence we have. Kelly's view is that the fact of our disagreement is not even relevant evidence here.[13]

In order to see how best to handle this sort of case, it will be useful to examine a different case in some detail. So let us look at what Kelly has to say about the Newcomb Problem.

II

Robert Nozick presented the Newcomb Problem, a problem in decision theory, in 1969.[14] There are two possible solutions to the Problem, the

---

[13] Kelly does, in addition, present an argument that, even if we were to count the fact of disagreement as relevant evidence, this would not rationally force us to suspend belief in the cases described ("The Epistemic Significance of Disagreement," 185–190). Nevertheless, his view is, as the quoted passage shows, that facts about disagreement are epistemically irrelevant to the issue under dispute.

[14] Robert Nozick, "Newcomb's Problem and Two Principles of Rational Choice," reprinted in Nozick, *Socratic Puzzles*, Harvard University Press, 1997, 44–73.

one-box solution and the two-box solution. The Problem arises because there is a highly intuitive argument for each of these incompatible solutions. As Kelly points out,[15] when Nozick first presented the Problem, he remarked[16] that opinion within the community of decision theorists seemed to be roughly evenly divided. Currently, however, Kelly notes that "the by-now over three decades of sustained debate ... has resulted in a significant shift in the original distribution of opinion in favor of Two-Boxing."[17] How should the distribution of opinion on this question affect our judgment about its proper resolution? Kelly's answer, as we have seen, is that we must look to the arguments on either side, and ignore the distribution of opinion.

Why should we ignore the distribution of opinion on this case? Kelly asks us to imagine a student studying the Problem at the time it was introduced; in talking to others, she discovers that opinion is evenly divided on the question. There are other possible worlds, however, in which everyone she meets is a One-Boxer. Is it rational to believe different things in these two worlds? Not according to Kelly.

> Should she take a different view about Newcomb's Problem in the other, unanimous world than she does in our fragmented and divided world? *Despite* the fact that she has access to exactly the same arguments in both worlds? This seems extremely dubious – after all, can't the student in the unanimous possible world simply look over at our own fragmented world, and realize that *here* she has epistemic peers who extol Two-Boxing?[18]

As Kelly notes, "whether there is any actual disagreement with respect to some question as opposed to merely possible disagreement might, in a particular case, be an extremely contingent and fragile matter."[19] But surely this leads, he argues, to the conclusion that the distribution of opinion should carry no weight for us.

Now I think it is significant that Kelly has chosen an example from decision theory. Areas of formal investigation within philosophy, such as logic, probability, and decision theory, are ones in which an extraordinary amount of progress has been made. There can be little doubt that there is as much reason for confidence in some of the results in these areas as there is in the empirical sciences. A look at the history of these fields, moreover,

---

[15] Kelly, "The Epistemic Significance of Disagreement," 182 n. 16.
[16] Nozick, "Newcomb's Problem and Two Principles of Rational Choice," 48.
[17] Kelly, "The Epistemic Significance of Disagreement," 182 n. 16.
[18] Kelly, "The Epistemic Significance of Disagreement," 183.
[19] Kelly, "The Epistemic Significance of Disagreement," 181.

shows some interesting trends.[20] As in mathematics, intuitions about results *and about arguments* in these areas are extremely unreliable at the early stages of investigation. It is only as theory advances that we come to be able to understand the fundamental concepts at issue in these fields, the kinds of intuitions that are genuinely insightful, and the kinds of arguments that are genuinely sound. To take a single example, Stephen Stich notes[21] that, as late as the end of the nineteenth century, one could find logic textbooks that defended the gambler's fallacy as a legitimate statistical inference. Diversity of opinion is a commonplace in these areas early on in the development of theory; as theory advances, the opinions of experts in the field tend to converge. Even among experts, of course, convergence of opinion is no guarantee of truth, but one would have to be a radical skeptic about mathematics, logic, probability, and decision theory to think that convergence of opinion is not, at this point in the history of these fields, evidence of truth. And at this point in the history of these fields, I think it is fair to say, radical skepticism is no longer a rational option.

Thus, as I see it, when we see that, after three decades of work on the Newcomb Problem, there is an emerging consensus on a solution, this is itself, given the history of the field, strong evidence that the consensus is correct. What should we make of Kelly's suggestion that we may always look over at other worlds in which the consensus is different, or in which there is no consensus? And what should we make of his suggestion that consensus may be "an extremely contingent and fragile matter"? I believe that these suggestions give a misleading view of the dynamics of consensus within formal fields in philosophy.

Let us consider, by way of contrast, views about the aesthetics of clothing. If I were to head off to buy a suit, I would find that there is some consensus in the fashion world about the proper width and shape of lapels. The consensus today is quite different from what it was five or ten years ago, and different still from what it was in the 1930s. Someone might argue that consensus among fashion experts is evidence of truth: the lapels currently approved of are ones, we should believe, that are aesthetically correct; the fashion world is converging on the timelessly right answer here. Whatever one thinks of the kind of realism about aesthetic value that such a view presupposes, it is surely unreasonable to think that consensus here is any evidence of truth at all. The history and dynamics of consensus in the fashion world are strikingly different from what one sees in

---

[20] See, e.g., Ian Hacking, *The Emergence of Probability*, Cambridge University Press, 1975.
[21] Stephen Stich, *The Fragmentation of Reason*, MIT Press, 1990, 83.

mathematics. In mathematics we see periods of disagreement followed, after intensive study, by a growing consensus; in the fashion world, we see a large consensus that simply changes from year to year. The second of these two patterns does not support any kind of confidence that this year's consensus is more likely to get it right than last year's consensus, or the consensus of the year before, or the year before that.

The consensus we find in the fashion world is one that we might accurately describe, to use Kelly's words, as "an extremely contingent and fragile matter." Although lapels of a certain width are currently in fashion, they might just as easily have been seen as evidence of bad taste. We need change little about the underlying dynamics of opinion about fashion if we are to imagine a world in which much broader or narrower lapels are approved of.

But now contrast this kind of case with cases of emerging consensus in formal areas of philosophy. Thus, consider the way in which a consensus was achieved following the publication of Gödel's result on the incompleteness of arithmetic. We can easily imagine worlds in which Gödel did not discover his proof, and in which no proof of incompleteness was discovered until much later, or at all. We can certainly imagine worlds in which someone else discovered the famous proof, or in which it was discovered earlier. Some of these worlds are not very different from our own. What would, however, be very much different from the world we inhabit is one in which Gödel discovers his proof, the very proof that he presented in the actual world; he presents it to the mathematical community, and a consensus emerges that it is mistaken. Such a world would be one that is very different from our own. It would be a world in which the abilities of mathematicians are utterly different from those in the actual world, and, as a result, one whose history would look entirely different from the history of mathematics as it has actually unfolded. The fact that we can imagine a world in which the people who are called mathematicians are all incompetent, and that they reach consensus in much the way that consensus about fashion is reached in the actual world, says nothing whatsoever about how we should allow consensus among actual mathematicians to affect our opinions.

Consensus in the mathematical community, except in rare cases, is not a fragile thing at all. When there is consensus in this community, the consensus is typically very robust: one could not easily change the consensus, or undermine it, without making very substantial changes in the underlying facts (for example, by changing the facts about what arguments are available on either side of an issue, or by changing the facts about the basic competence of the members of the community). The same is true within the scientific community. The fashion community, of course, is a different matter entirely.

So what should our student do when she examines the arguments for each side in the case of the Newcomb Problem? If she wants to understand anything about the Problem at all, she needs to examine the arguments on either side with tremendous care and try to figure out which of the two sides seems to have the better argument. And, if she wants to have any chance at all of advancing the community's understanding of the issues, she will, again, need to examine the arguments. But, if the question is, instead, what she is justified in believing when she knows that the community of experts is deeply divided on the issue, or, alternatively, what she is justified in believing when she knows that the community is unanimous in favor of one side rather than another, then the answer is that she should go with the community opinion.[22] And this is not simply true of students, who are not yet peers with the experts. It is true of the experts themselves as well.

Consider, once again, Christensen's restaurant case. In the simple version of the case, already discussed, you and I come to different opinions about how the bill is to be fairly divided. But Christensen also presents another restaurant case, in which I am dining with seventeen other people, each of whom is known to be as reliable at arithmetic as I, and each of whom has come to the same conclusion about the fair division of the bill, a conclusion different from my own. Clearly in this case, as Christensen argues, I should believe that it is I who have made the mistake. Things are no different if we move from dividing the bill at a restaurant to solving a problem in decision theory. If my views on a problem in decision theory are entirely at odds with the experts in the field, then, even if I am myself such an expert – well known to hold a minority position on this issue – I would not be justified in continuing to hold the belief in the face of such opposition.[23]

This is not, in many cases, how experts behave. Experts will often go on holding a view even when they know that they are in the minority. If we restrict ourselves to formal areas like mathematics, logic, probability, and

---

[22] I am assuming here that our student has not come up with a new argument, for in such a case our student is familiar with an argument that the other side has not yet considered. There are interesting questions about the extent to which one should be confident that one is right even in such cases, but I will not consider them here.

[23] Again, as in Note 22, I am assuming that I have not discovered some new argument in favor of my position that is as yet unknown to the other members of the community.

decision theory, however, or to the empirical sciences, then the long-run prospects for such dissenters is not very good. These are all areas in which there is a well-established track record of reliable results issuing from the community, and, although dissenters are sometimes proven right, these communities are sufficiently reliable, and have been so for long enough, that one would always be ill advised to bet on the dissenter in the face of an overwhelming majority opinion. My point is simply that this is something that dissenters should realize as well. If the question at issue is thus whether one is justified in siding with the dissenter in the face of an overwhelming majority, the answer is that one is not, and this is true not only of bystanders who seek to inform their opinions by looking to the experts; it is true of the dissenter him- or herself.

Kelly's suggestion then that we should look only to the arguments directly bearing on a disputed question, and simply ignore the distribution of opinion, cannot be sustained.

III

So let us return to the internalism/externalism dispute and the question, more generally, of what we should make of disagreement within philosophy outside of the most formal areas. I have been arguing that the distribution of opinion is, contrary to Kelly, importantly relevant to what we should think about disputed matters. In the case of the internalism/externalism dispute, I will suppose, what I believe to be in fact true, that there is not an overwhelming majority of opinion among the experts within epistemology as to which of these approaches is correct. If opinion is not evenly divided on this issue, there is certainly not an overwhelming majority of expert opinion on one side rather than the other. What is it reasonable then to believe about this issue, given the current state of play? I believe that we are justified in withholding opinion on this issue, and that one would not be justified in believing either that internalism is correct or that externalism is correct.

Suppose, first, that one thinks that the philosophical community is, in relevant respects, like the mathematical or scientific communities. Suppose, that is, that one believes that individual philosophers are, by and large, quite reliable in their opinions in matters that touch on their areas of expertise, and that the community, overall, has shown a long history of steady progress on the issues it addresses. If one were to believe this (and be justified in believing it), then, as I have argued, the distribution of opinion is straightforwardly relevant to what one should believe, and, when opinion is closely divided, one ought to suspend judgment. So, in this case, suspension of judgment would be mandatory.

But surely it is not reasonable to believe that the philosophical community is like the mathematical or scientific communities in relevant respects. We do not have a long history of steady progress on issues, and, as a result, the case for deferring to community opinion is thereby weakened. But this hardly strengthens the hand of those who would form an opinion one way or the other on matters such as the debate between internalists and externalists. When the community is composed of individuals each of whom is reasonably believed to be reliable, we must bow to majority opinion. But, if we do not have reason to believe that the community is composed of individuals who are reliable, if the history of the field gives us no reason for confidence in the judgment of individual practitioners, then this, by itself, gives us reason to suspend judgment on questions that confront the field. If the history of the field shows no track record of success in addressing the issues it confronts, the only conclusion we can reasonably reach is that there is no basis for opinion here on anyone's part at all. It certainly does not give one free rein to believe whatever one pleases.

The sad truth, it seems, is that the history of philosophy does not look remotely like the history of science or mathematics when it comes to the dynamics of consensus among its most esteemed practitioners, and this has a striking bearing on the question of its epistemic credentials. One might try to carve out a recent piece of this history, and some particular subject matter, where one believes that real progress is being made and that we are finally getting at the truth on some important issue. I must confess that, in my more optimistic moments, I find such a view tempting. But, if we are to take any such view seriously, and subject it to real scrutiny, we would surely find that this view of the particular question at issue is itself a subject of real controversy among acknowledged experts in the field, and so it too must be seen, on careful consideration, as an issue on which we ought to suspend judgment. The field of philosophy in general, outside of the more formal areas that are most akin to mathematics, simply does not have anything like the epistemic standing of the empirical sciences. So, much as we all find ourselves forming beliefs about disputed philosophical questions when we immerse ourselves in the arguments, we should acknowledge in quiet moments of reflection that these views we form are ones that are not epistemically justified. It would be as presumptuous to claim that we are justified here as it would in Christensen's restaurant case when we find that our mathematically reliable dinner companion has reached a different conclusion about the division of the check.

It is not my view that the distribution of opinion is all the evidence one needs to determine what one should believe on any given question; such a view is completely untenable. It must be acknowledged, however, that the distribution of opinion among acknowledged experts must carry a tremendous amount of epistemic weight, and anyone who would reject a consensus among experts, or adopt a specific view in the face of deep division among experts, faces a very large hurdle. One must show that, in such a case, there is independent reason to believe that a substantial group of experts have gone wrong on the disputed matter.[24] To take a purely imaginary case, one might be able to show that a large portion of some field of experts had been kidnapped and forced to express certain views at gunpoint, and, in such a case, one would be fully justified in ignoring the expressed consensus in the field. Here one's evidence of the kidnapping would be entirely independent of the disputed question within the field, and, once the expressed opinions of the kidnapped experts were thereby discounted, one might well be in a position to have confidence in one's own judgment. But here, too, one would need to attend to the opinions of the remaining experts, if any. And I think it is perfectly clear that the high hurdle that bucking the consensus of expert opinion presents us with, even when we are among the experts ourselves, is one we are rarely, if ever, in a position to meet. I have no reason to believe, for example, that internalist epistemologists have been defending their views under threat from subversive kidnappers.[25]

I am thus forced to conclude, very reluctantly, that the opinions I hold on most philosophical matters – and I have a great many of them – are not epistemically justified. Given the current state of the field, no one's opinions on these matters, it now seems to me, are epistemically justified.

---

[24] Christensen's discussion of this point about independence is particularly illuminating.
[25] This bears on a question addressed by David Lewis in "Academic Appointments: Why Ignore the Advantage of Being Right?," reprinted in his *Papers in Ethics and Social Philosophy*, Cambridge University Press, 2000, 187–200. Lewis notes the common practice, not only in philosophy departments, of bracketing the truth of a candidate's views in making judgments about whether the candidate should be offered a job. Why should we do this? Lewis's answer is as follows: "We ignore the advantage of being right because we comply with a tacit treaty to do so. It is reasonable for all of us to think that this treaty, and therefore our present compliance that sustains it, serves the advancement of knowledge" (p. 197). While I do not doubt that considerations of this sort may play a role, I suspect that this is not the major factor in explaining the practice, and that it is not the most important factor in explaining the legitimacy of the practice. Rather, in my view, it is a somewhat inchoate awareness of the weak epistemic standing of our opinions on disputed questions that both motivates and justifies the practice.

More than this, this conclusion seems to generalize quite broadly. There are, for example, a great many moral and political issues, issues about which I have, in some cases, rather strong opinions, that are subjects of dispute among very intelligent, thoughtful, and well-informed individuals. In some of these cases, we can explain away the disagreement of otherwise reasonable people by way of moves less desperate than the suggestion that our opponents have expressed their views only under threat by kidnappers. We do, after all, sometimes have good, independent reason to believe that someone who disagrees with us on a particular question is biased on that very question. We should, however, be wary of making this move too easily. The requirement of independence means that we cannot reject the opinions of our opponents as the product of bias merely on the basis of the view that their opinions are false – since they disagree with our own – and therefore must inevitably be due to some sort of biasing factor. What this means, in the end, is that this sort of maneuver will help us only rarely in dispensing with the challenge of disagreement from peers. And what follows from this, of course, is that a broad skepticism threatens.

This is not the sort of total skepticism of the Cartesian demon, but it would certainly force a radical revision in our body of beliefs.

IV

One might try to resist this conclusion, not, as Kelly does, by denying the relevance of the opinions of others, but, instead, by denying that giving others' opinions their due weight in the interesting cases of disagreement – in philosophy, for example, and on moral and political questions – forces such a broad withholding of opinion. On such a view, idealized cases like Christensen's restaurant example do genuinely show that one's own opinions should be given no more deference than the opinions of one's epistemic peers, but features of the more complex cases – somehow – allow one to avoid the unwanted and widespread change in our bodies of belief to which the general principle seems to lead. This, to be sure, is a consummation devoutly to be wished. It is, moreover, precisely the position defended by Adam Elga.[26]

As Elga points out, when you and I disagree about the fair division of the check at the restaurant, our disagreement is highly isolated. We do not disagree about arithmetical questions in general. Indeed, I count you as my arithmetical peer precisely because we agree so broadly on arithmetical

---

[26] Elga, "Reflection and Disagreement."

questions. More than that, it is not just that we agree. You and I might agree on some questions, knowing full well that we are rank amateurs in an area where others are far better informed. But this is not the case in the restaurant example. We not only agree. We have good reason to believe that we are as well informed as just about anyone when it comes to these sorts of questions. We are fully justified in believing that we are both highly reliable in forming judgments about simple arithmetical issues. We simply disagree about an isolated question within arithmetic when we are each able to assess the other's track record on arithmetical questions in general in a perfectly straightforward way.

This is not so, as Elga points out, in many other areas. Thus, Elga imagines two friends, Ann and Beth, who disagree about abortion. Their disagreement about abortion, if we are to make the case realistic, as Elga does, is not an isolated disagreement. Instead, there is a very wide range of related moral questions about which Ann and Beth disagree. But this is no minor complication, as Elga argues, for now the very basis each has for regarding the other as generally reliable on the kinds of questions at issue has been undermined. I may regard you as reliable about arithmetic even when we disagree about how to divide the check at the restaurant because we agree, it may be supposed, about every other arithmetical question we have ever jointly considered. But Ann and Beth cannot regard each other as reliable about moral matters generally precisely because their disagreement is so broad. We will regard others as suitably reliable only when they agree with us very broadly. It is for this very reason, Elga argues, that we may eat our cake and have it too: we may acknowledge that the opinions of our epistemic peers count just as heavily as our own antecedent opinions, and yet deny that in areas of moral and political dispute, for example, we must simply withhold opinion. Thus, Elga concludes, "with respect to many controversial issues, the associates who one counts as peers tend to have views that are similar to one's own. That is why – contrary to initial impressions – the equal weight view does not require one to suspend judgment on everything controversial."[27]

One might try, in response to this move, to think of the dispute between Ann and Beth not as one about abortion alone, but as one about a cluster of related issues that includes the abortion question. Ann and Beth, one might argue, regard themselves as reliable on issues outside this cluster, and it is for this reason that they are troubled by their disagreement about the cluster itself. They should regard each other as reliable on the

[27] Elga, "Reflection and Disagreement," 494.

basis of their agreement on issues outside the cluster surrounding abortion, and this then forms the basis for taking the disagreement over the cluster of issues surrounding abortion as seriously as they do. Once one views the disagreement in this way, it seems, the parallel with the restaurant case is restored.

> But Elga denies this.
> Contrary to what the objection supposes, Ann does *not* consider Beth a peer about that cluster [of issues related to the abortion question]. In other words, setting aside her reasoning about the issues in the cluster, and setting aside Beth's opinions about those issues, Ann does not think Beth would be as likely as her to get things right. That is because there is no fact of the matter about Ann's opinion of Beth, once so many of Ann's considerations have been set aside ... Once so much has been set aside, there is no determinate fact about what opinion of Beth remains.

Thus, according to Elga, once again, we see that the basis for seeing our opponents on moral and political matters as generally reliable, when our disagreements are very broad,[28] is undermined. And, once our judgment of the reliability of our opponents has been thus undermined, he argues, we are entitled to go on believing as we did before the disagreement was encountered.

I do not believe, however, that Elga is right about this. First, it seems to me that Elga's attempt to undermine Beth's and Ann's judgments about each other's reliability here is unsuccessful. It is true that, in the imagined case, there is a large cluster of moral issues about which Ann and Beth disagree. But we need not exaggerate their disagreement. Thus, for example, Elga describes Ann and Beth as being "at opposite ends of the political spectrum." So it would not be unfair to imagine Ann as, say, someone who characterizes herself as a typical American pro-choice Democrat, and Beth as someone who characterizes herself as a typical American pro-life Republican. They disagree, to be sure, on a wide range of moral and political issues. But, although Beth and Ann disagree about a great deal, their disagreement is not at all like their disagreement with, for example, Zena, a homicidal sociopath. Zena does not just disagree with Ann or Beth about the cluster of moral issues surrounding the abortion

---

[28] This is an important qualification, as Elga notes. On Elga's view, disagreement on these matters with those who see things largely in the way we ourselves do can serve as an important check on our own opinions. As Elga notes, this, by itself, if taken to heart, would force important revisions in our bodies of belief. It would thus be wrong to paint Elga as some sort of quietist. He is merely trying to resist the very sweeping withholding of belief on controversial matters that I am defending here.

question. She disagrees with them about virtually every moral question one might care to raise.

Now I think it is safe to say that neither Ann nor Beth will be much troubled by Zena's disagreement with them, nor should they. And the reason why they should not is precisely that, when we subtract the moral issues on which Ann or Beth disagree with Zena from the totality of moral issues, there is virtually nothing left at all on which they might base a judgment that Zena is, but for their little disagreement, generally reliable about moral issues. Here we may reasonably say precisely what Elga says about the disagreement between Beth and Ann: once we set aside the issues on which Beth and Ann disagree with Zena, there simply is no basis for forming an opinion about Zena's reliability on moral issues. When we set aside the areas of disagreement, after all, there are no moral issues that are left.

But this, it needs to be emphasized, is not at all the case with the disagreement between Beth and Ann. They disagree profoundly about an important range of moral issues, but neither regards the other as the moral equivalent of Zena. Indeed, it is because they do not regard each other as Zena's moral equivalent that they are so engaged, and so disturbed, by each other's opinions. Beth and Ann regard each other as basically decent, caring, thoughtful individuals whose opinions on a very wide range of moral matters, outside the sphere of issues most closely related to abortion, are trustworthy and insightful. While they rightfully dismiss Zena's moral views out of hand, they are in respectful agreement about a very wide range of moral issues. And it is on this basis that they regard each other as moral epistemic peers, something they simply cannot do with Zena. Given that they do, justifiably, regard each other as moral epistemic peers, their grounds for withholding belief on the cluster of issues on which they disagree is thereby restored.

Note that the same is true when we consider disagreement about philosophical questions. I disagree with others about the proper resolution of the internalism/externalism debate in epistemology. But this is not like the restaurant case, where there is a disagreement about a single claim against the background of complete agreement about all other issues on the same general subject. Rather, once again, we have a case like the abortion issue. Those who I disagree with about internalism and externalism are philosophers with whom I disagree about a wide range of related issues. Does this then mean that I am no longer in a position to see these philosophers as my epistemic peers, as Elga suggests is the case with Beth and Ann on the abortion issue? Not at all. Even these disagreements, broad as they are, take place against a background of very broad agreement, agreement about the important issues in epistemology, about which positions are worth taking seriously, about what counts for and against various views, and so on. In short, I view internalists in epistemology in much the same way that Ann views Beth; I do not view internalists in the way that Ann views Zena. What this means, of course, is that there is ample room to view such philosophers as my epistemic peers, which is, in fact, precisely how I view them.

Disagreement on a wide range of related issues, as in the abortion debate or the internalism/externalism controversy, is not automatically a bar to reasonably viewing one's opponents as one's epistemic peers. And it is for this very reason that, on many matters of great controversy, the only rational thing to do is to suspend belief.

V

It is worth thinking about these controversial matters from a somewhat broader perspective. Consensus and near-consensus on formal issues within philosophy is so weighty epistemically, as I have suggested, because there is a history within these formal areas of undeniable progress. Against that background, consensus among the experts is a formidable matter. By the same token, disagreement among experts in those fields must also carry great weight. The same is true, of course, in the empirical sciences. When we look at the track record of less formal matters in philosophy, however, or on matters of public controversy having to do with moral and political issues, the case for a well-established track record of progress is, to be sure, harder to make out. Without that background of long-standing progress, we must look at individual investigators quite differently. In the sciences, we have good reason to believe that individual experts are each highly reliable overall, and they should surely regard one another in this way. Their considered opinions should thereby be tempered when there is disagreement in the field. In philosophy, however, and the other areas of controversy we have been considering here, there is no such history of long-standing progress, and for that very reason we should not consider the experts in the field – including, of course, ourselves – to be highly reliable. The history of the field simply does not give any ground for credence in such a view. But it is then, for that very reason, that we must, in the end, withhold opinion on the issues under consideration.

I do not mean to suggest that we should stop thinking about these issues, or that thinking about them, and trying to work out tenable views, is not intellectually respectable. This is not my view at all. And, given the nature of human belief, I very much doubt that philosophers will stop forming views about the subjects they think about for so long and with such care. When we stand back, however, and reflect on our practice and on the beliefs that that practice generates, it seems to me that the history of our field makes epistemic modesty the only rational position available. We may hope that in trying to work out the views we are most sympathetic to that, in the long run, we may somehow contribute to an approach to philosophy that will look more progressive than any we have thus far seen. But, at the present time, we should all recognize that this is merely a hope, and that rational belief must be tempered by the facts about our current situation.

7

*Naturalism vs. the First-Person Perspective**

Quite a number of philosophers have discussed features of the first-person perspective that might seem to create problems for naturalism. According to some, it is qualitative character which creates a problem for the naturalist. According to others, it is consciousness itself which is the source of the real problem for naturalism. And according to still others, it is the fact that we are capable of thinking of ourselves from a first-person point of view which naturalists cannot capture. All of these suggestions create interesting problems for naturalism, and they have all been deservedly discussed at length. But I will not be discussing any of these problems here, for in this essay, I am not interested in the ways in which the first-person perspective might create problems for naturalism. I am interested, instead, in how it is that naturalism creates problems for the first-person perspective.

In my view, the first-person perspective gets far more respect than it deserves. There are serious problems with the view which the first-person perspective affords, and naturalism nicely brings these out. The first-person perspective needs to be taken down a notch, and naturalism is well-placed to do the job. Or so I will argue.

I

The case for the primacy of the first-person perspective finds its most vivid and uncompromising expression in the work of Descartes. On Descartes' view, epistemological questions are essentially first-personal questions. The most fundamental question in epistemology, for Descartes, is, "What should I believe?," but it is not the mere fact that this question is couched

---

* Versions of this essay were presented to the Jowett Society, University of Oxford; Western Michigan University; MIT; and the Pacific Division meeting of the American Philosophical Association. Discussion on those occasions was particularly helpful in putting together the final version of this essay. I am grateful as well to Allen Wood for detailed written comments.

in first-personal terms that makes Descartes' approach so distinctive. After all, I might approach the question about what I should believe by looking to various authorities about whatever issue I might be interested in, and simply defer to them. Alternatively, I might look to the best available work in experimental psychology to see what sorts of illusions and biases humans are most susceptible to, and what kinds of processes of belief acquisition are most reliable, and then attempt to draw on this work in conducting my inquiries. But both of these approaches, while they address the first-personal question about what I ought to believe, fail to adopt a first-personal approach in answering it.

When I examine the psychological literature which addresses the reliability of human belief-forming mechanisms, I adopt a third-person perspective on my own belief acquisition. I treat myself as one person among many, an embodied cognitive mechanism, and the method I make use of in examining that mechanism is the very same method I might adopt in examining anyone else's cognitive mechanism. It is also the same method that someone else might use in examining my cognitive mechanism. Indeed, the method of inquiry I adopt here, in which I treat my mental processes as objects of theoretical investigation, is no different from the method I might adopt in investigating non-mental features of the world. The fact that the object of investigation is mental, and, more importantly, that it is my mentality which is at issue, does not come into play. But this is just to say that this way of approaching things adopts a third-personal approach to my first-personal question. And the same is true, of course, when I simply consult with various experts. What is distinctive about Descartes' project is not just that he asks a question which is couched in first-personal terms, but rather that he insists upon a first-personal method for addressing it.

First Philosophy, for Descartes, is tied to the method of doubt: the idea that we must begin our epistemological investigations by suspending judgment on any claim about which mistake is so much as possible. This method embodies an approach which assigns an extremely heavy weighting to the epistemic disvalue of false belief, an extraordinary pessimism about the perils of belief unreflectively produced, and a remarkable optimism about the powers of introspection and reflection. Descartes' epistemological method is aided and abetted by a metaphysical view of the mind which places it outside the natural world, unconstrained by physical law, thus leaving Descartes himself unconstrained by the need to explain the workings of the mind in a way which answers to the usual standards of satisfactory explanations.

One cannot find contemporary philosophers, of course, who simply endorse the entire package of Cartesian views. Descartes' metaphysical views about the mind are almost universally rejected, as are his views about the infallibility of introspective belief. Nevertheless, the idea of the primacy of the first-person perspective is very much alive. Thus, for example, Richard Foley not only insists that the most fundamental question in epistemology is, "What am I to believe?," but he also insists that the proper approach to this first-personal question must itself proceed from a first-person point of view.

> I am to make up my mind by marshaling my intellectual resources in a way that conforms to my own deepest standards. If I conduct my inquiries in such a way that I would not be critical of the resulting beliefs even if I were to be deeply reflective, then these beliefs are rational for me in an important sense, an egoistic sense ... The basic idea is that if I am to be egoistically rational, I must not have internal reasons for retraction, ones whose force I myself would acknowledge were I to be sufficiently reflective.[1]

It is Foley's insistence that the appropriate standard here is set by reflection – the standards I would acknowledge if I were appropriately reflective – that commits him to the primacy of the first-person perspective.

Foley is certainly not alone in this. Laurence BonJour has long championed an internalist approach to questions about epistemic justification. Although he acknowledges the legitimacy of the kind of third-person approach to epistemological questions which is embodied in experimental investigations of psychological processes, BonJour wants to insist that any such investigation is essentially derivative.

> I want to insist that there is a clear way in which an internalist approach, in addition to being intellectually legitimate on its own, has a fundamental kind of priority for epistemology as a whole.[2]

For BonJour, as for Foley, it is the first-person approach to the question of what I should believe which is most fundamental.

It is, I suppose, unsurprising that internalists about epistemic justification should accept Cartesian views about the primacy of the first-person perspective.[3] But even many who say that they endorse some form of externalism about justification place a premium on the first-person

---

[1] "What Am I to Believe?," in Steven Wagner and Richard Warner, eds., *Naturalism: A Critical Appraisal*, University of Notre Dame Press, 1993, 148.
[2] "The Indispensability of Internalism," *Philosophical Topics* 29(2001), 62.
[3] See in addition, for example, Roderick Chisholm, *Theory of Knowledge*, Prentice-Hall, 1966, 1977, 1989; Earl Conee and Richard Feldman, *Evidentialism: Essays in Epistemology*, Oxford University

perspective. Thus, when Sinan Dogramaci addresses the question of why we're in a position to infer some deductive consequences of what we know, but not others, he insists that the question be posed in first-personal terms.[4] "I'm open to externalist views in the theory of justification," Dogramaci claims. "More specifically," he says,

> the view I'm open to is this: when one person calls another's belief unjustified (irrational, etc.), the attributed property is one that holds in virtue of conditions that are not always accessible to the subject of the evaluation.[5]

But in spite of this, Dogramaci insists that his question be posed from what he calls, "the subjective perspective"; it must be asked, and answered, from the first-person point of view. Why must the question be posed in this way?

> The fundamental reason for this is simple: I want to know about the epistemic justification I can, right now, claim for my beliefs. Anything inaccessible to me right now will not allow my claiming whatever justification it might generate.[6]

And as Dogramaci notes, this is a view he shares not only with Foley, but with Crispin Wright[7] and Christopher Peacocke.[8]

But why is what one may claim to be justified in believing so important? Dogramaci goes on,

> This question of one's first-personal claim to justification has a great deal of intrinsic philosophical interest and importance ... it derives importance from the fact that the first-personal claim to justification is partly constitutive of any non-skeptical and non-trivial worldview. Why? Well, if I cannot even judge that my beliefs are justified, then I will not be able to judge that my beliefs amount to knowledge, and that, I am worried, would almost already be to relinquish my beliefs altogether. I could try to hold on to my beliefs while foregoing the claim to justification, but that would be akratic, and, I suspect, psychologically unstable: the choice is thus either to not believe, or to believe with a claim to justification.[9]

Press, 2004; Richard Fumerton, *Metaepistemology and Skepticism*, Rowman and Littlefield, 1996, and *Epistemology*, Blackwell, 2006.

[4] "Intuitions for Inferences," *Philosophical Studies*, forthcoming.   [5] Ibid.   [6] Ibid.

[7] "On Basic Logical Knowledge," *Philosophical Studies* 106(2001), 41–85; "Warrant for Nothing (and Foundations for Free)?," *Aristotelian Society Supplementary Volume* 78(2004), 167–212; "Internal–External: Doxastic Norms and the Defusing of Sceptical Paradox," *Journal of Philosophy* 105(2008), 501–517.

[8] "Conscious Attitudes, Attention and Self-Knowledge," in Crispin Wright, Barry Smith, and Cynthia Macdonald, eds., *Knowing Our Own Minds*, Oxford University Press, 1998, 63–99.

[9] Op. cit.

So as Dogramaci would have it, even externalists, if they are not to be skeptics, must acknowledge the importance of the first-person perspective on one's justification. One finds similar sentiments expressed in the work of Selim Berker,[10] Adam Leite,[11] and Ernest Sosa.[12]

Let me be straightforward here. I don't agree with any of this. I believe that the first-person perspective is just one perspective among many, and it is wholly undeserving of the special place which these philosophers would give it. More than this, this perspective is one which fundamentally distorts our view of crucial features of our epistemic situation. Far from lauding the first-person perspective, we should seek to overcome its defects. We will only be able to understand our epistemic situation if we stop trying to view it from the first-person perspective.

Let me try to support these claims.

II

There is a good deal of work by experimental psychologists on what happens when we take the first-person perspective on our mental states and processes, and on the reliability of the beliefs which are produced under conditions of reflection.[13] I will focus here on our first-person view of the processes by which our beliefs are produced, since these beliefs play a crucial role in internalist epistemology.

The vast majority of our beliefs are formed unreflectively. Merely going about our lives, engaged in everyday tasks, we inevitably form beliefs about our surroundings without stopping to engage in any sort of reflective examination of the origins or epistemic credentials of those beliefs. But it is not merely beliefs about our surroundings which are typically formed unreflectively. New information we acquire is typically inferentially integrated with the rest of our beliefs without any need for reflective self-examination. Our mental mechanisms go to work producing beliefs in us without the intervention of first-person thought. For much of our lives, our focus is on the world around us, rather than the world within.

---

[10] "Epistemic Teleology and the Separateness of Propositions," *Philosophical Review*, forthcoming.
[11] "On Justifying and Being Justified," *Philosophical Issues* 14(2004), 219–253.
[12] I have in mind, in particular, Sosa's frequent emphasis on the importance of reflective knowledge in addition to animal knowledge. See the essays in *Reflective Knowledge: Apt Belief and Reflective Knowledge*, vol. II, Oxford University Press, 2009.
[13] I have discussed this work in some detail in my "Introspection and Misdirection," Chapter 1; chapter 4 of *Knowledge and Its Place in Nature*, Oxford University Press, 2002; and section 1.3 of *On Reflection*, Oxford University Press, 2012.

Nevertheless, we do, at times, stop to reflect on the contents of our own minds, and we sometimes stop to reflect on the origins of our beliefs as well as their epistemic status. When we are engaged in such reflective self-examination, we adopt the first-person perspective on our mental states and processes, and we are presented with a very vivid and compelling picture of our mental lives. If one stops to ask oneself what reasons one has for holding some particular belief, one frequently finds that an answer immediately suggests itself: one's reasons for holding that belief can, it seems, be quickly identified. More than this, one is frequently left with the powerful impression that one has not only identified the reasons one possesses, reasons which might serve to justify the belief in question if only they were, in fact, one's basis for holding that belief. One is also, in a great many cases, left with the powerful impression that one has identified the very basis on which one formed, or on which one currently holds, the belief in question. Our access to these facts seems to be non-inferential; we can just tell what the bases for at least a great many of our beliefs are.

How accurate is this view from the first-person perspective? Ziva Kunda nicely summarizes a very large body of psychological research on this issue:

> Our judgments, feelings, and behaviors can be influenced by factors that we have never been aware of and have only been exposed to subliminally, by factors that we were aware of at one time but can no longer recall, and by factors that we can still recall but whose influence we are unaware of.[14]

The first-person perspective thus inevitably leaves out a great many of the factors which are crucially involved in producing and sustaining our beliefs. Some of these factors are essential to explaining why it is that the beliefs formed on such a basis are so reliable. Others, of course, are sources of bias which, were we only aware of them, would allow us to recognize the unreliable bases on which many of our beliefs are held. The very nature of the process of first-person self-examination, however, makes these factors invisible to us, and, for that very reason, it simply will not do to suggest that we should introspect more carefully or at greater length in order to put ourselves in a position accurately to assess our epistemic situation.[15] The first-person perspective presents a partial and distorted view of the bases of our beliefs.

---

[14] *Social Cognition: Making Sense of People*, MIT Press, 1999, 308.
[15] Both Laurence BonJour and Richard Feldman have suggested that more careful introspection would be sufficient to address a good deal of this problem. See BonJour, "Kornblith on Knowledge and Epistemology," *Philosophical Studies* 127(2006), esp. 324–326; and Feldman, "Chisholm's Internalism and Its Consequences," *Metaphilosophy* 34(2003), 607.

It is worth enumerating some of the factors which come into play when we stop to reflect on our mental states and processes, if only to make more vivid just how deep this problem is. As Kunda points out, there are a very large number of subliminal factors which may play a role in belief formation. Many of these will rightly be viewed as non-cognitive. This is not to say that a proper assessment of the reliability of our belief-forming processes should omit these factors. Some of these factors, indeed, help to explain our reliability in forming judgments in a wide range of situations. Others, of course, serve to make us unreliable. I will focus here, however, on cognitive elements in first-person self-examination.

In cases where we have already formed some belief, and then stop to reflect on whether we do, indeed, have good reason to hold it, we will often stop to reflect on the evidence we have acquired over an extended period of time. If I stop to reflect on whether some belief I have about the current economic situation is justified, for example, I will recognize immediately that there is a very wide range of evidence which has come to my attention about this matter and I will endeavor to bring it to mind. It is well documented that our ability to recall relevant evidence in such a situation is deeply biased: we are far better able to recall evidence which confirms existing beliefs than evidence which counts against them.[16] The result, of course, is that although we recognize that, at times, there are good reasons to question the reliability of our processes of belief acquisition and retention, the biased manner in which we recall relevant evidence makes it likely that when we engage in reflective examination of our evidential situation, we will come to believe that the evidence we have provides strong support for the beliefs we have formed unreflectively. The understandable desire to engage in reflective checking on the reliability of our belief acquisition and retention is thereby undermined, ironically, by the unreliability of crucial features of the process of reflective checking.

This is but one element, of course, in the processes which come into play when we engage in reflection. It is important to point out, however, that reflective self-examination, contrary to what it seems from the first-person point of view, is not typically a process of directly registering various internal states and processes. Instead, there are rather elaborate inferential processes at work, processes which, in effect, attempt to reconstruct what must have been going on in us when, for example, we formed some particular belief. When we introspect and ask ourselves why it is that

---

[16] Richard Nisbett and Lee Ross, *Human Inference: Strategies and Shortcomings of Social Judgment*, Prentice-Hall, 1980, 180–183.

we hold some belief, we unknowingly engage in a process of confabulation, frequently attributing various beliefs to ourselves, beliefs which we take to have been instrumental in producing the very belief we are questioning, but which we did not hold prior to the exercise of self-examination. The process of reflection seems to provide us with direct acquaintance with our reasons for belief, but, instead, it involves an elaborate inference, postulating a variety of reasons we never had, and presenting them in a particularly vivid and compelling form.[17]

Now it may be tempting to suggest that we should never have thought that reflection on our reasons for belief would give us an accurate account of the factors which originally produced our belief, and, indeed, it is doubtful that anyone ever suggested that it might. Nevertheless, it will be suggested, reflection on our reasons for belief does give us an accurate account of the reasons for which we hold a belief at the time we stop to reflect.

Such a response would miss the point of the foregoing discussion in two different ways. The process of reflecting on our reasons for belief not only fails, quite frequently, to give an accurate account of the reasons for which we originally held the belief; it frequently fails to give us an accurate account of the reasons for which we hold the belief at the time of reflection. The processes which are responsible for belief retention are not available for direct inspection, much as it seems as if they are when we stop to reflect. We confabulate when we engage in reflection, and the reasons we come to endorse frequently fail to track, even approximately, the reasons for which we hold the belief at the time of reflection. The causal processes responsible for belief retention are extremely complex, and the reconstructive processes involved in confabulation do not reveal them to us.

Moreover, even if our reasons for belief were to shift as a result of reflection so that the factors holding a belief in place were to come to mirror the story we tell ourselves when we confabulate, this would surely be a pyrrhic victory for the advocate of reflection. What the psychological evidence about reflective processes reveals is that we are subject to a very strong confirmation bias: when we stop to reflect on the epistemic credentials of the beliefs we already hold, we are strongly biased toward believing

---

[17] See, for example, Richard Nisbett and Timothy Wilson, "Telling More than We Can Know," *Psychological Review* 84(1977), 231–295; Timothy Wilson, *Strangers to Ourselves: The Adaptive Unconscious*, Harvard University Press, 2002; Peter Carruthers, *The Opacity of Mind: An Integrative Theory of Self-Knowledge*, Oxford University Press, 2011, esp. 339–345.

that they are held for good reasons. What this means is that engaging in reflective self-examination is a particularly ineffective way to detect our own errors. Beliefs which were originally formed in an unreliable manner are not likely to be discovered by way of reflective self-examination. Indeed, quite the contrary: when we reflect on the epistemic credentials of these beliefs, we are likely to confabulate reasons for holding them, and thereby regard ourselves as holding beliefs which are likely to be true. If these beliefs are now firmly entrenched by the reflective process, this is surely not a victory for reflection. Reflection self-examination was supposed to make our beliefs more accurate, by providing us with an additional check on our reasons for belief. If, instead, the reflective process tends to make us more confident in the very beliefs we ought to be rejecting, then this is a serious problem with reflective self-examination, rather than something in its favor.

It is important to see that this is not just a problem about reflecting in a casual or ham-fisted manner. In particular, it won't do to point out that, of course, the friends of reflection all favor certain sorts of idealizing constraints on reflection; they are not simply in favor of any manner of reflection, however badly or haphazardly it may be carried out.[18] Descartes, for example, insisted that one reflect in such a manner as to "produce clear and distinct ideas." Idealizations consistent with the spirit of defenses of reflection, however, cannot accommodate the findings of the experimental literature. The problems that arise when we stop to reflect derive from features of the reflective process which are unavailable to the reflective agent. They are not a product of careless or insufficiently lengthy reflection. Instead, they are inevitable consequences of the manner in which these processes work. Idealization cannot address this kind of problem, since any such idealization would need to identify the proper sort of reflection in terms of features available to the reflective agent, and what the experimental literature shows is that the problems with reflection are not available to the conscientious agent in just this way.

The first-person perspective on our reasons for belief thus offers us an utterly misleading view. There is nothing at all wrong with the thought that it can be worthwhile to check on our unreflective processes of belief acquisition. After all, they are not uniformly reliable. The problems I have been detailing, however, suggest that reflective self-examination of the sort offered by a first-person perspective on our beliefs fails utterly to do the job of locating the errors which we unreflectively make. The important job of

---

[18] I am grateful to Brad Skow for pressing me on this point.

error detection cannot be effectively carried out by adopting the first-person perspective on our reasons and our reasoning.

III

If the first-person perspective on our reasons and our reasoning is so inaccurate, why is it that so many philosophers regard such a perspective as fundamental? Let us return to the justifications for treating the first-person perspective with such deference which were briefly surveyed at the beginning of this essay.

Although Sinan Dogramaci endorses an externalist account of justification, he insists that the first-person perspective is crucial for addressing certain questions about legitimate inference. Even if we concede to the externalist, as Dogramaci believes we should, that factors unavailable to the reflective agent may be crucial in determining whether a belief the agent holds is justified, the first-person perspective is relevant to what the agent may *claim* to be justified in believing. "Anything inaccessible to me right now," Dogramaci insists, "will not allow my claiming whatever justification it might generate." Thus, if an agent believes that p, then even if the agent is justified in holding that belief, it may yet be that the agent is not in a position to claim justification for that belief, for the simple reason that the agent lacks reflective access to the factors which make the belief justified. More than this, as Dogramaci sees it, what an agent may claim to be justified in believing is particularly important. If we imagine an agent with a justified belief that p, and yet without reflective access to the very features which make the belief justified, then the agent will be in a particularly unstable position: continuing to believe that p without being able to claim justification for one's belief would be "akratic." As Dogramaci sees it, "the choice is thus either to not believe, or to believe with a claim to justification." Belief without being able to claim justification is unstable, and being able to claim justification for a belief requires that it survive first-personal scrutiny. The importance of the first-person perspective is thereby assured.

Now I certainly understand why it is that those who favor an internalist account of epistemic justification should attach such importance to the first-person perspective. It is puzzling, however, why an externalist should do so. Dogramaci's argument turns on a view about when an agent may claim justification for a belief, and his standards here are straightforwardly internalist: the belief must pass reflective scrutiny; it must meet certain standards when viewed from the first-person perspective. Why, however, should an externalist about epistemic justification endorse such an internalist view about when an agent may claim justification? Someone who believes, for example, that a belief is epistemically justified just in case it is reliably produced or sustained might well think that one may claim justification for a belief in the very situation in which it is reliably produced or sustained: one may, in short, claim justification whenever one is, in fact, justified. Alternatively, an externalist might reasonably hold the view that one may claim justification for a belief just in case one's belief that the belief in question is justified is itself justified: thus, one's belief that one's belief is justified must itself be reliably produced or sustained. There are other externalist views available as well. There seems little motivation, however, once one is an externalist about epistemic justification, for holding internalist standards for claiming justification.

Anyone who is an externalist about epistemic justification must allow that there may be circumstances in which an agent is justified in holding a belief and yet that agent fails to meet internalist standards for justification. It is precisely such a situation which seems to animate Dogramaci. But externalists believe that the internalist standards for justification are simply mistaken; one needn't have introspectively accessible evidence which adequately supports a belief in order for that belief to be justified. Once one recognizes this, the discovery that one fails to have such introspectively accessible evidence, in a given case, should hardly be a source of instability.

One might nevertheless think that there is something odd, at a minimum, about being in a situation in which one holds a particular belief and yet believes oneself to be unjustified. There is even something odd, again, at a minimum, it seems, about holding some particular belief and recognizing that one has no view whatsoever about whether one is justified. But the externalist need not find himself in either of these positions when introspectively accessible evidence is lacking. An externalist should not hold his beliefs hostage to the dictates of introspectively available evidence. An externalist who believes that *p*, and yet finds, on reflection, that introspectively available evidence for *p* is lacking, might nevertheless find as well that he believes that he is justified in believing *p*. Would this latter conviction about the epistemic status of the belief that *p* itself be justified? According to externalism, it is indeed justified if, for example, it is produced or sustained by a reliable process. What is good for first-order beliefs is good for second-order beliefs as well. It is important to recognize that externalists are not externalists about first-order belief only while holding that second-order belief must meet internalist standards. Externalism is a view about justified belief of whatever order.[19]

There is nothing at all odd about an externalist finding himself in a situation of this sort. Many externalists have argued, after all, that internalism leads to skepticism. There simply isn't enough introspectively available evidence to satisfy internalist standards for justification even in simple perceptual situations. Externalists hold, however, that we are often sufficiently responsive to external facts, at times, so that our beliefs are produced in ways which make our beliefs justified. To take the simplest externalist view, our beliefs are sometimes reliably produced. But circumspect agents may also be sufficiently responsive to facts about their epistemic situation so that their beliefs about whether they are epistemically justified are themselves reliably produced, despite the lack of introspectively available evidence on the issue. No one who is an externalist should find this latter suggestion any more implausible than the former.

The worry that Dogramaci presents, that externalists must inevitably find themselves in the unstable and akratic position of holding beliefs which they themselves take to be unjustified, is thus entirely misplaced.[20] Reflective externalists need not, and should not, form beliefs about the epistemic standing of their first-order beliefs on the basis of internalist standards. There are interesting psychological questions about how it is that circumspect agents may come to be well-calibrated; that is, how such agents may come to be able to reliably register the epistemic standing of their beliefs. But just as externalists do not suppose that justified beliefs about the world outside our minds must come with

---

[19] The mistake Dogramaci makes here – and the points made against Dogramaci apply, *mutatis mutandis*, to the arguments of Wright and Peacocke in the works cited in Notes 7 and 8 – is quite similar to a mistake made by Barry Stroud and Laurence BonJour when they argue that externalists may only claim to have knowledge if certain conditions are met, but not claim to have knowledge *tout court*. See Barry Stroud, "Understanding Human Knowledge in General," reprinted in his *Understanding Human Knowledge*, Oxford University Press, 2000, 99–121; and Laurence BonJour, "The Indispensibility of Internalism," 47–65. I have replied to these arguments in detail in "Does Reliabilism Make Knowledge Merely Conditional?," *Philosophical Issues* 14(2004), 185–200.

[20] I don't mean to suggest that externalists could not find themselves in situations which raise concerns about epistemic akrasia. Indeed, I think that they can. But it is not at all clear that this is a problem unique to externalists. After all, on any fallibilist view about justification, whether internalist or externalist, it seems that there will be room for a gap between what one is justified in believing and what one is justified in believing that one is justified in believing. If this is right, then worries about epistemic akrasia, interesting as they are, cannot be used as a cudgel to beat externalists. Even if it should turn out, however, that there is some problem about epistemic akrasia which is unique to externalism, it cannot be the problem which Dogramaci raises above. I want to thank Sophie Horowitz for pressing me on this issue.

accessible justifiers, neither do they suppose that justified beliefs about the epistemic standing of our own beliefs must be accompanied by accessible justifiers.

Dogramaci's suggestion, then, that even externalists should recognize the importance of the first-person perspective relies on a failure to see what a thoroughgoing externalism really requires. In light of the facts about the unreliability of much of our reflective scrutiny of our reasons, it would be odd indeed if externalists were to pay a great deal of heed to the first-person perspective.

IV

There is a related case to be made for the importance of the first-person perspective, and it has to do with deliberation, whether about what to believe, or about what to do. We do, periodically, engage in deliberation, and we deliberate with a certain end in mind. At times, we wonder what it is that we ought to believe, and we deliberate with the intention of influencing our belief acquisition in constructive ways. By the same token, we deliberate about what to do, and the process of deliberation is undertaken with the intention of constructively affecting our actions. Deliberation is an activity which crucially involves a first-person perspective on our beliefs, desires, and activities. No one would suggest that we should cease to deliberate. So the importance of the first-person perspective seems assured.

Let us examine the two kinds of deliberation separately. I will begin with cases of deliberation about what to believe. Consider a situation in which a doctor – let's call her Mary – is attempting to diagnose a patient with a complicated set of symptoms. Mary has run the usual tests, and the results did not unequivocally point in any particular direction. This led Mary to run additional tests, and the results now begin to suggest a clearer picture. But Mary is a careful and circumspect diagnostician. She stops to reflect on what it is that she ought to believe in light of the full array of tests that she has performed. As she reflects about the upshot of the various test results, she self-consciously engages in various bits of reasoning. "These results seem to suggest Diagnosis A," she might think, "but these other results count against that diagnosis." At some point, she may form an all-in conclusion: "In light of the full array of test results, it now seems that Diagnosis B is what I ought to believe." Having come to this conclusion, Mary comes to believe that Diagnosis B is, in fact, correct, and she proceeds to act on that belief.

Naturalism vs. the First-Person Perspective

I want to ask a number of questions about what goes on when Mary deliberates, and what it is that Mary believes when she engages in deliberation. What is Mary's intention in deliberating? What does she believe is going on when she deliberates? To what extent does Mary actually achieve what she intends?

I think the question about Mary's intention is easily answered. Mary engages in deliberation because she believes that she is facing a complicated epistemic situation, and in such situations, she believes that she will be more reliable in coming to a conclusion if she deliberates than if she just forms a belief unreflectively. This is, I think, an utterly commonsensical idea, and it surely makes explicit the motivation which we typically have when we engage in deliberation.[21]

When Mary engages in deliberation, she self-consciously engages in reasoning. If we were to ask Mary what she is doing when she deliberates, no doubt she would tell us that she is focusing on certain bits of evidence, examining their relevance and probity, and drawing various conclusions. Subjects in situations like this confidently report on the reasoning that they have undertaken, and confidently explain exactly what the bases for their conclusions are.[22] Deliberation does not seem to involve some sort of passive awareness of processes going on within us.[23] It seems, instead, to involve an active undertaking, in which we draw conclusions from available evidence. When we are engaged in this activity, it seems, we know exactly what we are doing. We may not draw the proper conclusions from our evidence all of the time, but it surely seems that we know full well what conclusions we are drawing, and on what basis we are drawing them. The process of reasoning, it seems, when we engage in deliberation, is fully transparent to us.

---

[21] Thus, for example, consider Ernest Sosa's suggestion about the advantages gained by way of reflective examination of the source of one's belief and its reliability:

> Since a direct response supplemented by such understanding would in general have a better chance of being right, reflective knowledge is better justified than corresponding animal knowledge. ("Knowledge and Intellectual Virtue," in his *Knowledge in Perspective*, Cambridge University Press, 1991, 240)

[22] For an experimental examination of first-person accounts of deliberation, see K. Anders Ericsson and Herbert Simon, *Protocol Analysis: Verbal Reports as Data*, revised ed., MIT Press, 1993.

[23] It is for this reason that Stuart Hampshire and Richard Moran speak of self-knowledge in the deliberative situation as involving "a decision rather than a discovery." See Hampshire, *Freedom of the Individual*, Princeton University Press, 1975, and Moran, *Authority and Estrangement: An Essay on Self-Knowledge*, Princeton University Press, 2001. It seems doubtful to me that such a suggestion can form the basis for an account of self-knowledge for it seems to presuppose, rather than explain, our knowledge of our own decisions.

These commonsense claims about deliberation commit us to a host of empirical claims, and it is well worth asking to what extent they are true. The evidence quickly presented at the beginning of this essay provides us with part of the answer. The first point to make is that our reasoning is not transparent to us, even under conditions of deliberation. The factors which influence us when we reason are not all available to introspection, and our introspective judgments about our reasoning processes, as was pointed out earlier, frequently involve confabulation. Our judgments about which factors influence our judgments, and which do not, are quite unreliable. Much of the cognitive activity which plays a role in our deliberations simply does not make its presence felt to the first-person perspective. Our first-personal view of the deliberative process is not only quite partial; it is also not fully accurate, even as far as it goes.

Consider cases of inference to an explanation, such as the case of Mary's deliberation about a proper diagnosis. Subjects in cases like this are aware of considering a relatively small amount of data at a time; the capacity of working memory does not allow for large bodies of data to be brought to consciousness.[24] Nevertheless, information not present to consciousness plays a substantial role in the inferences we make. When alternative explanations of a body of data are considered, in the typical case, a relatively small number of such explanations come to mind. Why it is that these explanations are considered, rather than alternatives, is not, in the typical case, part of our conscious reasoning.[25] Nevertheless, there is, of course, a cognitive explanation for why it is that we consider the credentials of some explanatory hypotheses and not others. What we are aware of in deliberation, however, is nothing more than that we are considering some explanations and not others. The vast majority of our cognitive activity is not present to the first-person perspective.

The first-person perspective on our deliberations thus presents us with a vivid and compelling picture of our reasoning. We seem to have a direct awareness of all of the factors which are playing a role in the fixation of our beliefs, when, in fact, we are influenced by an extremely wide range of factors of which we are wholly unaware, while many of the factors we

---

[24] George A. Miller, "The Magical Number Seven Plus or Minus Two," *Psychological Review* 63 (1956), 81–97.

[25] I do not mean to suggest, of course, that this too cannot be an object of self-conscious deliberation. In many cases, however, it is not, and my point is simply that in these cases, a great deal of cognitive activity is taking place behind the scenes. More than this, the same is, of course, true when we self-consciously examine why it is that we consider some explanatory hypotheses and not others. The full picture of our cognitive activity is never present to consciousness.

believe to be influencing our belief fixation, in a wide range of cases, play no role in that process whatsoever. The perspective of the deliberating agent is grossly misleading.

Similarly, the intentions of the deliberating agent – namely, to provide some additional check on processes of belief acquisition which operate unreflectively, or, alternatively, to form beliefs in a more reliable way than would occur were belief acquisition to take place without self-conscious deliberation – are frequently frustrated, although the deliberating agent is blissfully unaware of this fact. Reflective checking on the epistemic status of one's unreflectively arrived at beliefs is frequently epiphenomenal with respect to belief fixation. The ways in which confirmation biases come into play when we stop to reflect on our already existing beliefs make it overwhelmingly likely, in a great many kinds of case, that these beliefs, whatever their epistemic status, will pass our reflective tests. What seems, from the first-person perspective, to be a careful and responsible additional check on our reasons and reasoning is, instead, in a great many cases, little more than a self-affirming pat on the back which does precious little to weed out beliefs which were the product of misguided inferences and unreliable processes. Deliberation where there is no pre-existing belief need not satisfy our intention to improve our reliability either. Deliberation sometimes improves our reliability, to be sure. It also often makes us less reliable than we otherwise would be,[26] and, in many cases, makes no difference at all.

From the first-person perspective, it seems just obvious that the process of deliberation is a vast improvement on belief unreflectively arrived at, but reflection does not have anything like such uniformly beneficial effects. The first-person perspective systematically misleads us about the epistemic value of reflective thought.

V

The case of deliberation about what to do raises a number of additional issues. As with the case of deliberation about what to believe, the deliberating agent is motivated to deliberate, in the typical case, by the thought that deliberation will improve the quality of decision-making. But the

---

[26] See, for example, Jamin Halberstadt and Timothy Wilson, "Reflections on Conscious Reflection: Mechanisms of Impairment by Reasons Analysis," in Jonathan Adler and Lance Rips, eds., *Reasoning: Studies of Human Inference and Its Foundations*, Cambridge University Press, 2008, 548–565.

value of deliberation about what to do is widely thought to go beyond the merely instrumental improvement of one's choice activity. Famously, Harry Frankfurt argued that it is our ability to deliberate about what to do which secures the possibility of freedom of the will.[27] Lower animals, who lack the ability to reflect upon their beliefs and desires, may act freely, according to Frankfurt; their actions may be informed by their beliefs and desires so that they act in ways which will secure them what they want, if only their beliefs are true. But this falls far short of the status that adult human beings have, for in our ability to reflect on our beliefs and desires, and thereby consider whether we want to be moved by our inclinations, we achieve the status of personhood, and thereby have the ability not only to act freely, but to manifest freedom of the will. Our ability to deliberate, on this view, which crucially involves our taking the first-person perspective on our choices, not only improves the quality of our decisions, but secures a kind of freedom unavailable to creatures who cannot take the first-person perspective on their mental states.

Those philosophers, such as Christine Korsgaard, who place heavy emphasis on the significance of reflective endorsement, see a similar import in the view of the deliberating agent. Thus, Korsgaard remarks,

> "Reason" means reflective success. So if I decide that my desire is a reason to act, I must decide that on reflection I endorse that desire.[28]

It is our reflective endorsement of action on the basis of particular desires, according to Korsgaard, that is essential to our freedom.

These views take the perspective of the deliberating agent, the first-person perspective on our decisions about what to do, far too uncritically. As Nomy Arpaly points out, the internal monologue of the self-controlled individual who decides to avoid a calorie-laden piece of chocolate cake may be no different from the internal monologue of the anorectic who slowly and systematically starves herself to death as a result of a compulsion.[29] Both reflectively endorse the action of eschewing the chocolate cake, and both reflectively rehearse the same considerations in its favor. But reflective endorsement is no hallmark of freedom, nor is it a hallmark of having a reason. What Frankfurt and Korsgaard are vividly aware of is that first-order desires may, at times, be somehow alien to the agent they reside in. Frankfurt's unwilling addict has a strong desire for drugs, and yet he wants

---

[27] "Freedom of the Will and the Concept of a Person," reprinted in his *The Importance of What We Care About: Philosophical Essays*, Cambridge University Press, 1988, 11–25.

[28] *The Sources of Normativity*, Cambridge University Press, 1996, 97.

[29] *Unprincipled Virtue: An Inquiry into Moral Agency*, Oxford University Press, 2003, 18.

not to be moved by that desire. This is certainly a familiar phenomenon, even apart from addiction. But just as first-order desires may, in an important sense, be alien to the individual who has them, the same is true of second-order desires. The mere having of a first-order desire does not legitimate it, and the same is true of the reflective endorsements of the deliberating agent. What makes a desire alien to an agent is a deep fact about that agent's psychology and the way in which the desire is embedded in it. The deliberating agent's reflective endorsements do not automatically track these facts.

I certainly do not want to deny that adult human beings are far more sophisticated creatures than animals which lack second-order mental states. Philosophers, such as Frankfurt and Korsgaard, who attach great importance to the perspective of the deliberating agent, however, treat that perspective with far too much deference. If we are to understand the nature of intentional action, and the process of deliberation itself, then it will be imperative that we have an accurate view of the psychological processes which inform both intentional action and deliberation. The perspective of the deliberating agent does not provide us with such a view.

Just as in the case of deliberation about what to believe, deliberation about what to do typically is motivated by the thought that such deliberation will improve our performance. Deliberation can, of course, have such an effect. Such a positive effect, however, is no more uniformly associated with deliberation about what to do than it is with deliberation about what to believe.[30] Here too, the effects of deliberation are decidedly mixed. It may enhance one's performance by allowing one more effectively to recognize which actions best satisfy one's desires and conform to one's values; but it may also degrade one's performance, either by misleading one about the best course of action or by impairing one's ability to act on one's decisions. Finally, just as in the case of deliberation about what to believe, it may leave things just as they would have been without deliberation, while simultaneously leaving one with the impression that one has improved the quality of one's decision.

Deliberation does, of course, crucially involve taking a first-person perspective on one's beliefs or one's actions, but the first-person perspective we take during deliberation does not play an unqualifiedly positive role. The first-person perspective is fraught with limitations and distortions. The act of deliberation does not somehow sidestep these features of

---

[30] Here too, see Wilson, *Strangers to Ourselves*; and Halberstadt and Wilson, "Reflection on Conscious Reflection."

that perspective. Instead, if we are properly to understand how deliberation works, we must recognize it as a product, in part, of these very shortcomings.

VI

It is, perhaps, a professional liability of philosophers to overvalue reflective thought, and with it, the first-person perspective which is an essential part of it. The recognition that beliefs unreflectively acquired may be unreliable, and that actions unreflectively taken may fail to answer to our concerns, seems to motivate a more reflective approach to belief acquisition and action. If unreflective activity is fraught with the possibility of error and misjudgment, the thought goes, reflective checking can surely provide the solution. Commonsensical as such a thought may be, it is utterly misguided. Just as unreflective thought is subject to the possibility of error, reflective checking is as well. Reflective checking does not automatically improve one's situation merely in virtue of one's good intentions. Moreover, as we have seen here, this worry does not present some mere logical possibility. The limitations and distortions of the first-person perspective are, indeed, substantial. This, together with the fact that unreflectively acquired belief and unreflective action are, in a very wide range of cases, quite reliable and effective, significantly circumscribes the appeal of reflective thought.

Indeed, the situation is worse than this. If the original motivating thought was that belief unreflectively acquired is just irresponsible, precisely because of the concern about its reliability, then the appeal to reflection offers a solution which could not possibly address the problem. If first-order beliefs unreflectively acquired are just irresponsible precisely because they are not reflected upon, then reflecting upon them will only leave us with second-order beliefs which have the same problem. We must stop reflecting somewhere, and, on this line of thought, our stopping place will leave us believing irresponsibly. The same is true, of course, in the case of action. Reflection is asked to do something here which simply cannot be done.

A great deal of thought about reflection, and the first-person perspective which is an essential part of it, presents it as a kind of mystical phenomenon. If one is worried about the reliability of unreflective belief acquisition, one should appeal to reflection to solve the problem: introspect and take a first-person look at one's beliefs and the logical relations among them, and the worries one had about unreflectively acquired belief will drop away. If one is worried that unreflective creatures are simply pushed around by their beliefs and desires and so lack some important sort of freedom, one should stop to reflect on one's desires – take the first-person perspective – and in reflectively endorsing action on the basis of one's preferred desire, a higher freedom will be achieved. Reflection and the first-person perspective cannot achieve these kinds of results, of course, because nothing can.

Once we treat reflection and the first-person perspective as natural phenomena, just as unreflective belief and action are, we will no longer be tempted to see them as some sort of universal solvent which may be applied to do away with our philosophical problems in one fell swoop. A demystified view of reflection, and the first-person perspective, are sorely needed if we are to understand these phenomena for what they are, and if we are to recognize not only the benefits, which they surely do, at times, provide us with, but their very real limitations as well. This is precisely what a naturalistic account promises to provide us with, and it is for this reason that I believe we are unlikely to revise, or correct, or defeat naturalism by way of insights gained from the first-person perspective. We shall, instead, come to understand the first-person perspective for the first time when we take a naturalistic approach to examining it.[31]

---

[31] I have tried to provide the beginnings of such an examination in *On Reflection*.

8

Is There Room for Armchair Theorizing in Epistemology?

Quine argued, of course, for the rejection of the very notion of the a priori,[1] and in "Epistemology Naturalized," in 1969, he argued for a general approach to epistemological questions which would be straightforwardly empirical.[2] Precisely what that program might be, however, was very much in dispute, among both those who wished to reject it and those who were eager to sign on. In the 1980s and 1990s, largely under the influence of Alvin Goldman,[3] the possibility of a thoroughly empirical approach to epistemology once again rose to the fore, and the question of whether epistemological theorizing might profitably be approached a priori, and what, if anything, the empirical sciences might contribute to epistemology, was much discussed.[4] Those who wished to defend traditional approaches to epistemological questions typically acknowledged the relevance of empirical results to certain questions about knowledge, but then went on to minimize the importance of this fact. Richard Feldman, for example, is typical here. He comments,

> Obviously, empirical work is relevant to "the study of human knowledge." But this shows its relevance to epistemology only if epistemology is as broad as the study of human knowledge. The complete study of human knowledge would, presumably, include historical studies of what people knew

---

[1] See especially, "Truth by Convention" (originally published in 1935) and "Carnap and Logical Truth" (originally published in 1954), both reprinted in Quine's *The Ways of Paradox and Other Essays*, revised and enlarged ed., Harvard University Press, 1976; and "Two Dogmas of Empiricism" (originally published in 1951), reprinted in Quine's *From a Logical Point of View*, Harper Torchbooks, 1961.
[2] In *Ontological Relativity and Other Essays*, Columbia University Press, 1969, 69–90.
[3] See especially "Epistemics: The Regulative Theory of Cognition," *Journal of Philosophy* 75(1978), 509–523; the papers collected in his *Liaisons: Philosophy Meets the Cognitive and Social Sciences*, MIT Press, 1992; and *Epistemology and Cognition*, Harvard University Press, 1986.
[4] See also the papers collected in Hilary Kornblith, ed., *Naturalizing Epistemology*, MIT Press, 1st ed., 1985; 2nd ed., 1994. My own approach to these issues is presented and defended in *Inductive Inference and Its Natural Ground*, MIT Press, 1993, and *Knowledge and Its Place in Nature*, Oxford University Press, 2002.

when; studies in neuroscience concerning the ways the brain processes information, sociological studies about the ways knowledge is transmitted in societies, and so on. While some philosophers may think that they have something to say from their armchairs about many of these topics, no sensible person could think that all such inquiries can succeed without scientific input. So it is hard to imagine any disagreement with the view that methodological naturalism is true given such a broad interpretation of what counts as epistemology.[5]

As Feldman went on to suggest, however, epistemology need not be understood as nearly so broad an enterprise, and, as Feldman urged, one might not need experimental input to epistemological issues more narrowly – and plausibly – conceived.

Feldman's response here, which was not at all atypical,[6] involves two points which deserve to be separated. First, there is the point about the breadth of epistemology properly speaking. But second, Feldman no longer talks about whether epistemological theorizing is a priori. Instead, he talks about whether epistemology might profitably be pursued from the armchair. This is an important distinction.

Thus, for example, in Timothy Williamson's recent book, *The Philosophy of Philosophy*,[7] Williamson sets out to defend an armchair approach to philosophical questions. As Williamson is eager to point out, however, this does not mean that empirical information is not relevant here. Indeed, Williamson rejects the a priori/a posteriori distinction, although for reasons importantly different from those of Quine.[8] More than this, Williamson is at pains to reject what he calls "philosophical exceptionalism," the view that proper methods in philosophy are different in kind from other sorts of inquiry. Nevertheless, Williamson, like Feldman, wishes to defend the integrity of philosophy as an armchair discipline. When we theorize from the armchair, our empirical beliefs will inevitably and properly play some non-trivial role in the conclusions which we reach. Nevertheless, there is a real difference between armchair theorizing and the straightforwardly empirical work which one sees, for example, in experimental psychology or experimental physics. Williamson, like Feldman, is concerned to defend the legitimacy of armchair methods in philosophy

---

[5] "Methodological Naturalism in Epistemology," in John Greco and Ernest Sosa, eds., *The Blackwell Guide to Epistemology*, Blackwell, 1999, 171.
[6] For similar sorts of remarks about the importance of externalism, and the way in which empirical information is thereby brought to center stage in epistemology, see Laurence BonJour, "The Indispensability of Internalism," *Philosophical Topics* 29(2001), 47–65.
[7] Blackwell, 2007.   [8] See *The Philosophy of Philosophy*, chapters 3 and 4.

generally, and especially in epistemology. So the issue about the status of epistemological theorizing seems to have changed. Many defenders of traditional methods in epistemology no longer seek to defend these traditional methods as a priori; instead, it is the integrity of theorizing from the armchair which is now seen as the real issue.

One further trend in recent philosophy should be mentioned, by way of introduction. One of the salient alternatives to the armchair method, in recent years, is the newly emerging field of so-called experimental philosophy. I say "so-called" not because I believe that the label is not apt, let alone in order to somehow cast aspersions on this approach, but rather to indicate that this label is a name and not a description. Experimental philosophy is not merely an approach to philosophical questions which attempts to draw on experimental work of whatever kind. Rather, this approach, championed in work by Stephen Stich, Jonathan Weinberg, Joshua Knobe, Shaun Nichols, and a host of others, seeks to cast light on philosophical issues by way, typically, of questionnaires which probe our folk conceptions of various key philosophical notions.[9] This is, beyond doubt, an experimental approach to philosophical questions, but it is not at all the kind of empirical work which was suggested by Quine or Goldman as forming the basis for a properly scientific epistemology. Much of the recent discussion of armchair methods in philosophy has focused, unlike the earlier periods in which this issue was prominently discussed, on the question of whether the approach of the experimental philosophers is likely to shed light on issues of real philosophical importance.

Let me lay my cards on the table. I will argue here that armchair methods are unlikely to shed real light on central issues in epistemology. Without direct and substantive input from experimental work, I will argue, we are likely to remain ignorant of, or to misunderstand, the very nature of epistemological problems and their likely solution. The source of real enlightenment here, as I see it, is not likely to come from the work of experimental philosophers, but rather from more traditional work in the cognitive sciences, work not directed at our folk conceptions of anything. My complaint about work by experimental philosophers will not, of course, be an objection to the idea that empirical work might shed light on philosophical problems, but rather that much (though not all) of the

---

[9] See, for example, Jonathan Weinberg, Shaun Nichols, and Stephen Stich, "Normativity and Epistemic Intuitions," *Philosophical Topics* 29(2001), 429–460; *Midwest Studies in Philosophy* 31 (2007), *Philosophy and the Empirical*; Joshua Knobe and Shaun Nichols, eds., *Experimental Philosophy*, Oxford University Press, 2008.

work that experimental philosophers have done and wish to do is misdirected, indeed, that it is misdirected in much the same way, I believe, that a good deal of armchair theorizing in philosophy is. So I will be arguing in defense of a thoroughly empirically informed approach to epistemology, but one which is fundamentally different from that pursued by the experimental philosophers.

I

While questions about the relevance of psychology to epistemology have been much discussed in the recent literature, they were not a subject of discussion at all among the philosophers of the seventeenth and eighteenth centuries. Descartes, Locke, Hume, and Kant, for example, would not likely have understood the question of whether they were engaged in philosophical theorizing or psychological theorizing. The discipline of psychology did not emerge as an independent discipline until the late nineteenth century, but, more than that, the epistemological views of all of these philosophers were clearly influenced by their views about psychology. For them, an epistemology which was not informed by a theory of mind would have been inconceivable.

Of course, the view of the mind which these philosophers had was not informed by experimental results in psychology, since there was no such thing as experimental psychology at the time. Rather, these philosophers all held that introspection and reflection together provided the key to understanding the mind, and thus, even though beliefs arrived at by way of introspection are not a priori justified,[10] the use of introspection is clearly an armchair method of investigation. If we can understand the features of the mind which are needed for a fully informed epistemology entirely from the armchair, then armchair methods may well be all that is needed once one turns more directly to epistemological questions themselves.

These philosophers were right, I believe, to think that an understanding of the way the mind works is a prerequisite for constructing a reasonable epistemology, but they were mistaken, of course, in thinking that we might understand the relevant features of the mind by way of armchair investigation. It is not just that experimental work in psychology has proven necessary to fill in minor gaps in the view which introspection

---

[10] At least in the typical case. There is some real disagreement about whether certain judgments arrived at by way of introspection are a priori justified. For a particularly useful discussion of this issue, see Philip Kitcher, "A Priori Knowledge," *Philosophical Review* 89(1980), 3–23.

provides us of the mind, or that experimental work is needed to correct some small errors around the edges, so to speak, of an otherwise largely accurate picture provided by armchair methods. Rather, it has turned out that on issue after issue, we cannot even begin to understand how the mind works without extensive experimental work, and the picture of the mind which armchair methods provide us with is fundamentally flawed from beginning to end. Let us consider a number of topics here which will prove to be especially important when we turn from the nature of mind to epistemology.

Descartes held, famously, that introspection provides us with a picture of our current states of mind which is both infallible and complete; in a word, the mind is wholly transparent to itself. Such a view is no longer defended these days, but the extraordinarily vivid picture which introspection provides of our own mental states and processes is an important part of the armchair view of the mind. Consider, for example, the manner in which epistemological problems are often introduced. Chisholm suggests, in a discussion which is in many ways quite typical, that we should engage in Socratic questioning. Introspect, and you will detect a large number of your beliefs. Choose one of these and ask yourself, "Why do I hold this particular belief?" At least in the typical case, you will note that the initial, target belief is one which you hold for various reasons: that is, you hold it on the basis of still other beliefs. And then we may ask about each of these why you hold it. We may continue this process, Chisholm argues, until we arrive at beliefs which provide some sort of appropriate stopping place for inquiry.[11]

Let us leave aside the Chisholmian defense of foundationalism. When we engage in the kind of Socratic questioning which Chisholm encourages, introspection not only provides us with a view of our beliefs, but it provides us with a view of the source of our beliefs. Thus, when I consider some belief A of mine, and I ask myself why it is that I hold it, introspection seems to reveal to me why it is that I currently believe A: I believe it, say, because I believe B and C. Vivid and powerful as this introspective view of the source of our beliefs may be, we may ask how accurate the impressions are which introspection conveys. This is an issue which social psychologists have investigated in some detail.

---

[11] To my mind, Chisholm's best presentation of this way of thinking about epistemological questions is to be found in the second edition of his *Theory of Knowledge*, Prentice-Hall, 1977, chapter 2.

Much of what introspection seems to reveal, when we engage in this sort of exercise, amounts to little more than confabulation.[12] What appears in introspection to be the direct apprehension of causal relations among our mental states is really, at bottom, the result of a process of rational reconstruction: we are actually engaged in a subconscious process of theorizing about what the source of our beliefs must have been. More than this, this process of reconstruction is, in a wide range of cases, not terribly accurate. A good many of our beliefs are formed in ways which are not at all reasonable, but it seems that in reconstructing what our reasons were, we help ourselves to a crucial minor premise: that whatever it is we believe, we probably came to believe it on the basis of good reasons.[13] It should thus come as no surprise that, when we turn reflective and scrutinize the reasons for which we hold various beliefs, by and large it turns out that we find that our reasons pass muster. What looks, from the point of view of introspection, like a responsible, extra check on our first-order unreflective processes of belief acquisition turns out, in fact, to be little more than an exercise in self-congratulation. But this is not something which we can tell from the armchair. Indeed, there is a powerful illusion which arises precisely from the use of armchair methods of investigation. Unless we get up and out of the armchair, we are likely to misunderstand the sources of our beliefs.

Much of our belief acquisition is unreflective. For example, when I walk into my office, I inevitably come to believe that there is a desk in front of me. I don't stop to reflect about whether such a belief is justified given my evidence. And in this respect, this particular belief of mine is not unusual; most of my beliefs are formed unreflectively. Moreover, this is not some peculiarity of mine; the vast majority of beliefs are formed unreflectively. Nevertheless, we do, at times, stop to reflect and ask ourselves what it is that we ought to believe. When we do so, we have the distinct impression of epistemic agency. Forming beliefs, at least on these reflective occasions, seems to be something that we do rather than something that merely happens to us.[14]

---

[12] See especially Richard Nisbett and Timothy Wilson, "Telling More than We Can Know: Verbal Reports on Mental Processes," *Psychological Review* 84(1977), 231–259; Richard Nisbett and Lee Ross, *Human Inference: Strategies and Shortcomings of Social Judgment*, Prentice-Hall, 1980, chapter 9; Timothy Wilson, *Strangers to Ourselves: Discovering the Adaptive Unconscious*, Harvard University Press, 2002.

[13] I have argued for this at some length in chapter 4 of *Knowledge and Its Place in Nature*, Oxford University Press, 2002.

[14] A number of authors have attached a great deal of significance to this fact. See, for example, Christine Korsgaard, *Source of Normativity*, Cambridge University Press, 1996, chapter 3; Richard Moran, *Authority and Estrangement: An Essay on Self-Knowledge*, Princeton University Press, 2001.

To what extent should this impression of agency be taken at face value? In order to answer this question, we need to get out of the armchair and look to experimental work in social psychology. In general, our judgments about our own agency are not terribly reliable. People who are emotionally healthy tend to have an exaggerated impression of their own efficacy in a great many areas of life.[15] In addition, the idea that there is some deep asymmetry with respect to agency when it comes to the difference between reflective and unreflective belief acquisition is one which does not survive careful scrutiny. While unreflective belief acquisition is, of course, mediated by a host of mental processes which operate at the sub-personal level in ways of which we are typically unaware,[16] the same is quite clearly true of reflective belief acquisition. We are no more aware, through introspection, of the full range of mental processes at work in reflective belief acquisition than we are in the unreflective case. Finally, the fact that our introspective judgments about the source of our beliefs turn out largely to be a matter of after-the-fact rationalization rather than genuinely contemporaneous monitoring shows, at a minimum, that the deliverances of introspection greatly exaggerate the extent to which we play an active role in forming our beliefs when we stop to reflect.[17] An accurate understanding of the extent to which we are genuine agents in reflective belief acquisition cannot be achieved from the armchair.

The workings of some of the most fundamental processes underlying cognition are not only invisible to introspection, but they work in ways which are strikingly different from the armchair view which we have of them. Thus, for example, the operation of memory leaves little by way of introspective trace. When memory is operating most efficiently, we may be aware of forming a memory belief, but nothing more than the belief itself is available to introspection. The armchair view of memory is simply that we initially gain beliefs by other means – for example, by way of perception – and then these beliefs are stored in memory; later, on suitable occasions, they are brought out of storage and made available to introspection. But this very simple picture of the working of memory is entirely inaccurate. The initial process of encoding, the storage process, and the

---

[15] See, for example, Shelley Taylor and Jonathan Brown, "Illusion and Well-Being: A Social Psychological Perspective on Mental Health," *Psychological Bulletin* 103(1988), 193–210, and Shelley Taylor, *Positive Illusions: Creative Self-Deception and the Healthy Mind*, Basic Books, 1989.

[16] Ernest Sosa makes this point in an attempt to support the idea that "reflection aids agency." See Sosa, "Replies," in John Greco, ed., *Ernest Sosa and His Critics*, Blackwell, 2004, 292.

[17] I have discussed these issues in greater detail in "The Myth of Epistemic Agency," manuscript.

retrieval process all involve a great deal of construction and reconstruction. Genuine human memory is nothing at all like the process of taking a picture and entering it into a file, only to bring it out of the file on subsequent occasions when it might be needed.[18]

Much the same may be said about our responsiveness to testimony. Introspection reveals little if anything about the cognitive processes which go on when a speaker states that p and we, immediately thereafter, come to believe that p. Armchair theorizing about the process has led to a variety of accounts, some of which suggest that very little actually goes on here in the typical case; the transmission of information involves nothing more than "content preservation."[19] On other views,[20] there is a certain amount of screening that goes on to check, for example, for the speaker's sincerity and capacity to know whereof he or she speaks. But the empirical literature on such screening reveals features of the situation which armchair methods could not begin to detect.[21] We do indeed screen testifiers for sincerity on the basis of a variety of observable cues, and there are, as a matter of fact, a number of behavioral cues which are reliable indicators of insincerity; unfortunately, the cues we tend to rely on are not the ones which reliably indicate whether the testifier is genuinely sincere. The psychological and epistemological situations here are highly complex,[22] and they are complex in a way that introspection and armchair methods cannot reveal.

The content and format of our concepts plays an important role in a variety of epistemological issues, but the character of our concepts cannot be settled from the armchair.[23] The classical view of concepts has it that concepts are represented by a set of necessary and sufficient conditions in

---

[18] David Christensen and I have discussed this in "Testimony, Memory and the Limits of the A Priori," *Philosophical Studies* 86(1997), 1–20. For an extremely useful review of the psychological literature, as well as a discussion of its philosophical implications, see K. Michaelian, "Generative Memory," manuscript.

[19] The phrase comes from Tyler Burge, "Content Preservation," *Philosophical Review* 102(1993), 457–488. I should make clear that it is not Burge's view that, in the typical case, little more goes on beyond content preservation.

[20] See, for example, Elisabeth Fricker, "Against Gullibility," in B. K. Matilal and A. Chakrabarti, eds., *Knowing from Words*, Kluwer, 1994, 125–161. For a sampling of the (now very large) epistemological literature on testimony, see J. Lackey and E. Sosa, eds., *The Epistemology of Testimony*, Oxford University Press, 2006. As is typical of this body of literature, the essays in this last anthology do not engage with the relevant empirical literature on the subject.

[21] Here I rely on K. Michaelian, "In Defence of Gullibility: The Epistemology of Testimony and the Psychology of Deception Detection," *Synthese*, forthcoming. I have also benefited from reading a manuscript on this topic by Joseph Shieber.

[22] Again, see the papers by Michaelian and Shieber cited in Note 21 .

[23] For a discussion of these issues, see Alvin Goldman, "Philosophical Intuitions: Their Target, Their Source, and Their Epistemic Status," *Grazer Philosophische Studien* 74(2007), 1–26; and Hilary Kornblith, "Naturalism and Intuitions," *Grazer Philosophische Studien* 74(2007), 27–49.

much the same format as traditional philosophical analyses. Thus, for example, the concept of a bird might be represented as an animal with a beak, wings, and two feet. Following work by Eleanore Rosch,[24] it has been suggested that the format in which concepts are represented, however, might be quite different. Instead of a set of necessary and sufficient conditions in the standard format, a concept might be represented by way of a prototypical case, together with a set of dimensions of similarity such that any object sufficiently similar to the prototypical case falls under the concept.[25] And there are other accounts as well.[26] Indeed, it is not at all clear that our concepts are represented in any single format. Not only may different concepts be represented in different formats; one and the same concept may well be represented in more than one format.[27] However concepts may be represented, it is perfectly clear that we cannot determine the format of their representation by way of introspection. Nothing short of experimental work can be of use in addressing this issue.

Issues about the large-scale structure of the mind have been an important focus of work in philosophy from the time of Plato to the present day. Here, as elsewhere, armchair theorizing has been replaced by work which is empirically informed. Issues about modularity, and related concerns about domain-specific inference, can only be profitably addressed by way of experimental work. At this late date, how things seem from the first-person point of view or how they seem from the armchair are no more relevant to these inquiries than they are for an investigation of the mechanisms involved in digestion.

The same is true about the role of emotion in cognition. Introspection provides us with a vivid impression of our emotional states and their effects. Armchair views about these issues based on this introspective picture may be of interest to cognitive anthropologists or sociologists, but they are simply irrelevant to an inquiry into the actual effects of emotion on cognition. If we want to understand how the mind actually

---

[24] "Principles of Categorization," in Eleanore Rosch and B. B. Lloyd, eds., *Cognition and Categorization*, Laurence Erlbaum Associates, 27–48.

[25] It is, of course, a mistake to say that this kind of format for the representation of concepts does not provide necessary and sufficient conditions for falling under the concept. Any account of what concepts are will inevitably provide necessary and sufficient conditions. What is at issue is whether those necessary and sufficient conditions are presented in the kind of format characteristic of traditional philosophical analyses.

[26] For a useful collection of essays on these issues, see Eric Margolis and Stephen Laurence, eds., *Concepts: Core Readings*, MIT Press, 1999. For a very helpful discussion of the literature, see Gregory Murphy, *The Big Book of Concepts*, MIT Press, 2002.

[27] See Joachim Horvath, "Conceptual Analysis and Naturalized Epistemology," manuscript; and Daniel Weiskopf, "Atomism, Pluralism and Conceptual Content," *Synthese*, forthcoming.

works, our introspective view of things is not only not the last word on these matters; it is no longer seen as even the first word. A proper investigation of these phenomena does not begin with our introspective view of them, or our armchair view, and then proceed to make corrections where needed. The armchair view of these matters is simply irrelevant to a serious inquiry into the workings of the mind.

II

What has any of this to do with epistemology? Understanding how the mind works, it may be granted, cannot be achieved from the armchair. At the same time, epistemology is not a simple investigation of how it is that the mind operates. Even if we grant, then, as of course we must, that psychology cannot profitably be pursued from the armchair, what bearing does this have on the methodology of epistemology?

I will begin to address these questions by way of examples. I will argue that a number of issues central to epistemology cannot profitably be addressed without the kind of direction and constraint which experimental work offers. This will leave open, of course, the question of whether there are other issues within epistemology which might usefully be addressed without the aid of experimental work. I will have something to say about this question as well.

Consider, then, the debate between internalists and externalists in epistemology.[28] Internalists and externalists disagree about the determinants of justification: the features which make a belief justified, internalists insist, must, in some important sense, be internal to the agent; externalists deny this. Thus, for example, access internalists insist that the features of a belief which make it justified must be accessible to introspection or reflection. Some internalists, such as Laurence BonJour, argue that beliefs which are justified in the internalist sense are more likely to be true than beliefs which fail to meet internalist standards.[29] Once one has an internalist account of justification on the table, so to speak, BonJour's requirement makes an empirical claim: that beliefs which meet those standards are more likely to be true than beliefs which don't. Since there is a great deal of empirical research on what happens when we introspect and reflect, this experimental work becomes relevant to examining BonJour's claim. And

---

[28] For a collection of some of the central essays on this issue, see Hilary Kornblith, ed., *Epistemology: Internalism and Externalism*, Blackwell, 2001.
[29] *The Structure of Empirical Knowledge*, Harvard University Press, 1985, 8.

much as we have an armchair view about what happens when we engage in introspection and reflection, this armchair view, as I've pointed out above, is not at all accurate. So in order to examine whether BonJour's claim is actually true, and not just whether it seems true from the armchair, we need to take a serious look at the empirical research here. The view from the armchair gives us a thoroughly misleading picture.

Now BonJour is, admittedly, an unusual internalist in that he wants to identify the property of being justified with an internally recognizable property, while, at the same time, insisting that beliefs which have this property are likely to be true. Not all internalists want to make this second claim, a claim which amounts to insisting that internally justified beliefs are reliably produced. But the empirical research on the mechanisms involved in introspection and reflection is not, for that reason, entirely irrelevant to the claims of these other internalists. If, as I've argued, the empirical literature shows that the very procedures which internalists view as a kind of check on unselfconscious processes of belief acquisition do not effectively carry out any such check, then the motivation for identifying justification with such internal monitoring is, at a minimum, severely compromised. Internalism gains a specious plausibility from the fact that an armchair view of introspection and reflection generates the illusion that such checking procedures are genuinely effective.

The same is true, of course, of a good deal of the discussion of epistemic responsibility. A variety of claims are made about what it is that an epistemically responsible agent must do in order to make it likely that his or her beliefs be true, but most of the literature on epistemic responsibility is nothing more than armchair theorizing. The empirical literature on the actual effects of the very checking procedures which armchair theorists insist constitute epistemically responsible behavior can be quite salutary.[30] It is, of course, always open to such theorists to insist that they are not identifying epistemically responsible belief acquisition with reliable belief acquisition, and, indeed, that they are not committed to the view that responsibly acquired belief tends to be reliable. All of this is true, but it does not by any means show that the empirical results are irrelevant to the evaluation of claims about epistemic responsibility. At a minimum, the empirical results place a certain pressure on these theorists, for the very

---

[30] I first addressed this issue in my "Introspection and Misdirection," Chapter 1. In addition to chapter 4 of my *Knowledge and Its Place in Nature*, see also Michael Bishop, "In Praise of Epistemic Irresponsibility: How Lazy and Ignorant Can You Be?," *Synthese* 122(2000), 179–208, and Michael Bishop and J. D. Trout, *Epistemology and the Psychology of Human Judgment*, Oxford University Press, 2005.

procedures which they insist are definitive of responsible epistemic behavior turn out, on empirical examination, to do little more than increase the confidence of already benighted agents. Depending on the details of the particular view about epistemic responsibility, the empirical results need not constitute any kind of conclusive refutation of them, but it would surely be a mistake to view such information as irrelevant to a full evaluation of these claims. The results are deeply surprising, and they are surprising because they contradict our armchair view of these matters. But it was precisely the armchair view which made the claims about epistemic responsibility appear plausible in the first place.

There is a long tradition in epistemology of offering epistemic advice, that is, suggestions about how it is that one ought to go about arriving at one's beliefs if one's goal is to gain true beliefs. Talk of "rules for the direction of the mind" was once common, and, in recent years, epistemologists have discussed at some length the extent to which an account of justified belief should provide some sort of guidance to the concerned epistemic agent. As with the discussion of epistemic responsibility, it is quite clear that the empirical literature on the effects of introspection, reflection, and various inferential strategies is directly relevant here. And, again, precisely because this body of literature has regularly produced surprising results – results which directly contradict the way things seem from the armchair – it is clear that these issues cannot profitably be addressed in ways which are not informed by experimental work.

Many philosophers believe that proper method in epistemology, and in philosophy more generally, is a matter of conceptual analysis, and Ed Gettier's famous counterexample[31] to the suggestion that knowledge might be identified with justified, true belief is seen as a model of how such conceptual analysis might be carried out. On this view, the target of philosophical analysis is seen as a concept, and armchair methods are seen as the means for eliciting the content of our concepts.[32] So there is a large body of philosophical literature which attempts to provide an account of the content of various philosophically interesting concepts. There is, moreover, a standard format in which these analyses proceed, namely, by providing necessary and sufficient conditions of a certain sort. There is also a large body of literature in psychology which investigates the content and format of our concepts, and this literature has produced a body of

---

[31] "Is Knowledge Justified True Belief?," *Analysis* 23(1963), 121–123.
[32] For a defense of this approach, see, for example, Frank Jackson, *From Metaphysics to Ethics: A Defence of Conceptual Analysis*, Oxford University Press, 1998.

interesting and surprising results. The format in which our concepts are mentally represented seems to be quite different from the format of traditional philosophical analyses, and the content of our concepts is also quite different from the way it appears from the armchair.[33] How should we regard the relationship between these two investigations? How, if at all, does the experimental investigation of our concepts bear on the armchair inquiry?

Alvin Goldman has argued that the armchair investigation is a kind of proto-scientific version of the experimental work engaged in by psychologists.[34] Goldman argues that, as a matter of fact, armchair methods turn out to be fairly reliable in giving us information about the content of our concepts, although experimental work may certainly provide a needed check on our results, and, on occasion, a source of correction for the armchair view. On this view, armchair methods give us a fairly accurate account of the content of our concepts, but they need to be supplemented by experimental work. Others are less sanguine about the extent to which armchair methods here will approximate the results achieved by careful experimentation,[35] and this has led many experimental philosophers to suggest that the task of conceptual analysis needs to be pursued, not from the armchair, but from the psychological laboratory. But the difference between Goldman and these experimental philosophers is just a matter of degree. They are in full agreement that the target of philosophical analysis and the target of experimental inquiry are one and the same, and they agree, as well, that experimental inquiry is the most reliable means for pursuing this inquiry. In particular, when armchair methods and experimental methods yield different results, it is the experimental methods which are to be trusted.

What is difficult to defend, I believe, is any attempt to insulate the philosophical project of conceptual analysis from the results of the experimental investigations. It is not, after all, just an orthographic accident that both philosophers and psychologists refer to the object of their investigation as a concept. This is surely not a simple case of homonymy, as with "bank" and "bank." Both the object of philosophical investigation and the object of psychological investigation are thought to be implicated in explaining the content of our thoughts, the kinds of inferences we are inclined to make, and our classificatory behavior. Given this extensive

---

[33] See work cited in Note 26.
[34] "Philosophical Intuitions: Their Target, Their Source, and Their Epistemic Status."
[35] I present reasons for doubting that Goldman is right in "Naturalism and Intuitions."

overlap in the causal and explanatory endeavors which talk of concepts is meant to engage with, it surely looks for all the world as if the objects of study in these two investigations are identical. At a minimum, if some case can be made out that there are real differences here, it will still be hard to see how the results of the experimental investigation could possibly be irrelevant to an understanding of the object of philosophical analysis. Given, once again, the extent to which the experimental results turn out to be surprising – that is, given that the experimental results are so deeply at odds with the view we have from the armchair – this raises a serious challenge to armchair methods in epistemology.

There is another way in which experimental results bear on the project of conceptual analysis as traditionally conceived. Most epistemologists reject skepticism, and their rejection of skepticism is quite a deep commitment.[36] They offer analyses of justification and of knowledge, and they believe that these accounts serve to explain why it is that we are justified and why it is that we know in various paradigmatic cases. So it is an important part of the defense of these analyses that paradigmatic cases of justification and knowledge turn out to fit their analyses. An account of justification, or an account of knowledge, which has the consequence that we have little if any justified belief or knowledge, is, for that very reason, held to be implausible. But now the psychological facts about belief acquisition and retention are directly relevant to the evaluation of philosophical analyses, even on the most traditional conception of the project of analysis. Most accounts of knowledge, for example, include some sort of basing requirement, and this basing requirement is typically explained in causal or counterfactual terms: one belief cannot be based on another unless the first is caused by the second, or unless one would not have the first were it not for having the second.[37] Our armchair understanding of causal and counterfactual dependencies among beliefs, however, is notoriously deficient. Thus, in order to see whether paradigm cases of knowledge actually meet the conditions laid out in our analyses, we need to leave the armchair and

---

[36] My remarks here apply equally to contextualists. Thus, although contextualists will want to allow that skepticism is true in high-standards contexts, they will also want to insist that skepticism is false in everyday contexts. The kinds of concerns I address here would raise worries about everyday contexts.

[37] See, for example, Richard Feldman and Earl Conee's discussion of well-foundedness in their essay "Evidentialism," in their *Evidentitialism: Essays in Epistemology*, Oxford University Press, 2004, 83–107, especially 92–93.

enter the psychological laboratory.[38] The same is true of accounts of justification. In the case of doxastic justification, a basing requirement is as essential a feature as it is in accounts of knowledge. But even accounts of propositional justification must come to terms with their consequences for paradigmatic situations. An account of propositional justification which had the consequence that most people rarely meet its conditions would, for that very reason, be extremely implausible. But whether the conditions are in fact met in real-world situations cannot be determined from the armchair.

This point, I believe, has very broad implications. Consider some of the central terms of epistemological discourse: perception, memory, testimony, reasoning. These terms seem to pick out various real-world phenomena, and there is a great deal of psychological work that goes on in figuring out just what these phenomena come to. Side by side with this psychological work, we see philosophers attempting to offer analyses of these fundamental epistemological notions, and these analyses are often presented in isolation from, and, indeed, in ignorance of, the psychological literature. Epistemologists are interested in these topics, however, because they are interested in the nature and scope of human knowledge. A philosophical analysis of these notions which fails to fit with the real-world phenomena is, for that very reason, missing its target. Just as in the case of knowledge and justification, there is a serious problem with any account of perception, memory, testimony, or reasoning which has the consequence that there isn't very much of it going on. The fit, however, between philosophical analyses and real-world phenomena cannot be determined from the armchair. This is not just a worry in principle. Some of these phenomena – particularly memory, as I noted above – turn out to be quite a bit different than they seem from the armchair. Armchair analyses of such phenomena thus run a serious risk of simply failing to capture the very phenomena they seek to analyze. The analogue of skepticism here is eliminationism, the claim that it really turns out that there is no perception, memory, testimony, or reasoning; and eliminationism is about as plausible as skepticism. When the phenomena of cognition turn out to be quite different from what we thought they were – that is, when

---

[38] I don't mean to suggest that philosophers need to carry out experiments themselves. In most cases, philosophers simply lack the relevant training to carry out experiments properly, and one does no better to engage in philosophical theorizing by way of amateurish experimentation than by way of armchair theorizing. What is needed, however, and what I mean to be claiming here, is that philosophical theorizing must be informed by experimental work, whether done by (appropriately trained) philosophers or by psychologists.

Is There Room for Armchair Theorizing in Epistemology? 171

our armchair view of these phenomena is deeply mistaken – we cannot allow our epistemology to be built around our armchair misconceptions. But just as elsewhere in science, psychology periodically reveals that our armchair view of things is not merely incomplete or mistaken in detail; our armchair view of psychological phenomena is, at times, extremely wide of the mark. It would be a very bad mistake to engage in epistemological theorizing in ways which simply ignore this fact. But this means that we cannot rest content with an epistemology conducted from the armchair.

If this argument is accepted, as I believe it should be, then it counts against seeing our concepts as the target of epistemological analysis.[39] It is not our concept of knowledge, or justification, or reasoning, or memory which is the target of philosophical analysis; it is knowledge, justification, reasoning, memory, and so on themselves. Just as we may mentally represent such things as gold and water in ways which fail to do justice to the substances themselves, we may mentally represent the objects of epistemological investigation in ways which build in substantive misunderstandings. We are interested in certain real phenomena – human knowledge, for example – and there is little point in elucidating, in however great detail, what our personal or folk conception of those phenomenon are. For this reason, I am no more sympathetic to the work of the experimental philosophers than I am to those who practice conceptual analysis in a more traditional manner. It is true, as the experimental philosophers have argued, that if one wants to get at what our concepts are, then one must proceed experimentally. The traditional methods of conceptual analysis amount to little more than social psychology done badly. But while the experimental philosophers respond to this problem by trying to do the social psychology well, it seems to me that they have addressed the wrong problem here. Doing a better job at getting at our concepts does not constitute progress, in my view, since the proper target of philosophical analysis is simply not our concepts. Our concepts are the vehicles by way of which we represent the target of philosophical analysis, but this is altogether different from taking the concepts themselves to be the object of study.

There are thus a great many central projects in epistemology which would be dramatically affected by experimental results from the cognitive

---

[39] I have presented this argument at length in *Knowledge and Its Place in Nature*. Timothy Williamson defends this view as well, in a somewhat different way, in *The Philosophy of Philosophy*, Oxford University Press, 2007. Williamson and I disagree about the upshot of this thesis for the use of armchair methods in philosophy.

sciences. Our armchair view of psychological phenomena is often deeply mistaken, and these mistakes are then incorporated into our philosophical analyses if we rely on nothing but armchair methods. The subject matter of epistemology is so closely tied to these psychological phenomena, and our armchair view of them is so badly skewed, that our epistemological theories will inevitably suffer if they are insulated from experimental results. But it is not just a handful of, admittedly important, epistemological projects which need to be informed by laboratory work. The very phenomena which epistemologists seek to illuminate are ones which are the object of experimental study, and this experimental work has often led to surprising results. We ignore this work at our peril. When philosophical theories in epistemology are constructed from the armchair, they run a serious risk of being divorced from the very phenomena they seek to illuminate. The only way to assure that we do not build elaborate castles in the air, unconnected to the real-world phenomena which motivated our work in the first place, is to base our work on the best available experimental understanding of those phenomena. Any such empirically informed epistemology will inevitably leave the armchair very far behind.

III

Although Timothy Williamson and I agree on a great deal about philosophical method,[40] there is also a good deal about which we disagree. Williamson is far more optimistic about the prospects for philosophy generally, and epistemology in particular, as carried out from the armchair.[41] Now Williamson remarks that, "The legitimacy in principle of experimental philosophy does not make armchair philosophy illegitimate in principle."[42] This is quite right, of course, and no one has argued that it does. My argument here, as elsewhere,[43] is not that armchair methods might, in principle, lead to errors and omissions, but rather that, in actual

---

[40] See my "Timothy Williamson's *The Philosophy of Philosophy*," *Analysis* 69(2009), 109–116; and Williamson's "Replies to Kornblith, Jackson and Moore," *Analysis* 69(2009), 125–135.
[41] Thus, Williamson remarks, "I expect armchair methods to play legitimately a more dominant role in future philosophy than [Kornblith] expects them to – of course, such difference in emphasis can result in widening differences in practice." "Replies to Kornblith, Jackson and Moore," 126.
[42] Ibid., 126.
[43] In "The Role of Intuition in Philosophical Inquiry," in M. DePaul and W. Ramsey, eds., *Rethinking Intuition*, Rowman and Littlefield, 1998, 129–141; in *Knowledge and Its Place in Nature*; in "Appeals to Intuition and the Ambitions of Epistemology," in Stephen Hetherington, ed., *Epistemology Futures*, Oxford University Press, 2006, 10–25; in "Naturalism and Intuitions"; and in "Timothy Williamson's *The Philosophy of Philosophy*."

practice, armchair methods have regularly led to very substantial errors in epistemology. The features of cognition which are most directly relevant to epistemology are ones which we badly misunderstand when we remain in the armchair. It is for this reason that I worry about formal models designed to square with our armchair view of matters. It is not that I think there is something wrong with developing formal models – very far from it. As Williamson rightly points out,[44] formal modeling and experimental methods need not be seen as rivals; in the ordinary practice of science, they are, quite typically, mutually beneficial. Experimental input provides useful data to inform our formal models; formal modeling provides useful information about where best to test our available theories. What I object to, then, is not formal modeling per se, but rather formal models in epistemology which do not have the benefit of this substantive interaction with experimental data. When the input to our formal models comes from the armchair rather than the laboratory, and when the output of our formal models is not used to inform experimental tests but, instead, merely to prompt more interactions with the view from the armchair, the resulting epistemological theories are likely to be badly mistaken. Even when this method does not result in errors, it is a method in which we should not place our confidence. Formal modeling uninformed and unchecked by experimental results makes for bad epistemology.

No one could reasonably object to the use of armchair methods as a component of philosophical methodology. After all, we do need, at times, to step back from the data which have been collected, and the theories we have constructed on that basis, and think about their implications. From the armchair, we can construct various formal models and examine their consequences. But to acknowledge this is to say no more than that philosophy, like any intellectual activity, involves thinking things through. What is at issue between those who are optimistic about the prospects of armchair methodology in philosophy and those who are more pessimistic is not whether stopping to think can be a good idea. It is, instead, a question of what we need to bring to the armchair to think about. Those who favor a thoroughgoing armchair methodology believe that no special experimental input is really necessary for at least a good deal of philosophical theorizing. Those of us who are more pessimistic about this sort of methodology believe that experimental data are needed to keep us in touch with the phenomena we seek to understand.

---

[44] "Replies to Kornblith, Jackson and Moore," 128.

IV

There is one more motivation for adopting armchair methods in epistemology which I want to discuss. Many philosophers have the conviction that the most fundamental questions of epistemology are, at bottom, questions that must be asked from the first-person point of view, and, to the extent that they are convinced of this, they will see armchair methods as essential to the pursuit of fundamental epistemological questions. Thus, for example, Richard Foley argues that a particularly fundamental question for epistemology is, "What am I to believe?," and although he acknowledges that there is a way to answer such a question from a third-person perspective, by, for example, engaging in psychological research about the reliability of one's own processes of belief acquisition, such an investigation would not approach this question in the way that treats it as the fundamental epistemological question he has in mind. The approach he favors, one which respects the fundamental nature of the question, is as follows.

> I am to make up my mind by marshaling my intellectual resources in a way that conforms to my own deepest standards. If I conduct my inquiries in such a way that I would not be critical of the resulting beliefs even if I were to be deeply reflective, then these beliefs are rational for me in an important sense, an egoistic sense ... The basic idea is that if I am to be egoistically rational, I must not have internal reasons for retraction, ones whose force I myself would acknowledge were I to be sufficiently reflective.[45]

So armchair reflection plays an essential role in addressing a fundamental epistemological issue, and any attempt to answer a question which sounds like Foley's, by third-person means, simply fails to get at the issue about which he is concerned.

Laurence BonJour says something quite similar. Although he allows that there may be a perfectly legitimate externalist notion of justification, and of knowledge – and that accounts of these notions would make no special appeal to the first-person perspective or to armchair reflection – nevertheless, there is also a legitimate internalist notion of justification, and a notion of knowledge which requires such justification. Such a notion requires that "what is appealed to for justification must be *internal to the individual's first-person cognitive perspective.*"[46] Moreover, BonJour insists, these two notions of justification, and of knowledge, are not on a par.

---

[45] "What Am I to Believe?," in Steven Wagner and Richard Warner, eds., *Naturalism: A Critical Appraisal*, University of Notre Dame Press, 1993, 148.
[46] "The Indispensability of Internalism," 54.

I want to insist that there is a clear way in which an internalist approach, in addition to being intellectually legitimate on its own, has a fundamental kind of priority for epistemology as a whole.[47]

So for both Foley and BonJour, there are fundamental questions about what we ourselves should believe, and the most fundamental way to pursue such questions must itself be from the first-person perspective. This will inevitably involve reflecting on our beliefs, and their sources, and the relationship among them. In order to answer the fundamental questions of epistemology, armchair reflection will need to play a leading role.

Debates about which questions in a discipline are really the most fundamental can often seem terribly unproductive, with members of each side of the debate doing little more than insisting that it is their preferred approach which really gets to the bottom of things. But that is not the case here. There are arguments for the priority of the first-person perspective, and if these arguments are successful, then justification and knowledge will inevitably involve a heavy dose of armchair reflection. Let us look at how these arguments play out.

While some internalist epistemologists characterize internalism by way of a metaphysical distinction – e.g., that the justificatory status of a person's beliefs depends exclusively on states of the person which are, in some suitable sense, internal (in the way that, say, mental states are)[48] – BonJour rightly rejects this way of thinking about internalism. While it is certainly true that for Descartes, as clear a case of an internalist epistemologist as one might try to find, the justificatory status of a person's belief did have to supervene on features of that person's mental state, this is only because Descartes held a view which made this metaphysical distinction – the distinction between things internal to the mind and those external to it – correspond to an important epistemological distinction: namely, the distinction between those things which are known directly and with certainty, as opposed to those things which are known only indirectly and fallibly. For those who reject the claim that the metaphysical distinction between mental and non-mental items tracks this epistemological divide – as everyone now must – it must therefore be acknowledged that the metaphysical distinction does not capture, and is not even

---

[47] "The Indispensability of Internalism," 62.
[48] This is the way that Conee and Feldman characterize internalism. See *Evidentialism: Essays in Epistemology*, Oxford University Press, 2004, 56: "The justificatory status of a person's doxastic attitudes strongly supervenes on the person's occurrent and dispositional mental states, events, and conditions."

extensionally equivalent to, any epistemological distinction at all. There are some mental states, such as the early states of perceptual and linguistic processing – to which our epistemological access is extraordinarily indirect.[49] We have far better cognitive access to many states of the so-called external world than we do to some of the states of our own psychology. And, finally, even mental states to which we seem to have some sort of direct access of a sort which would license claims about certainty turn out, on further examination, not to answer to that description. When internalists talk about things internal to us, they need to have an epistemological notion in mind rather than a metaphysical one.

What is this epistemological notion of the internal, a notion which will illuminate the fundamental nature of the question both Foley and BonJour wish to address? BonJour, I believe, is especially helpful here.

> A person's conscious mental states play the role that they standardly do in internalist conceptions of justification, I would suggest, *not* simply because they are internal to him or her in the sense merely of being his or her individual states, but rather because it is arguable that some (but not all) of the properties of such states, mainly their specific content and the attitude toward that content that they reflect, are things to which the person has a first-person access that is direct and unproblematic, that is, that does not depend on other claims that would themselves have to be justified in some more indirect way.[50]

BonJour thus rightly gives an epistemological characterization of the features which make an internal state internal: it must be a state to which one has "first-person access that is direct and unproblematic." Internalism is thus defined in terms which assure the importance of reflection, for first-person access here just is the sort of access that armchair reflection affords.

Why should we think, however, that armchair reflection affords access which is unproblematic? It is clear enough that, when we reflect, the access which reflection affords us to various features of our mental life certainly *seems* unproblematic from the first-person perspective. What reason do we have, however, for taking such appearances at face-value?

Notice, first of all, the context in which BonJour speaks of our access to certain features of our mental life[51] as unproblematic. BonJour comes to

---

[49] This is going to be so on any way that one tries to make sense of the direct/indirect distinction. I do not mean to be endorsing any particular way of making out such a distinction, or, indeed, even the claim that we can make good sense of it.
[50] "The Indispensability of Internalism," 54.
[51] And various extra-mental items as well. BonJour rightly points out that, on standard internalist accounts, we have such unproblematic access by way of reflection to at least some a priori knowable

talk about unproblematic access in the context of raising the problem of radical skepticism.⁵² The same is true of Foley; his question about what one is to believe is presented, unsurprisingly, as a distinctively Cartesian question, one which serves to make vivid the problem of skepticism. And Sosa too, in recent work, sees an important connection between the importance of reflective knowledge and the traditional project of responding to the skeptic.⁵³ So how is it that our access to certain features of our mental life is supposed to be unproblematic in the context of responding to radical skepticism?

There is no denying that one can raise a skeptical challenge to knowledge of the physical world by granting, for the sake of argument, that we have perfect access to (at least some features of) our mental states. We can raise skeptical challenges of all sorts, by granting, for the sake of argument, that certain sorts of knowledge are unproblematic. Thus, for example, we might grant, for the sake of argument, that we have unproblematic knowledge of the behavior of others, and then ask, in the light of this knowledge, how knowledge of their mental states is possible. Or we might grant, again, for the sake of argument, that knowledge of the observable features of the world is unproblematic, and then ask how knowledge of unobservables is possible. We can raise all sorts of skeptical challenges in this way. When we do so, however, the knowledge that we take as unproblematic is not, automatically, unproblematic *tout court*. At least without additional argument, to say that a certain body of knowledge is unproblematic for the purposes of raising a skeptical problem is simply to allow that, within a certain dialectical situation, we are not going to raise challenges to that sort of knowledge. But this shows nothing at all about the epistemic status of the knowledge which we agree not to challenge. What BonJour, and Foley, and Sosa need to show, if they are to secure the importance of the first-person perspective, and the importance of armchair reflection which goes with it, is that our first-person access to relevant features of our mental life is unproblematic in a far more substantive way.

---

truths. "The Indispensability of Internalism," 55. I will focus in the text, however, on our access to relevant features of our mental lives. If internalists cannot secure this, then internalism is committed to an extremely broad skepticism, and, indeed, the coherence of the entire position is threatened. More than this, there is every reason to believe that the kind of argument I make against unproblematic access to mental items can easily be generalized to cover the cases in which BonJour believes we have unproblematic access to a priori knowable truths. I have discussed these problems about the a priori in "The Impurity of Reason," *Pacific Philosophical Quarterly* 81 (2000), 67–89. It would take us too far afield from the issues under discussion here to pursue these questions about the a priori.

⁵² "The Indispensability of Internalism," 53.   ⁵³ "Replies," 292.

But this is just what they cannot do. One can raise skeptical worries about features of one's mental life just as easily as one can raise worries about our knowledge of the physical world. Descartes prepared the ground for skepticism about the physical world by, initially, pointing out that we do in fact make mistakes about various features of the external world. This is enough to show that there is not only in principle, but, at times, in practice as well, a gap between how the world actually is and how we represent it in our beliefs. This is all that is needed to generate the skeptical worry: What reason is there to believe that the world is anything like the way we represent it to be?

But the very same strategy will generate a skeptical worry about our access to our mental states. As we have already seen, there is not only in principle, but, at times, in practice as well, a gap between how our mental life actually is and how it is presented to us when we engage in armchair reflection. Considerations of cases involving self-deception show that we may, at times, be mistaken about what it is that we believe, so here too, there is, not only in theory, but in practice as well, a non-trivial gap between appearance and reality. And it is the possibility of such a gap which raises the skeptical worry: What reason is there to believe that our mental life is anything like the way it appears to us when we reflect on it?

I am not, in any way, a radical skeptic. These considerations are not meant to provide support for radical skepticism. What they do show, however, is that the sense in which the beliefs about our mental life which are generated from the first-person perspective – that is, the beliefs which result from armchair reflection – are not unproblematic in any way that matters to epistemology.[54]

The idea that the first-person point of view presents some sort of neutral and unproblematic starting point for epistemological inquiry is, to my mind, a product of two not unrelated facts. First, there is an important historical tradition in epistemology, a tradition of which Descartes is the

---

[54] BonJour seems to come quite close to acknowledging this. At one point he remarks that,

> Certainly it would be a very unusual brand of scepticism which would challenge whether my belief that B is justified by raising the issue of whether I do in fact accept B, the normal sceptical claim being precisely that certain beliefs which are in fact held are nonetheless unjustified. (*The Structure of Empirical Knowledge*, 81)

But claims about which skeptical challenges are common in the history of philosophy, or which are unusual, tells us nothing about which kinds of claims are unproblematic *tout court*. And it is this sense of what is unproblematic, rather than the dialectical sense, which is epistemologically relevant.

preeminent representative, according to which the way the mind is presented to us in reflection genuinely is unproblematic: it is unproblematic because it is absolutely certain and utterly resistant to any sort of skeptical doubt whatsoever. Second, there is the psychological fact that when we do reflect on our own mental states, we are presented with a view of our mental life which we tend to find utterly compelling. Neither of these facts, however, should convince us that the access to our mental life which reflection provides and which is represented in our first-person perspective on our mental lives genuinely is unproblematic. Descartes' views about the powers of reflection are, for very good reason, no longer accepted, and without them, the claim that reflection provides an unproblematic view of our mental life is wholly undermined. The psychological fact about the compelling nature of the first-person perspective is itself put in proper perspective by the surprising experimental results which we have surveyed. Viewed in this light, there is nothing epistemically unproblematic about the first-person perspective or the epistemological projects which flow from treating it as if it were.

V

I have argued that it would be a mistake to pursue epistemological theorizing entirely from the armchair. Let me end, however, on a conciliatory note. Philosophy is a cooperative enterprise. Just as there is a division of labor in physics, with some physicists actively engaged in laboratory work, and others, more theoretically inclined, engaged in armchair theorizing, there is obviously room for such a division of labor in philosophy, even on my view. This is not to say that any old armchair theorizing, however, is likely to be constructive. The physicists who engage in armchair theorizing do not do so in splendid ignorance of the work of their experimental colleagues. Armchair physics carried on in ignorance of experimental results would be entirely worthless. When we talk about the actual phenomenon of armchair theorizing in physics, then, what we have in mind is not work that is wholly independent of experimental results. Instead, talk of theorizing from the armchair in physics amounts to a simple acknowledgment of the diverse interests and talents of those who contribute to physical theorizing, together with a recognition that progress in physics is not typically attributable to individuals acting in perfect isolation, but is instead the product of a community of investigators. The same is true, in my view, of epistemology. Individual theorists may pursue their work in constructive ways from the armchair, so long as they are part of a community which keeps them in touch with real epistemological phenomena by way of experimental work. We misunderstand the role of armchair theorizing, in my view, if we think that it is possible to make progress in epistemology without experimental work playing this important role.[55]

---

[55] I am indebted to Timothy Williamson for conversations on this topic on a number of occasions. In addition, I have presented versions of this essay at Fortaleza, Brazil; the University of St. Andrews; and the University of Cincinnati. I am grateful to audiences on all of these occasions for helpful comments and criticisms. Thanks too to Matthew Haug for helpful suggestions.

9

*The Role of Reasons in Epistemology**

The nature of reasons, and of good reasons, is utterly central to a great deal of epistemological theorizing. How, after all, could it be otherwise?

There are some commonsense distinctions which, it seems, any plausible epistemological theory will need to preserve. When Jack believes that it will rain tomorrow because he noticed that his tea leaves were wetter than usual, while Jill believes that it will rain tomorrow because she carefully examined the local weather patterns, the obvious thing to say is that Jill has good reasons to believe as she does, while Jack does not. We need to preserve the distinction between beliefs like Jack's and beliefs like Jill's lest we lapse into a view which sees all beliefs as epistemologically on a par, and the obvious way to draw this distinction is just the way we do in everyday parlance: Jill holds her belief for good reasons, while Jack does not. Without talk of reasons, it seems, we cannot distinguish between the cases of Jack and Jill.

There is also another distinction which common sense draws. When Jack falls down and hits his head on a rock, and then, on returning to consciousness, holds a belief which he never held before – that he is the present King of France, say – we need to contrast this case, and cases like it, with beliefs such as Jill's, that Jack has had a concussion, and that it would be wise for him to seek medical attention immediately. Jill's belief is based on reasons, and good ones at that, but Jack's belief is not based on reasons at all, not even bad ones. His belief was caused, to be sure; it was caused by his unfortunate encounter with the rock. But there is a distinction, it seems, between coming to believe for reasons, whether good or

---

* Versions of this essay were presented to the Fordham Epistemology and Ethics Workshop; as a Brown Bag Work in Progress Talk at UMass, Amherst; and at the 10th Anniversary *Episteme* Conference in San José, Costa Rica. I am extremely grateful for much helpful discussion on these occasions, and especially to Louise Antony, Nathan Ballantyne, Stephen Grimm, Joe Levine, Howard Robinson, and my commentator in San José, Baron Reed.

bad, and merely being caused to believe. We need to advert to reasons, of course, to make this important distinction. Any plausible epistemological theory, it seems, should thus incorporate such a distinction, and give us an account of it.

Given the importance of these commonsense distinctions, it is unsurprising that talk of reasons is found at the center of many epistemological theories. Wilfrid Sellars,[1] famously, drew a distinction between "the space of reasons" and "the space of causes," and many contemporary philosophers influenced by Sellars, including Robert Brandom,[2] John McDowell,[3] and Michael Williams,[4] make this distinction central to their epistemological views. Internalist accounts of knowledge typically define "knowledge" in terms of good reasons, or instead, what seems to be a mere terminological variant, in terms of adequate evidence.

But not all epistemological theories are like this. Thus, consider reliabilist theories of justification and knowledge.[5] Reliabilists about justification do not explain what it is for a belief to be justified in terms of reasons, or evidence, or the like. Rather, they explain justification in terms of the reliability of the process by which the belief was formed, and nothing about reasons, or evidence, or the like, comes into play. The same is true, of course, of reliabilist theories of knowledge, whether they make justification a necessary condition for knowledge, and then explain justification in terms of reliability, or, instead, simply do away with justification as a necessary condition for knowledge. What is true of reliabilist theories seems to be true of naturalistic accounts of knowledge and justification generally: these theories tend to explain knowledge and justification in terms of some naturalistic relation between belief and world. At least in their accounts of knowledge and justification, these views leave talk of reasons completely out of the picture.

What should we make of this? Does the fact that certain theories of knowledge and justification make no mention of reasons show that these theories are committed to an epistemology which simply leaves reasons

---

[1] "Empiricism and the Philosophy of Mind," reprinted in his *Science, Perception and Reality*, Routledge and Kegan Paul, 1963.
[2] E.g., in *Making It Explicit*, Harvard University Press, 1994.
[3] E.g., in *Mind and World*, Harvard University Press, 1994.
[4] E.g., in "Is Knowledge a Natural Phenomenon?," in R. Schantz, ed., *The Externalist Challenge*, de Gruyter, 2004, 193–209.
[5] See, e.g., Alvin Goldman, *Epistemology and Cognition*, Harvard University Press, 1986.

entirely out of the picture? I think it is clear that the answer to this question is, "No."⁶

One might, for example, be a reliabilist, and explain both justification and knowledge in terms of reliability, and yet hold, as well, that there is an important place in epistemological theorizing for talk of reasons. On such a view, talk of reasons should not be eliminated from epistemological theorizing; rather, reasons themselves can be explained in naturalistic terms, thereby making good naturalistic sense of talk of reasons, rather than eliminating such talk altogether. Nothing in the reliability theory of justification or knowledge, or in causal theories, or in the very commitment to naturalism, rules out such a view.

But there is, as well, of course, a more radical possibility. The very fact that naturalists can offer prima facie plausible theories of knowledge and justification without adverting to reasons raises the possibility that one might be able to accomplish everything an epistemological theory needs to accomplish without the notion of a reason playing any role in the theory whatsoever. Such a theory would offer a kind of eliminationism about reasons, something far more radical, I believe, than any would-be naturalistic reduction of reasons.

What I have in mind here is not a view which does away with beliefs, although there are certainly naturalistic accounts which propose to do exactly that. Reliability accounts of justification and knowledge – and I will use such accounts as paradigmatic examples of a naturalistic epistemology in what follows – do not propose to do away with beliefs, or intentional states generally. The kind of eliminationism that I have in mind is far more narrowly focused: it seeks to do away with reasons, while leaving belief and knowledge entirely intact. Such a view is far less radical than those epistemologies which would have us do away with intentional states, but I think it is clear that many will certainly regard it as far too radical nonetheless. Epistemology without reasons, they will say, is no epistemology at all.

---

⁶ Laurence BonJour seems to disagree:

> Certain recent philosophers have questioned, or seemed to question, this requirement for knowledge [HK: that a person must have reasons for a belief if it is to count as knowledge], arguing instead that knowledge requires only that the process leading to the acceptance of the belief in question be *reliable*, i.e., that it in fact produce or tend to produce true beliefs, even though the person in question may have no reason of any sort for thinking that this is so (where this variant requirement may be presented as either a competing account of justification or an alternative to the justification requirement). (*In Defense of Pure Reason*, Cambridge University Press, 1998, 1)

I believe that the eliminationist position deserves far more discussion than it has thus far received. Indeed, I believe that many who have expressed an allegiance to reliabilism have left completely open the question of whether one should hope to achieve some sort of naturalistic reduction of reasons, or, instead, a more radical and thoroughgoing elimination.

In considering the role which reasons should play in epistemology, it should be clear that we are not presented with a simple dichotomy according to which we must either defend the utter centrality of reasons in epistemological theorizing, or else eliminate reasons wholesale. Talk of reasons has had a long and complicated history. One might well think that a proper approach to this issue will result in a defense of certain applications of the notion of a reason, while taking an eliminativist approach to others. There is thus a spectrum of possible views on this topic, rather than a simple choice between defending and eliminating all talk of reasons. What I will argue is that, wherever one's view falls on this spectrum, a proper defense of that view will need to draw on information about the psychology of belief fixation. The discussion of reasons in epistemology has not, to my mind, been sufficiently informed by the psychological facts, relying far too often, instead, on the phenomenology of deliberation. The role of reasons in epistemological theorizing provides us with one more venue in which experimental psychology may play an important role in revising and informing folk epistemological theories and categories.

I

It will be obvious that the first of the two commonsense distinctions I introduced above – the distinction between the status of Jack's belief that it will rain tomorrow on the basis of his soggy tea leaves, and the status of Jill's belief that it will rain tomorrow on the basis of her meteorological investigations – can easily be accommodated by the reasons eliminationist. Jill's belief is reliably formed, and, if we accept a reliabilist account of justification, it is therefore justified; Jack's belief is unreliably formed, and so it is unjustified. Those who wish to talk about reasons here are proposing an account of the substance of the distinction between beliefs such as Jack's and those such as Jill's, but there should be no question that the reasons eliminationist can recognize that there is an important distinction here, and the eliminationist has an account of it as well.

The second commonsense distinction – the distinction between Jack's belief that he is the present King of France, which he formed as a result of a bump on the head, and Jill's belief that Jack needs to see a doctor, which she formed on the basis of hearing Jack claim that he is the King of France – is importantly different. The reasons eliminationist will recognize, of course, that Jack's belief is unreliably formed, and so unjustified, while Jill's belief is reliably formed, and so justified, but this second distinction was supposed to be different from the first. After all, the defender of reasons will want to say that in our first pair of cases Jack has bad reasons while Jill has good reasons, but in the second pair of cases, Jack has no reasons at all while Jill has good reasons. If the reasons eliminationist views the second pair of cases as just another example of the way in which some beliefs are reliably formed, while others are not, then the eliminationist is unable to make a distinction which the defender of reasons, and common sense as well, it seems, is committed to making.

The reasons eliminationist will insist, and rightly so, that it is not always an advantage of a theory that it commits us to additional distinctions. The defender of reasons sees a continuum of cases, starting with beliefs formed on the basis of excellent reasons and proceeding through weaker and weaker reasons down through cases in which beliefs are formed on the basis of pathetically weak reasons; but then, it will be insisted, there is a sharp break. There is a difference in kind, and not just in degree, according to the defender of reasons, between forming a belief on the basis of terribly weak reasons – such as Jack's belief about the weather formed on the basis of tea-leaf reading – and beliefs formed for no reasons at all – such as Jack's belief that he is the present King of France. For the reasons eliminationist, on the other hand, we simply have a single continuum of cases, differing only in degree of reliability. There is no difference in kind, on this view, between Jack's belief about the weather and Jack's belief that he is royalty. Indeed, as the reasons eliminationist sees it, we should not assume that beliefs which are formed, as the defender of reasons would describe things, on the basis of no reasons at all are automatically lower down on this continuum than any of the beliefs which are formed on the basis of weak reasons.

Notice how each of these views would describe these cases. For the defender of reasons, there is a difference in kind between forming beliefs on the basis of reasons, however weak those reasons may be, and cases like Jack's belief that he is French royalty. In the former kind of case, there is a psychological explanation for the origin of the belief in question. Jill's belief that Jack has a worrisome medical problem is caused by another belief she has: that Jack is making utterly crazy claims. Her belief about Jack's medical problem is thus a result of an inference, and Jill's psychology thus includes some inferential mechanism which takes her belief about what Jack has said as input and produces her belief that Jack has a medical problem as output. If we are reliabilists, and the defender of reasons may in fact be a reliabilist, then we may go on to assess the reliability of such an inferential mechanism. But Jack's belief that he is the present King of France is quite different; it is not formed by inference. There is, plausibly, no psychological explanation for Jack's forming this belief. Instead, we must descend to the neural level to explain how this particular belief came about, and, for the defender of reasons, this makes this case fundamentally different in kind from the former case.

The reasons eliminationist sees things differently. After all, we sometimes form beliefs, quite reliably, in ways that do not have any psychological origin. Explaining the origin of these beliefs requires that we descend to the physiological level, just as we did in the case of Jack's bump on the head. Proprioception is arguably like this. We each have beliefs about the orientation of our bodies. There is a physiological explanation of how these beliefs are produced, but that may well be all of the explanation that there is of them. Let us suppose, for the sake of argument, that such an account is correct. Beliefs produced by proprioception, we are assuming then, are not just different from inferential beliefs; they are not based on sensory experience either. What is interesting about the case of proprioception is that, unlike ordinary perceptual beliefs, there seems to be no sensory experience mediating between neural input and belief. This is, at least, what I want to assume here.

Now if this is the right account of the origin of proprioceptive beliefs, the defender of reasons will have to assimilate them to Jack's belief that he is the King of France, for these beliefs are not based on reasons of any kind; they operate merely in "the space of causes," as Sellars would put it. And since these beliefs are not based on reasons, and the defender of reasons sees justification, and thus knowledge, as demanding a basis in reasons, these beliefs are unjustified, and so cannot constitute knowledge. But for the reasons eliminationist, the proper way to think about cases like this is quite different. We merely need to ask ourselves how reliable the process is by which such beliefs are formed. If it is a reliable process, as proprioception in normal conditions certainly is, then the resulting beliefs are justified, and typically cases of knowledge as well. From an epistemological point of view, the reasons eliminationist will insist, these beliefs are more like Jill's belief that it will rain tomorrow, and her belief that Jack has a serious problem as well, than they are like Jack's belief that he is the King of France. In order to see things properly, the reasons eliminationist will insist, we must do nothing more than look at questions of reliability, and let reasons drop out of the picture entirely. If we insist on classifying these cases as the defender of reasons would have it, we don't just add an unnecessary distinction to our epistemological picture. We do something far worse than that. By viewing these cases in terms of reasons, the reasons eliminationist will insist, we are led to misjudge the epistemological status of the beliefs under discussion.

It is no small cost to reject the possibility of justified belief and knowledge on the basis of proprioception. The defender of reasons seems forced, however, to just such a position, while reasons eliminationism treats proprioception as a source of justified belief and knowledge. This surely seems to be an advantage for the reasons eliminationist.

II

Simple perceptual beliefs raise a host of complex issues for those who put reasons at the center of their epistemological theories. If we examine the etiology of perceptual beliefs, then in the typical case, although beliefs about sensory experience do not come into play, sensory experience itself is surely found in the causal chain that leads to belief. My belief that there is a tree just outside the window in front of me is caused, in part, by a sensory experience which I currently enjoy. As Sellars famously argued, however, those who favor some sort of foundationalist account of justification face a troubling dilemma: either my experience itself should be understood as having propositional content, in which case it too, like my perceptual belief, stands in need of further justification, or the sensory experience fails to have propositional content, and can thus do no justificatory work.

Foundationalists have not been silent on this problem. They have, of course, had a great deal to say about it. Some have sought to show how propositional content may be assigned to experiential states in a principled way, and then show just how such states may play a justificatory role in perceptual belief. Others have tried to slip, somehow, between the horns of the dilemma, allowing sensory states to play a justificatory role even without assigning them any propositional content. Still others have attempted to show, instead, that sensory states, when properly understood, should be seen as playing a causal role in the production of perceptual belief, without thereby playing any justificatory role at all. But it is surely no exaggeration to say that each of these approaches faces serious problems, and it is for this reason that none of them has won general assent.

The reasons eliminationist proposes a simple solution. We should stop talking about reasons here, and, in so doing, the Sellarsian dilemma goes away. When we look at the etiology of perceptual belief, it is certainly true that sensory states seem to play an important causal role. If we wish to know about the justificatory status of these beliefs, all that is relevant is the reliability of the process which produces them. If our psychological theories tell us that there is theoretical work to be done by assigning propositional content to sensory states, then we should do that. But if, on the other hand, our best theories of the origin of perceptual belief assign no propositional content at all to sensory states, that is no problem either. Whichever way our psychological theory goes, the only issue for our theories of justification and knowledge is whether the processes which produce perceptual beliefs are reliable. And there can be little doubt that in a great many cases, such beliefs are indeed reliably produced. The relationship between sensory states and perceptual belief thus understood fails to raise the issues which give rise to the Sellarsian dilemma because we no longer seek to explain the epistemological status of these beliefs in terms of reasons. There are no puzzles about how it is that sensory states, whether they have propositional content or not, may play a crucial role in processes which reliably lead to true belief. As the reasons eliminationist sees it, the Sellarsian dilemma is the product of a mistaken picture about the nature of justification and knowledge: the view that these central epistemological notions should be explained in terms of the having of reasons.

A similar issue arises for the defender of reasons who is committed to the existence of a priori justification and knowledge. Let us suppose, for the sake of argument, that some of our beliefs are, in fact, a priori justified. Some of these beliefs, it seems, are arrived at by way of inference, and the defender of reasons will explain why it is that they have the epistemological status they do by appealing to the way in which proper inference may transmit justification. Thus, for example, if I come to believe that the Pythagorean theorem is true by recognizing the soundness of a standard proof of it, there is an obvious way in which, it seems, we may explain the epistemological status of the resulting belief in terms of the reasons I have for believing it. But not all apparently a priori beliefs are arrived at, it seems, by way of inference. Consider a candidate for such non-inferential a priori status: the belief that nothing may be red and green all over at the same time, or the belief that the law of the excluded middle is true, or the belief that the sum of one and one is two. What, according to the defender of reasons, is the source of the justificatory status of such beliefs? A variety of accounts have been offered here, involving, among other things, appeals to intuition or intellectual seemings. Such approaches face the very same problem which the status of sensory experience gave rise to: either intuitions or intellectual seemings, or what have you, have propositional content, in which case they stand in need of further justification themselves, or they lack propositional content, in which case they seem incapable of playing a justificatory role. Any account of a priori knowledge which explains the epistemological status of our beliefs in terms of reasons will face just such a Sellarsian dilemma about basic a priori beliefs.

Now many epistemologists of a naturalistic turn of mind will simply reject the a priori/a posteriori distinction. It is certainly true that, under Quine's influence, the rejection of the a priori was long seen as a hallmark of a naturalistic approach to epistemological issues. But those times are now long past, and many naturalistic epistemologists have argued that there is a perfectly coherent distinction to be made among reliably formed beliefs between those which are the product of experiential input to belief-forming mechanisms and those which are formed without any such input.[7] Naturalists who wish to preserve talk of reasons in their account of key epistemological distinctions will need to face the Sellarsian dilemma for a priori belief just as much as those who reject naturalism. But the reasons eliminationist will urge that we may avoid the dilemma entirely, just as we did in the case of perceptual belief, by doing away with talk of reasons. If some of our beliefs are reliably formed without any experiential input, then those beliefs are thereby justified and so candidates for knowledge as well. We may look to experimental work in psychology to see if there any beliefs which answer to such a description, as some philosophers and psychologists have urged is quite plausible, but the epistemological status of such beliefs raises no special problems at all. For example, if part of our native intellectual equipment includes some inferential tendencies which reliably track some basic deductive rules, and if these inferential tendencies may produce some beliefs about logic without involving any experiential input, then the reliability of the processes producing these beliefs is thereby assured, while at the same time, assuring the a priori status of those beliefs.[8] All of this may be easily explained without appeal to talk of

---

[7] See, e.g., Philip Kitcher, "A Priori Knowledge," *Philosophical Review* 89(1980), 3–23; Georges Rey, "The Unavailability of What We Mean: A Reply to Quine and Fodor and Lepore," *Grazer Philosophische Studien* 46(1993), 61–101, and "A Naturalistic A Priori," *Philosophical Studies* 92 (1998), 25–43; Alvin Goldman, "A Priori Warrant and Naturalistic Epistemology," *Philosophical Perspectives* 13(1999), 1–28; and Louise Antony, "A Naturalized Approach to the A Priori," *Philosophical Issues* 14(2004), 1–17.

[8] Such a view is defended by Lance Rips in *The Psychology of Proof*, MIT Press, 1994.

reasons. As the reasons eliminationist sees it, talk of reasons here is nothing but a source of apparently unsolvable problems. It is a mistake to try to address these problems head-on, as the defenders of reasons seek to do. What we should do, instead, according to the reasons eliminationist, is reject the very picture which gives rise to these problems. We should stop trying to explain justification and knowledge in terms of the having of reasons. An epistemology without reasons allows us to do precisely that.

III

While the Sellarsian dilemma focuses our attention on the premises from which our inferences proceed, it should not be assumed that the status of inference itself is unproblematic for the defender of reasons, if only the legitimacy of those premises can be explained. Inference itself raises problems for the defender of reasons, problems which may simply be sidestepped if we endorse reasons eliminationism.

There is a traditional picture of how it is that legitimate inference may play a justificatory role according to which our most basic inferential principles are a priori justified. Simple deductive principles, according to this picture, such as modus ponens, may be recognized a priori as licensing inference because they are truth-preserving. Such an account, of course, requires that we successfully address the Sellarsian dilemma for a priori justification, but the defender of reasons had to face that problem anyway. But deductive inference, by itself, cannot possibly define the limits of legitimate inference, and on the traditional picture, there are also certain non-deductive principles, such as those involved in inductive inference, or inference to an explanation, whose legitimacy needs to be explained as well. Here too, on the traditional picture, it will be claimed that such inferences are a priori legitimate, although here, of course, this cannot be explained by appeal to their truth-preserving character, since non-deductive inference is not truth-preserving. On the standard view, it will be claimed that we may know a priori that good principles of inference are justification-conferring, despite the fact that they are not truth-preserving, and this has led to a wide variety of arguments which attempt to show, a priori, how certain non-deductive principles of inference meet this standard. The history of attempts to give such a priori defenses of various inductive principles, however, has not been salutary.

Notice that it will not do, of course, simply to show that, given one's other epistemological commitments, such principles of inference had better be a priori defensible or else an untenable skepticism will result.

Although a number of philosophers have made such arguments, what is needed here is something which provides a certain amount of epistemological illumination: if we are committed to an account of justification or knowledge which explains these notions in terms of reasons, we will need to know how it is that we have good reason to make inferences which accord with the principles in question. The insistence that, if we are to reject a very broad skepticism, the legitimacy of such principles must be knowable a priori does not provide the needed illumination. To put the point slightly differently: the fact that defenders of a reasons-based approach to epistemology seem committed to showing a priori that basic inferential principles are legitimate need not be taken as an argument for such a priori legitimacy; it may, instead, be taken as an argument against the reasons-based approach itself.

Reliabilists who wish to maintain the reasons-based approach may object here. While it is certainly true that internalist epistemologists are committed to the a priori defensibility of basic principles of inference, the philosopher who wishes to reconstruct reasons talk in terms of reliability has no such commitment. A reliabilist may view principles of inference as legitimate to the extent that they are reliable, whether they are a priori defensible or not. One belief provides good reason for another just in case the second belief may be reached from the first by way of a reliable principle of inference. On such a view, good reasons may be explained in terms of reliability, and good inference as well; reliability may be seen, on such a view, as a way to resuscitate the notion of reasons, rather than a way to undermine it. Such a reliabilist will think that it is a certain traditional internalist account of reasons which needs to be given up, but we need not give up the very idea of good reasons.

Such a view certainly deserves to be taken seriously, but I believe that reasons eliminationism deserves a serious hearing as well. There are a number of considerations which suggest that a reliabilist should not very quickly commit to a reliabilist reconstruction of talk about reasons. Discussions of the epistemology of inference often begin with very simple examples, as I myself did above, involving applications of modus ponens. But as Gilbert Harman has long argued, modus ponens is not a principle of inference.[9] That q is entailed by p, and *if p, then q*, does not tell us what

---

[9] "Induction. A Discussion of the Relevance of the Theory of Knowledge to the Theory of Induction (with a Digression to the Effect That Neither Deductive Logic nor the Probability Calculus Has Anything to Do with Inference)," in Marshall Swain, ed., *Induction, Acceptance, and Rational Belief*, Humanities Press, 1970, 83–99.

we should infer if we believe both *p* and *if p, then q*. It may be that we should infer *q*, but it may also be that we should give up either *p*, or *if p, then q*, or both. Inference, as Harman argued, is more holistic than the simple examples would suggest.

Exactly how holistic inference actually is is a difficult question about human cognition. More than this, there are difficult questions about how such belief change is to be explained. It could be that inference proceeds by way of fairly local principles of inference, where these principles are not a priori defensible, but are, instead, often reliable in the environments in which they are used. If this were the case, the effect of the workings of such inferential principles would be to produce the appearance of some holistic process – since the individual inferences would typically be reliable, and a body of truths is, of course, coherent. Something very much like coherence would thus be achieved not by way of inferential principles which are especially sensitive to coherence, but instead as a by-product of the reliability of the individual inferences. If our minds work in ways like this, then although we need to depart from the internalist picture which has our inferences licensed by their a priori defensibility, it might still be appropriate to talk of reasons for belief.

Alternatively, it might be the case that belief change is achieved by way of principles of inference which genuinely operate holistically. Exactly what such holistic inferential principles might look like is not at all clear, especially since any attempt to spell out a set of workable principles of this sort would need to take into account problems of computational complexity, but we need not suppose that any such principles would have to be a priori defensible. It would surely be good enough if we were able to discover principles of belief change of this sort which operated reliably within the kinds of environments we tend to inhabit. So long as belief change is carried out by way of inferential principles, however, whether local or more holistic, it seems quite natural to explain it in terms of reasons. Admittedly, if the actual processes of belief revision involve holistic principles of inference, then the illustrations we typically use in epistemology, involving, for example, applications of modus ponens, are horribly oversimplified, and the way in which we typically talk of reasons for belief is horribly oversimplified as well, but, all the same, on this picture, there seems a place for talk of reasons, rather than their wholesale elimination.

There is, however, another possibility. It may be that belief change is not achieved by way of principles of inference at all, whether a priori defensible or otherwise. Change of belief may be a product of neural processes which do not implement anything like inferential principles, but which operate, instead, by various sorts of activation systems, as defenders of parallel distributed processing have typically suggested.[10] While some who have defended accounts of this sort have sought to do away with not only talk of inference, but talk of belief as well, this is not universally true. On many such accounts, the notion of belief survives our understanding of cognitive change, even if the notion of inference needs to be given up. The very idea of inference, on such a view, involves a vast oversimplification of what goes on in belief change. When we see belief change for what it is, it will be argued, all talk of inference drops out of the picture, and once we give up on the notion of inference, the very idea of reasons is seen to be mistaken as well.

One need not be committed to such an account of belief change in order to think that we should adopt an epistemology without reasons. If an account of belief change without inference is even a live possibility, we should not adopt an epistemology which presupposes that it is mistaken. One might thus favor an epistemology which does not commit to the importance of the category of reasons unless and until we can be quite sure that an account of change of belief which does away with inference is mistaken. An epistemology which distinguishes good belief change from bad belief change in naturalistic terms, as reliability theories do, can remain neutral on the question of whether talk of reasons is genuinely illuminating, or, instead, simply misleading.

IV

Those who wish to defend the place of reasons in epistemology may seek to avoid getting involved in discussions of cognitive architecture. The distinction between "the space of reasons" and "the space of causes," it may seem, is extremely robust, and far more secure than any current account of the mechanisms of belief change. In order to defend the importance of this distinction, one need not hold, of course, that reasons for belief are not causes. The suggestion that there is a robust distinction

---

[10] Some will regard these accounts as offering non-classical views of inference rather than simply doing away with inference. Precisely how these accounts are best conceptualized is exactly what is at issue here. If the right way to think about these accounts is that they involve belief change without inference, then this lends support to some sort of reasons eliminationism. The right way to conceptualize this issue, on my view, will flow directly from our best available psychological theories.

here worth defending merely involves the idea that there is a distinction in kind between a reason for belief and a mere cause.

Let us return to the case introduced at the beginning of this essay. When Jack hits his head on a rock and comes to believe, as a result of his injury, that he is the present King of France, his belief is caused, but he lacks any reason for holding it. And this case seems different in kind, and not merely in degree, from cases in which Jack forms beliefs for good reasons, or even for very weak reasons. The importance of the distinction seems clearest in cases of self-conscious deliberation. Jill sees Jack lying on the ground with a slight head wound. There's some blood, and he's briefly knocked unconscious. When he comes to, he takes himself to be the King of France. And perhaps Jill wonders, "Can I safely walk down the hill with Jack and get him to a doctor, or do I need to call an ambulance immediately?" In situations like this, people like Jill may self-consciously ask themselves about the reasons they have for various beliefs. They consider the reasons on either side of an issue, and they try to figure out what to believe. There seems no other way to describe this situation without invoking the notion of a reason. More than this, such situations of doxastic deliberation seem quite central to epistemology. On some views, the most fundamental questions which epistemology can address concern the guidance we might offer to agents in these situations, and it is hard to see how we might perspicuously parse such guidance without making use of the notion of a reason for belief.[11]

No one should dispute this account of the phenomenology of doxastic deliberation. We seem to be capable of making decisions about what to believe, and we certainly do, at times, self-consciously consider the strength of our reasons. The important questions for epistemology, however, are not about the phenomenology of doxastic decision-making. They concern, instead, questions about the nature of justified belief and knowledge, about the nature of epistemic normativity, and about the extent to which the phenomenology of doxastic decision-making actually tracks the psychology of belief acquisition and change. It is only in the light of a clear understanding of these issues that we may hope to determine whether the notion of a reason should play a central part, or, indeed, any part at all, in epistemological theorizing.

---

[11] See, e.g., Richard Foley, "What Am I to Believe?," in Steven Wagner and Richard Warner, eds., *Naturalism: A Critical Appraisal*, University of Notre Dame Press, 1993, 147–162; and Laurence BonJour, "The Indispensability of Internalism," *Philosophical Topics* 29(2001), 47–65.

There can be no question at all, in particular, that the phenomenology of doxastic decision is deeply misleading about the actual processes that go on when we wonder about what to believe.[12] Our beliefs, even when we reflect, are influenced by a wide variety of factors which are unavailable to the reflective agent. Factors which seem to influence us when we reflect may, in fact, play no causal role in determining what we come to believe. Although the reflective agent seems to have some sort of direct grasp of the cognitive processes which take place in doxastic decision-making, the appearances here are deeply deceiving. Reflective agents have only a very partial view of the processes that go on during reflection, and even that partial view is not entirely accurate as far as it goes. The perspective of the reflective agent who considers what to believe is thus extraordinarily misleading. It is not even clear that we should be talking about agency here at all.

What this means, of course, is that even if the notion of reasons for belief is essential to the way in which individuals conceive of what they are doing when they are engaged in doxastic deliberation, this need tell us nothing at all about the extent to which an epistemological theory should take this notion seriously. After all, the fact that sincere participants in religious rites conceive of what they are doing in ways which make ineliminable appeal to the notion of a deity does not provide us, by itself, with a quick argument for theism. Since we are well aware that there are a variety of illusions about mental states and processes which the first-person perspective is subject to, we need to be especially careful here.

A number of factors combine to provide the doxastic deliberator with a vivid, though illusory, picture of the mental processes which lead to belief fixation. First, the capacity of working memory is quite small, and thus, when we try to bring to mind the considerations which bear in favor and against adopting a particular belief, it is inevitable that only a tiny fraction of the relevant considerations will be brought to consciousness. Second, as was briefly mentioned above, even apart from considerations of the size of working memory, many of the relevant considerations are simply inaccessible to reflection. The result, then, of self-conscious consideration of what to believe is that we end up focusing our attention on a very small, and unrepresentative, set of considerations which might bear on our doxastic

---

[12] I have discussed the issues raised in this paragraph at length in my "Introspection and Misdirection," Chapter 1; *Knowledge and Its Place in Nature*, Oxford University Press, 2002, chapter 4; *On Reflection*, Oxford University Press, 2012, chapters 1, 3, and 5; and my "Naturalism vs. the First-Person Perspective," Chapter 7.

decision. Although these considerations do not, in the typical case, even approximate a good deductive or inductive argument either for or against the claim which is under consideration, it is easy to turn any set of such considerations into a valid deductive argument by adding appropriate conditional beliefs. Thus, for example, if in trying to decide whether to believe p or *not-p*, I attempt to bring to mind the considerations which bear on this issue, and the considerations I can think of amount to q, r, and s, considerations which jointly seem to count, however, inchoately in favor of p, then I may turn these considerations into a valid deductive argument for p by accepting the claim that *if q and r and s, then p*. There is a good deal of psychological evidence that, in the situation described, the conditional will strike me as plausible. The act of reflection will thereby provide me with a valid deductive argument in favor of a particular conclusion. When I come to believe that very conclusion in such a situation, it thereby seems that I have formed the belief on the basis of just that argument. Talk of reasons for belief seems a natural way to characterize the influence of such considerations on the resulting belief.

The fact that the considerations which count in favor of a belief may be so easily put in the form of a valid argument, or, at a minimum, a convincing non-deductive argument, is a product of the forces which go to work when we stop to reflect on what we should believe, rather than some real insight into the considerations which move us. Our ability, under conditions of reflection, to put these considerations in the form of a tidy argument makes it seem natural, and utterly perspicuous, to regard the premises of such arguments as reasons for our beliefs, and the rules of inference which are needed to get from premises to conclusion as the ones which guide our reasoning.[13] But this is an utterly inaccurate view of the fixation of belief, even under conditions of reflection, and to the extent that conceptualizing this whole process in terms of reasons for belief is funded by this inaccurate view, the very idea of reasons for belief is thereby called into question.

It is tempting to think that we can settle the issue about the importance of reasons without getting into difficult questions about the mechanisms of belief fixation only because the phenomenology of doxastic decision provides us with such a vivid picture of precisely how belief fixation takes places under conditions of reflection. We know too much, however, about

---

[13] I have referred to views which regard justification in this way as endorsing the "Arguments-on-Paper Thesis." See "Beyond Foundationalism and the Coherence Theory," *Journal of Philosophy* 77(1980), 597–612.

the processes which go on during reflection to take this phenomenology at face value. And this surely suggests that if we are to understand the place of reasons in epistemological theorizing, we cannot avoid addressing the difficult psychological questions about how belief fixation actually occurs.

V

I want to look at one last attempt to secure the place of reasons in epistemological theorizing which bypasses the kinds of psychological questions on which I have been focusing. I have been assuming throughout this essay that if my belief that q is part of my reason for believing that p – and here I am concerned with the reasons which provide my doxastic justification for believing that p, and not just the propositional justification for that belief – then my belief that q must be part of the cause, or part of what causally sustains, my belief that p. If the two beliefs are causally independent of one another, then neither can be a reason – in the doxastic justification sense of reason – for the other. It is this causal requirement that allows experimental results from psychology to get their purchase on these issues. There can be no doubt that psychological results give us real insight into the causal relations among our mental states, and well-confirmed theories in psychology are far more deserving of our credence than the deliverances of phenomenology.

But some will insist that this way of thinking of things fundamentally misunderstands the nature of reasons. As some philosophers would have it, my reflectively believing that *q is my reason for believing that p* is what constitutes my believing that p on the basis of q.[14] There is no further fact which my reflective belief, or as some would put it, my reflective endorsement of believing one thing on the basis of another, attempts to record. On this view, since the reflective belief is what constitutes my believing on the basis of a reason, it is not the sort of belief which even could be mistaken. To think that the psychological facts about causal relations among beliefs are even relevant to evaluating the truth of the reflective belief, on this view, simply fails to recognize what believing on the basis of reasons consists in. If this sort of view is correct, then facts about our

---

[14] See, e.g., Christine Korsgaard, *The Sources of Normativity*, Cambridge University Press, 1996, lecture 3; Richard Moran, *Authority and Estrangement: An Essay on Self-Knowledge*, Princeton University Press, 2001; and Nishi Shah and Ekaterina Vavova, "Review of *On Reflection*," *Ethics* 124(2014), 632–636. Adam Leite holds a view very much like this as well: "On Justifying and Being Justified," *Philosophical Issues* 14(2004), 219–253, as does Earl Conee, "Against Debasing Skepticism," manuscript.

reasons for belief are wholly insulated from any facts about the etiology of belief, and we need not worry, therefore, that the place of reason in epistemology may somehow be undermined by discoveries in empirical psychology.

Let us consider, then, a particular example. Suppose Jim is part of a faculty search committee, and he is reading over dossiers of applicants. A woman who has applied, with some undeniably strong credentials, is favored by some members of the search committee, but Jim has placed her file in the reject pile. When asked why he found her candidacy unacceptable, Jim cites a number of features of her record. These, he says, are the reasons he believes that she is an unacceptable candidate.

Now I simply want to stipulate that Jim is entirely sincere in stating his reasons. He has not passed over this file lightly, since he knew that some of his colleagues favored the candidacy of this particular woman, and he sincerely believes that the reasons he cites are the reasons for which he is dismissing her candidacy. Since he reflectively believes that these are his reasons, then on the view we are considering, this thereby constitutes his reason for believing that her candidacy is unacceptable.

Imagine that, at this point, one of Jim's colleagues brings up a number of studies in social psychology which show that when one and the same set of credentials was presented to subjects to be evaluated for faculty positions, some labeled with male names, and others labeled with female names, the male "applicants" were consistently rated more highly than the female "applicants," despite the fact that their credentials were identical. Such studies seem to show, it has been argued, that the very items cited as reasons for the ratings given simply could not be the actual reasons for which the female "candidates" were rated lower than their male counterparts.[15]

When presented with studies of this sort, some people tough it out: "that may be true of the subjects in those studies," they say, "but I'm not like that." "I'm not moved by those kinds of things." "I'm not prejudiced in that way." "They haven't studied me."

Given the robustness of the results in these studies, many of us may find such responses unconvincing. But what is interesting about the constitutive view of reasons under consideration here is that, on this view, Jim need not resort to such special pleading in order to defend the integrity of

---

[15] See, e.g., R. Steinpreis, K. Anders, and D. Ritzke, "The Impact of Gender on the Review of the Curricula Vitae of Job Applicants and Tenure Candidates: A National Empirical Study," *Sex Roles* 41(1999), 509–528.

his assessments. What Jim should reply is not that he is immune to influence of the sort uncovered by the psychological research, but rather that the etiology of his belief is simply irrelevant to the issue of the reasons for which he holds his belief. The claim about Jim's reasons is simply a claim about the reasons he endorses under conditions of reflection. As such, the fact that he does endorse a certain claim about his reasons, a claim which has nothing to do with the gender of the candidate, thereby guarantees that his reasons have nothing whatever to do with the fact that the candidate is a woman.

Implausible as the various sorts of special pleading are in cases like this, the claim of the constitutivist about reasons seems even more implausible. If one wishes to define justification in terms of the having of reasons, then doxastic justification requires that the reasons for which one holds a belief meet certain standards. The fact that one sincerely believes that one's reasons are of a certain sort does not in any way assure that one's reasons are of that very sort, as cases like this clearly show. If the reasons one sincerely cites are actually good reasons for belief, but they are not the reasons which causally produced or sustained one's belief, then one is not doxastically justified. The attempt to identify reasons for belief with higher-order beliefs about one's reasons, or reflective endorsements of reasons, is extraordinarily implausible.

The attempt to insulate particular claims about one's reasons from the psychological facts about a belief's etiology cannot be sustained. Once we allow these facts to play a role in our understanding of the epistemologically relevant features of belief, however, we need to take seriously the possibility that the etiology of belief may be quite different from the way in which we pretheoretically believe it to be. As I have argued, this is not merely some logically possible situation in some world which we know to be very distant from our own. It is, instead, a way that belief fixation in our world might actually occur. Whether we should think of the epistemological status of a belief in terms of reasons at all, however, depends on these difficult issues about the origins of our beliefs.

VI

Let me sum up. The view that the notion of reasons is central to epistemological theorizing is undeniably attractive. It seems, indeed, unavoidable, but that appearance of unavoidability may well be a product of the phenomenology of doxastic decision-making. This is, however, a poor basis for determining just how a defensible epistemology ought to be conceptualized. We know that phenomenology gets crucial features of psychological processes fundamentally wrong. This is no less true in doxastic decision than it is elsewhere. Any attempt to insulate central concepts of epistemology from the psychological facts seems doomed to failure. But when we take a serious look at the processes involved in belief fixation, it is no longer obvious that we will find a place for a distinction between "the space of causes" and "the space of reasons." Giving up such a distinction would not mean that we would regard all beliefs as epistemically on a par. What it suggests, instead, is that the best way to make the epistemological distinctions which are needed may not involve the notion of a reason at all.

Even if the psychology of belief fixation does not lead us to give up the notion of reasons entirely – and I should say here that I expect that it will not – it may well lead us to modify our pretheoretical ideas about just where talk of reasons should prove to be illuminating. Exactly how large a role talk of reasons should play in epistemology, and, indeed, whether it should play any role at all, must be settled by our understanding of the psychological facts.

10

Doxastic Justification Is Fundamental

Epistemologists typically distinguish between propositional justification and doxastic justification. Roughly, one is propositionally justified when one has good reasons for believing a proposition; one is doxastically justified when one holds a belief on the basis of good reasons.[1] More than this, the standard view here is that propositional justification is the more fundamental notion. An account of propositional justification will tell us what it is to be a good reason for belief; doxastic justification is then defined in terms of propositional justification.[2]

This is, I believe, a terrifically commonsensical approach, and it conforms to a traditional understanding of the nature of the philosophical enterprise. The requirements for propositional justification belong to the domain of philosophy proper, on this view. Exactly what the relationship must be between a set of reasons and the proposition for which they provide adequate support is a question which may be answered a priori, involving considerations of logic and probability theory, among others.

---

[1] As John Turri rightly points out ("On the Relationship between Propositional and Doxastic Justification," *Philosophy and Phenomenological Research* 80(2010), 312–326), more than this is needed for doxastic justification. In addition, the belief must be based on those reasons *in the right way*. Given that basing is typically (and rightly, to my mind) understood causally, this further requirement should come as no surprise. Causal accounts of various philosophical notions need to rule out deviant causal chains, and the "right way" requirement does exactly that. Turri argues that this, by itself, shows the fundamentality of doxastic justification, but this seems to ignore a natural move on the part of those who see propositional justification as fundamental: they may simply say that one is doxastically justified in a belief when one holds it on the basis of good reasons *in the right way*, with the notion of good reason being provided by one's account of propositional justification. As I see it, the issue of which notion of justification is fundamental is tied in with a wider range of issues than Turri considers.

[2] I do not mean to be endorsing the idea that either of these notions should be explained in terms of reasons. I raise some doubts about whether this is the right way to conceptualize issues about justification and knowledge in "The Role of Reasons in Epistemology," *Episteme* 8(2011), 38–52. There is, however, no completely neutral way to explain the propositional/doxastic distinction, and the explanation in terms of reasons certainly does a good job of fixing attention on the phenomenon at issue, even if, in the end, a proper account of it may need to be given in other terms.

Whether a particular belief is doxastically justified, on the other hand, cannot be settled a priori, since the issue of what a belief is based upon involves a psychological component. Doxastic justification may be a requirement for knowledge, but the real philosophical issue about justification lies on the propositional justification side of the ledger.

One of Alvin Goldman's most important contributions to epistemology, in my view, was to reverse the order of explanation here. Goldman is widely, and rightly, given credit for introducing reliabilism, and developing it in extraordinary detail.[3] He is similarly, and rightly, given credit as one of the most important and earliest defenders of externalism in epistemology.[4] But the importance of seeing doxastic justification as fundamental is comparable, in my view, to these other contributions, and I do not believe that this has been adequately appreciated. I hope to remedy that oversight here.

I

The distinction between propositional and doxastic justification, or propositional and doxastic warrant, as he termed it, was introduced by Roderick Firth in 1978.[5] As soon as he introduced the distinction, Firth provided an argument for the fundamentality of propositional justification.

> Since doxastic warrant has this ultimate importance for theory of knowledge [namely, as a necessary condition for knowledge –HK], it is tempting to suppose that we can analyze propositional warrant in terms of doxastic warrant.

---

[3] Thus, for example, Michael Williams writes, "Since the 1960s, Anglophone epistemology has undergone a paradigm-shift: 'the Reliabilist Revolution.' The revolutionary-in-chief has been Alvin Goldman" ("Internalism, Reliabilism, and Deontology," in Brian P. McLaughlin and Hilary Kornblith, eds., *Goldman and His Critics*, Blackwell, 2016, 3). Goldman introduced reliabilism in his 1979 paper, "What Is Justified Belief?," reprinted in his *Liaisons: Philosophy Meets the Cognitive and Social Sciences*, MIT Press, 1992, 105–126, and he developed it in detail in *Epistemology and Cognition*, Harvard University Press, 1986.

[4] Goldman's earliest papers presenting the externalist approach were "A Causal Theory of Knowing" (1967) and "Discrimination and Perceptual Knowledge" (1976), both of which are reprinted in *Liaisons*, 69–83 and 85–103, respectively. Other important early externalists were D. M. Armstrong, in his *Belief, Truth and Knowledge*, Cambridge University Press, 1973, and Fred Dretske, whose externalism was most explicit in his *Knowledge and the Flow of Information*, MIT Press, 1981, although the foundation for it had been laid in a series of earlier papers, reprinted in his *Perception, Knowledge and Belief: Selected Essays*, Cambridge University Press, 2000.

[5] "Are Epistemic Concepts Reducible to Ethical Concepts?," in Alvin Goldman and Jaegwon Kim, eds., *Values and Morals: Essays in Honor of William Frankena, Charles Stevenson, and Richard Brandt*, Reidel, 1978, 215–229.

But how could this be done? From the fact that a proposition *p* is warranted for a person [i.e., is propositionally justified –HK], together with the fact that *S* believes *p*, we cannot infer that *S* arrives at his doxastic state in a rational way. The two facts are compatible with the supposition that *S* believes *p* for the wrong reasons or even as a consequence of hypnotic suggestion. Thus we cannot hope to reduce propositional warrant to doxastic warrant by using a hypothetical statement in the subjunctive mood. We cannot say that "*p* is warranted for *S*" [i.e., *p* is propositionally justified for *S* –HK] is short for "If *S* were to believe *p* then *S* would be warranted [i.e., doxastically justified –HK] in believing *p*." For if *S* were to believe *p S* might not do so rationally. And no elaboration of this formula is going to help. For in assessing doxastic warrant we must employ as a standard of rationality the very standard that we employ in assessing propositional warrant.[6]

Once the distinction was drawn, the idea that propositional justification is the more fundamental notion was immediately attractive to most epistemologists. Frege's insistence that epistemological notions be divorced from psychological considerations, and the development of this way of thinking under the guidance of the logical positivists, still held considerable sway at the time of Firth's writing.[7] When philosophers prior to Firth attempted to provide analyses of justified belief, they were quite clearly thinking of propositional justification, the notion which might be explained in suitably apsychologistic terms. They thus needed little in the way of argument to view propositional justification as the more fundamental of the two notions. Firth's distinction quickly became a mainstay of epistemological discussions, but it did little to change the course of epistemological theorizing. Most epistemologists went on much as they had done before, focusing attention on propositional justification, adding little more than a brief acknowledgment that knowledge required still more than this; it required not only that one's belief be propositionally justified, but that one hold the belief on the basis of the reasons in virtue of which it is so justified.[8]

A notable exception to this tendency was found in Alvin Goldman's "What Is Justified Belief?" Goldman's paper presents, for the first time, his reliabilist account of justified belief, an account which made a radical break

---

[6] Ibid., 219–220.
[7] For an extremely useful history of these ideas in the development of twentieth-century epistemology, see Philip Kitcher, "The Naturalists Return," *Philosophical Review* 101(1992), 53–114.
[8] Typical here is the discussion of well-foundedness in Richard Feldman and Earl Conee's "Evidentialism" (1985), reprinted in their *Evidentialism: Essays in Epistemology*, Oxford University Press, 2004, 83–107. The discussion of well-foundedness is located at 92–93.

from the apsychologistic and internalist approach then characteristic of analytic epistemology. But what goes without mention in that paper, until three paragraphs before its end, is the distinction between propositional and doxastic justification,[9] and the fact that Goldman is reversing the traditional order of explanation. Goldman's paper was devoted to providing an account of doxastic justification, the notion he saw as more fundamental. The final few paragraphs of the paper show how propositional justification may be explained in terms of it:

> Person S is [propositionally justified] in believing p at t if and only if there is a reliable belief-forming process available to S which is such that if S applied that operation to his total cognitive state at t, S would believe p at t-plus-delta (for a suitably small delta) and that belief would be [doxastically] justified.[10]

Doxastic justification is, famously, defined in terms of the reliability of the process which produces S's belief.

Without any fanfare, Goldman thus showed that Firth had failed to consider any but the simplest attempt to explain propositional justification in terms of doxastic justification. Firth's additional one-line argument – that any account of doxastic justification must incorporate a prior account of propositional justification – simply begs the question at issue. So one might think that at this point we have a standoff: we may take propositional justification as the more fundamental notion, and there is an obvious way to define doxastic justification in terms of it; or we may take doxastic justification as the more fundamental notion, and we may define propositional justification in terms of it. Indeed, at this point in the discussion, one might wonder what difference it makes which of these two strategies one adopts. What, after all, is the substantive issue at stake here? Is there, in fact, any substantive issue at stake? I believe there is.

II

Let us consider some of the accounts of propositional justification which have been offered by philosophers who take such justification to be the more basic notion.

Thus, for example, Roderick Chisholm explains that his approach to constructing an epistemological theory begins with three presuppositions:

---

[9] Goldman uses different terminology, referring to *ex ante* and *ex post* justification. "What Is Justified Belief?," 124–125.
[10] Ibid., 124.

> We presuppose, first, that there *is* something that we know and we adopt the working hypothesis that *what* we know is pretty much that which, on reflection, we think we know ...
>
> We presuppose, second, that the things we know are justified for us in the following sense: *we* can know what it is, on any occasion, that constitutes our grounds, or reason, or evidence for thinking that we know ...
>
> And we presuppose, third, that if we do thus have ground or reasons for the things we think we know, then there are valid general principles of evidence – principles stating the general conditions under which we may be said to have grounds or reasons for what we believe.[11]

Chisholm's first presupposition expresses his commitment to a non-skeptical account of knowledge, and the second expresses his commitment to an internalist account of justification. The third presupposition, as it plays out in Chisholm's work, involves a commitment to the a priori knowability of the principles of evidence. When Chisholm says that "there are valid general principles of evidence – principles stating the general conditions under which we may be said to have grounds or reasons for what we believe," what he has in mind is that such principles must be knowable independent of any experience. In giving his account of what he calls "a theory of evidence," Chisholm thereby provides an account of propositional justification, and the commitment to the a priority of any such account assures that contingent features of human psychology will be irrelevant here.[12] In particular, if an individual has certain psychological limitations which prevent him from seeing the relevance of some body of claims to a given proposition, that has no bearing whatsoever on the theory of evidence, and thus no bearing on what it is that is propositionally justified for that individual. Similarly, if there are psychological limitations which humans in general should have, this too is irrelevant to the theory of evidence, and thus has no bearing on what it is that is propositionally justified for humans. By the same token, should some individual, or humans in general, have some native reliable psychological mechanism which tends to draw a certain conclusion from a given body of beliefs – for example, a tendency to conclude that there is fire on the basis of the presence of smoke – this too would simply be irrelevant to an account of propositional justification. What makes a claim propositionally justified is a set of a priori certifiable features of the claim and its relation to potential

---

[11] *Theory of Knowledge*, 2nd ed., Prentice-Hall, 1977, 16–17.
[12] I do not mean to be assuming here that there can be no contingent a priori claims. Rather, it is simply implausible that the relevant contingent features of human psychology are themselves a priori knowable.

justifiers. The peculiarities of human psychology, whether limitations, or truth-conducive adaptations, have no bearing on such an account. Such is Chisholm's view of the matter.

Nor is Chisholm's view on this matter unusual for traditional epistemologists, especially those of an internalist bent. Matters of propositional justification are typically regarded as wholly independent of the vagaries of human psychology.

Formal epistemologists see matters in much the same way. Formal accounts of justification are, of course, accounts of propositional justification, and they are elaborated in terms of probabilistic relations among sets of propositions. Formal accounts inevitably abstract away from the psychological peculiarities of individual agents, as well as the psychological peculiarities of human beings in general. This is, of course, regarded as a feature, rather than a bug: such accounts are typically presented as theories of ideal rationality, and formal ideals must leave room for the possibility that individuals or entire species may fall quite short of the ideal. As David Christensen remarks, "We should accept with good grace that the limits of good human thinking need not be the limits of goodness for all thinking."[13] Similarly, propositions which fail to have the preferred formal relations to one's body of beliefs fall short of the epistemic ideal, even if there should be reliable psychological processes available which would produce beliefs in those propositions. It is not just human limitations or deficiencies which are irrelevant to formal accounts of justified belief, but reliable adaptations which fail to mirror formal relations as well. The account of propositional justification inherent in formal epistemologies makes features of human psychology, whether good, bad, or indifferent, simply irrelevant.

When the order of explanation is reversed, however, and propositional justification is defined in terms of doxastic justification, psychological matters become directly relevant to matters of propositional justification. If I have some psychological peculiarities which you lack, then even if you and I share all of the same beliefs, and all of the other non-belief potential justifiers as well, assuming there are such justifiers, a different set of propositions may be propositionally justified for the two of us. Similarly, what is propositionally justified for typical humans, given a certain body of potential justifiers, may be quite different from what is propositionally

---

[13] *Putting Logic in Its Place: Formal Constraints on Rational Belief*, Oxford University Press, 2004, 177–178.

justified for typical members of a different species with the very same body of such justifiers. When doxastic justification is viewed as fundamental, psychological matters become relevant not only to doxastic justification, as they are on all views; they become relevant to the realm of propositional justification as well. The pristine realm of propositional justification, long viewed as amenable to a priori investigation, is informed – or, some would say, corrupted – by empirical matters, if Goldman's approach is correct. And this, it seems, is a matter of the first importance.

The question of whether propositional justification is the more fundamental notion, as tradition would have it, or, instead, doxastic justification is more fundamental, as Goldman suggests, thus seems to involve a substantive issue. Before I turn to addressing that issue, however, we will need to examine one way in which one might attempt to avoid this issue entirely.

III

As I have presented matters thus far, there appears to be a substantive issue which separates Goldman from more traditional epistemologists, and it concerns the nature of propositional justification. On traditional views, the nature of propositional justification has nothing to do with the psychology of epistemic agents, and it is susceptible to a priori investigation. On Goldman's view, propositional justification is inevitably entwined with psychological matters, and a proper understanding of it will thus require empirical investigation. One might attempt to avoid this dispute, however, by drawing a distinction here, and presenting the two sides as simply talking past one another.

Instead of seeing the two sides of this dispute as disagreeing about a single phenomenon – propositional justification – one might draw a distinction. We may introduce two notions of propositional justification – propositional justification$_G$ and propositional justification$_T$ – each of which is a wholly legitimate subject of inquiry. Propositional justification$_G$ is, indeed, infused with psychological content, and must be investigated empirically. Propositional justification$_T$ concerns a priori knowable relations among potential justifiers, and psychological matters are irrelevant to it. Goldman is right about propositional justification$_G$, but wrong about propositional justification$_T$; traditional epistemologists are right about propositional justification$_T$, but wrong about propositional justification$_G$. On this way of seeing things, there is no substantive dispute between Goldman and the tradition, simply a failure to recognize that there are two equally legitimate notions of propositional justification when we had all thought that there was only one.

Formal epistemologists especially might find this solution appealing. Indeed, formal epistemologists tend not to use the term "justification" at all, and the suggestion that this is no accident, and that they are, indeed, investigating a phenomenon quite different from the one which Goldman sees as derivative from doxastic justification, may strike many, if not most, of them as entirely unsurprising. Such epistemologists need not deny the legitimacy of the category of justification which Goldman seeks to investigate, a notion of propositional justification which has distinctively psychological content. They need only insist that their formal notion of justification, or ideal rationality, or whatever one wants to call it, is no less legitimate.

And this kind of approach need not be restricted to formal epistemologists. Consider what Laurence BonJour has said about the debate between internalists and externalists about justification. After years of arguing that externalists are simply mistaken about justification,[14] BonJour had a change of heart. Externalists, he came to argue, have a perfectly legitimate notion of justification, and the kinds of investigations which externalists are engaged in are equally legitimate.

> Neither I nor any reasonable epistemologist should have any quarrel with any of this. Such investigations are obviously legitimate and valuable, and also obviously of epistemological, though not merely epistemological, significance.[15]

Externalism and internalism, on this view, are not rival views of a single phenomenon; instead, they are properly viewed as equally correct accounts of two different epistemic phenomena.[16] As BonJour remarked,

---

[14] See especially "Externalist Theories of Empirical Knowledge," *Midwest Studies in Philosophy* 5 (1980), 53–73; *The Structure of Empirical Knowledge*, Harvard University Press, 1985; and *In Defense of Pure Reason*, Cambridge University Press, 1998, where he remarks, on the first page, speaking of externalism, "My conviction is that views of this kind are merely wrong-headed and ultimately uninteresting evasions of the central epistemological issues."

[15] "The Indispensibility of Internalism," *Philosophical Topics* 29(2001), 50.

[16] BonJour, of course, is not the only one to hold such a view. Ernest Sosa's distinction between animal knowledge and reflective knowledge embodies a similar idea. See especially "Knowledge and Intellectual Virtue" (1985), reprinted in his *Knowledge in Perspective: Selected Essays in Epistemology*, Cambridge University Press, 1991, 225–244; and also *Virtue Epistemology: Apt Belief and Reflective Knowledge*, volume I, Oxford University Press, 2007; and *Reflective Knowledge: Apt Belief and Reflective Knowledge*, volume II, Oxford University Press, 2009. Views of this sort are now quite widely held.

Though I never expected to find myself paraphrasing Chairman Mao in an epistemological context, why not let many epistemological flowers bloom?[17]

One might, it seems, with no less reason, adopt a similar strategy in the debate over the status of propositional justification. Why shouldn't we see two different epistemic phenomena here, with the two disputant parties each correct about one of the phenomena? Isn't there room in an epistemological theory for a notion of propositional justification which is divorced from features of an epistemic agent's psychology, and another, equally legitimate notion of propositional justification, which incorporates such features? If so, there is no substantive dispute left to be resolved about which notion of justification – propositional or doxastic – is the more fundamental.

There is one way to defend this move which, I believe, many will find tempting. Formal epistemologists may argue that just as the legitimacy of logic as an area of inquiry is hardly in need of defense, the legitimacy of inquiry into formal approaches more generally, including, but not restricted to, Bayesian methods, should be equally uncontentious. We may thus define a notion of propositional justification in these formal terms, if we like, even if, in doing so, we in no way dispute the legitimacy of other notions of propositional justification. It would be folly to suggest that these formal areas of inquiry are illegitimate, so the psychology-free notion of propositional justification should be seen as inheriting the legitimacy of formal methods generally.

If this argument is successful, even those who favor more traditional, informal approaches to epistemology may make a similar move. Chisholmians, for example, might argue that they too may introduce their own stipulated notion of propositional justification, and once this is done, there are a variety of perfectly legitimate questions which arise internal to the Chisholmian system. And so too for any other psychology-free notion of propositional justification. Once a term is defined, we may legitimately investigate how it interacts with other notions within the domain of our theorizing. Drawing out the consequences of one's stipulations is a familiar, and clearly legitimate, part of intellectual inquiry.

It would, indeed, be folly to deny the legitimacy of formal methods, or to attack the integrity of investigating the consequences of one's stipulations in the course of theoretical investigations. Nevertheless, the

---

[17] Ibid., 63.

legitimacy of a psychology-free notion of propositional justification is not so easily defended as this argument would suggest. It does not follow from the intellectual legitimacy of formal investigations that such investigations have anything to do with epistemology,[18] let alone that any particular stipulated definition of 'propositional justification' is itself intellectually legitimate. And the same applies, as well, to less formal approaches to epistemology, and any would-be stipulations there. It is, of course, intellectually legitimate, and, indeed, important to investigate the consequences of well-motivated stipulations within the development of well-motivated theoretical views. But there is a great distance between this obviously true claim and the suggestion that it is intellectually legitimate to investigate the consequences of any stipulation whatever. If the intellectual legitimacy of a psychology-free notion of propositional justification is to be defended, more will be needed than to point out the legitimacy of formal inquiries, or the need, in the course of well-motivated inquiries, for an investigation of the consequences of one's stipulations. An argument is needed to show the epistemological relevance of a psychology-free notion of propositional justification. I will briefly return to this issue in Section V below.

Rather than canvas attempts to show the legitimacy, and the epistemological relevance, of an apsychological notion of propositional justification, I will turn instead to Goldman's preferred view of propositional justification and argue for its legitimacy and epistemological importance. I will then argue that the reasons which count in favor of such a notion of propositional justification give us reason, as well, for rejecting any apsychological notion. The view that there are two equally legitimate epistemological notions here is, in my view, a mistake.

IV

Chisholm's first presupposition in epistemological theorizing, namely, his anti-skepticism, is hardly unique to him. Almost all contemporary epistemologists have a similar starting point, and Goldman is no exception. There surely seems to be a robust phenomenon of human knowledge, and it is this very phenomenon which has been the object of philosophical reflection for as long as philosophers have engaged in epistemological

---

[18] Relevant here, for example, is Gilbert Harman's argument that deductive logic and probability theory have nothing to do with inference. See his "Induction: A Discussion of the Relevance of the Theory of Knowledge to the Theory of Induction (with a Digression to the Effect That Neither Deductive Logic nor the Probability Calculus has Anything to Do with Inference)," in Marshall Swain, ed., *Induction, Acceptance, and Rational Belief*, Reidel, 1970, 83–99.

theorizing. The same is true, it seems, of justified belief. There is an awful lot of justified belief out there, as it were, and it is the phenomenon of justified belief which has prompted philosophical reflection about its nature.

Chisholm's first presupposition is not merely anti-skeptical, however. He adopts as a working hypothesis not only the claim that we know, and justifiedly believe, a great many things, but also that we know, and justifiedly believe, roughly what we pretheoretically take ourselves to know, and justifiedly believe. So we are in a position at least roughly to recognize much of our knowledge and justified belief.[19] And this too is a common starting place for almost all contemporary epistemologists, including Goldman. So we begin with the working assumption that there is a robust phenomenon of justified belief, and, given that doxastically justified belief is a necessary condition for knowledge,[20] this means that there is a robust phenomenon of doxastically justified belief as well.

Of course, since doxastically justified belief requires propositional justification, this means, in addition, that there is a robust phenomenon of propositional justification. But there is a sense in which doxastically justified belief is more easily available to us for inspection. The phenomenon of doxastic justification involves belief states and their bases, items which are susceptible to straightforward empirical investigation. Propositional justification involves relations between a proposition and would-be justifiers, where the proposition at issue need not be believed, and the would-be justifiers are abstract objects rather than psychological states of individuals which have these abstract objects as their contents.

Now some will think my suggestion that psychological states and their bases are somehow more easily available to us for investigation than the abstract objects at issue in propositional justification displays nothing more than a naturalistic prejudice. On certain views, our access to abstract objects in general should be viewed as entirely unproblematic, indeed, as far less problematic than our access to items located in the physical world.[21] Perhaps there are abstract objects to which we have especially easy access, but what I want to argue here is that, whatever one's views on

---

[19] For an empirical defense of this claim, see Kenneth Boyd and Jennifer Nagel, "The Reliability of Epistemic Intuitions," in Edouard Machery and Elizabeth O'Neill, eds., *Current Controversies in Experimental Philosophy*, Routledge, 2014, 109–127.

[20] I have, at times, expressed some doubts about whether this is actually true. See my "Knowledge Needs No Justification," in Quentin Smith, ed., *Epistemology: New Essays*, Oxford University Press, 2008, 5–23. I bracket such doubts here.

[21] BonJour's *In Defense of Pure Reason*, loc. cit., is an especially important version of such a view.

the accessibility of abstract objects in general, when it comes to the case of doxastic justification and propositional justification, it turns out that it is doxastic justification which is the more easily accessible phenomenon.

Experimental work on human inference, beginning with Wason and Johnson-Laird,[22] Tversky and Kahneman,[23] and the entire heuristics and biases tradition which they founded, presented epistemologists with a difficult problem. These psychologists identified a number of inferential heuristics which, it seemed, were typically involved in human inductive inference, and which seemed, on their face, to be normatively unacceptable. Tversky and Kahneman remarked in one paper that "intuitive expectations are governed by a consistent misperception of the world."[24] Nisbett and Borgida commented that this work had "bleak implications for human rationality."[25] This work, if taken at face value, seemed to reveal the manner in which human inductive beliefs are typically based, and the basis for our beliefs failed to live up to the kinds of standards for propositional justification which philosophers had typically appealed to. Indeed, Tversky and Kahneman explicitly compared the inferential heuristics they found to be at work in human inference with what they referred to as "the logic of statistical inference"[26] and found us wanting. As they colorfully remarked,

> The law of large numbers guarantees that very large samples will indeed be highly representative of the population from which they are drawn ... People's intuitions about random sampling appear to satisfy the law of small numbers, which asserts that the law of large numbers applies to small numbers as well.[27]

What this work seemed to show is that the anti-skeptical presupposition which Chisholm and so many others took as a working hypothesis was, at least with regard to inductively based beliefs, largely mistaken.

---

[22] Peter Wason and Philip Johnson-Laird, *Psychology of Reasoning: Structure and Content*, Harvard University Press, 1972.
[23] For a selection of papers, both by Tversky and Kahneman themselves, and others working in that tradition, see Daniel Kahneman, Paul Slovic, and Amos Tversky, eds., *Judgment under Uncertainty: Heuristics and Biases*, Cambridge University Press, 1982; and Thomas Gilovitch, Dale Griffin, and Daniel Kahneman, eds., *Heuristics and Biases: The Psychology of Intuitive Judgment*, Cambridge University Press, 2002. For an important early review of the literature, see Richard Nisbett and Lee Ross, *Human Inference: Strategies and Shortcomings of Social Judgment*, Prentice-Hall, 1980.
[24] "Belief in the Law of Small Numbers" (1971), reprinted in Kahneman, Slovic, and Tversky, op. cit., 31.
[25] "Attribution and the Psychology of Prediction," *Journal of Personality and Social Psychology* 32 (1975), 935.
[26] "Belief in the Law of Small Numbers," loc. cit., 31.   [27] Ibid., 25.

But another possibility soon emerged.[28] Instead of holding on to the traditional a priorist ideas about the standards for propositional justification and giving up the view that much of our inductively based belief is indeed doxastically justified, one could reexamine one's ideas about the appropriate standards for propositional justification in the light of the discoveries about the psychological bases of our inductive beliefs. This would allow one to maintain the view that our inductively based beliefs are indeed doxastically justified at the cost – if, in the end, it is properly viewed as a cost – of adopting a psychologistic notion of propositional justification.

Such a move might seem, at least as thus far described, as nothing more than a cynical attempt to move the goal posts. If we are found not to meet appropriate standards for doxastically justified belief, these philosophers and psychologists seem to be saying, we can just redefine our standards downward until we reach a standard that we do, in fact, meet. It is easy to maintain our anti-skeptical views about our inductive beliefs if we show enough flexibility in revising our standards for propositional justification.

But this is not at all the right way to view this move. The psychologization of propositional justification is not a cynical attempt to maintain an optimistic view about the status of our inductive beliefs by dumbing down the standards for propositional justification. Instead, the psychological investigation of the bases of our inductive beliefs showed that a certain commonsense view of how inductive inference works, and how it must work if it is to be normatively acceptable, is simply mistaken. The idea that the laws of logic served to define, at least in part, the laws of proper inference is one which has been a common theme in the Western philosophical tradition at least since Aristotle, and with the advent of the probability calculus, this natural idea was expanded to include it. Boole, famously, saw the laws of logic and the probability calculus as the laws of normatively acceptable thought.[29] So natural was this idea that it was easy to miss the fact that it involves a highly non-trivial move from talk of laws

---

[28] See the later papers by Tversky and Kahneman in Kahneman, Slovic, and Tversky, op. cit., and Gilovitch, Griffin, and Kahneman, op. cit.; Nisbett and Ross, op. cit., esp. chapter 11; Hilary Kornblith, *Inductive Inference and Its Natural Ground*, MIT Press, 1993; Edward Stein, *Without Good Reason: The Rationality Debate in Philosophy and Cognitive Science*, Oxford University Press, 1996; Gerd Gigerenzer, Peter Todd, and the ABC Research Group, *Simple Heuristics That Make Us Smart*, Oxford University Press, 1999; Michael Bishop and J. D. Trout, *Epistemology and the Psychology of Human Judgment*, Oxford University Press, 2005; Daniel Kahneman, *Thinking, Fast and Slow*, Farrar, Straus and Giroux, 2011.

[29] *An Investigation of the Laws of Thought on Which Are Founded the Mathematical Theories of Logic and Probabilities*, Dover, 1958.

of logic and probability to talk of laws of inference. But inference, is, of course, a psychological process, and there is a substantive question as to whether it is, or should be, governed by the laws of various mathematical formalisms. When one views the realm of propositional justification in apsychologistic terms as susceptible to a priori investigation, one takes a stand on this important issue. And it is just this position that the heuristics and biases literature forces us to reexamine.

The kinds of inductive inferences humans tend to make do not answer to the standards of traditional a priorist ideas about propositional justification, nor do they often approximate them. But, at least in many cases, they are none the worse for that. Indeed, it is useful to compare the ways in which inductive inference works with a familiar feature of our perceptual mechanisms. These mechanisms are well adapted to certain stable features of the environment. They would not work in all logically possible environments, or even in all physically possible environments. Rather, as our susceptibility to visual illusions illustrates, the visual system is able both quickly and easily to identify external objects by presupposing that the source of our visual stimulation has certain very general features. The presupposed features are, indeed, features of normal environments, and thus when we find ourselves in just such environments, the visual system quickly produces accurate judgments. When we find ourselves in non-standard environments, on the other hand, these false presuppositions result in illusory appearances, and, in many cases, false judgments as well. Given that normal environments vastly predominate, such a system is highly reliable. More than this, a visual system which made no such presuppositions would be entirely unworkable. The input to our visual system so vastly underdetermines the external facts that it would be impossible, without any presuppositions about the environment, to reach any conclusions about it at all.

What the heuristics and biases literature reveals about human inference is that, structurally, a good deal of it seems to work in much the same way. Our inductive tendencies do not conform to the probability calculus, nor to any system which would even seem to satisfy a priori standards for propositional justification. Just as with our perceptual processes, our inductive heuristics build in certain presuppositions about the environment, presuppositions which are, indeed, true of the typical environments in which we tend to be found. It is for this reason that these heuristics work so well so often. Of course, these presuppositions are just straightforwardly false about non-standard environments, and when we are in such surroundings, unless we knowingly compensate for that fact, our typically reliable inferential heuristics will lead us astray. But these inferential heuristics are exceptionally effective in providing us with true beliefs about the world around us.[30]

The impression persists, among many philosophers, that a good deal of human inference can be properly explained as legitimate by appeal to a priori principles. Just as a non-deductive argument can easily be turned into a valid deductive argument by adding an appropriate conditional premise, a formally unacceptable non-deductive argument can be turned into an acceptable one through the judicious addition of further premises. Philosophers who favor a psychologized notion of propositional justification will see human inference as governed by inferential principles which are not formally legitimate, but are instead well adapted to stable features of human environments. Those who favor an apsychological notion of propositional justification may seek to defend the legitimacy of human inference by claiming that, when appropriate background knowledge about our environment is included in our body of beliefs, we are shown to have the requisite background knowledge to ground the inferences we make even against traditional a priorist standards.

There are two problems with such a move. First, although epistemologists themselves may often have the requisite background knowledge about normal environments to fill out the premises they would need to appeal to in justifying many of their inferences, this kind of abstruse background knowledge is not in the purview of most human knowers. We are extraordinarily sensitive to a wide range of both perceptual and inferential cues about which we do not have explicit knowledge. The fact that by adding claims about these cues, and about normal environments, to standard bodies of belief would then allow for the construction of good formal inductive arguments would, at a minimum, leave the vast majority of believers out in the cold. If we wish to avoid a broad inductive skepticism, this move will not provide the requisite relief.

More than this, however, there is reason to think that appealing to this body of abstruse information, even in the case of those who are knowledgeable about such things, will not get the epistemology right. Having taken a few courses in linguistics, and read a bit of the linguistics literature, I have some explicit knowledge of the syntactic rules of English. But this explicit knowledge of syntactic rules, of course, has nothing to do with my ability to speak and understand English. My linguistic performance is not

---

[30] I have defended this view at length in *Inductive Inference and Its Natural Ground*.

governed by my explicit knowledge of these syntactic rules, as is easily proven by the fact that I was a competent speaker of English even before taking courses in linguistics. From the point of view of my linguistic performance, explicit knowledge of syntactic rules is entirely epiphenomenal: it plays no role whatsoever in linguistic processing (which, of course, is just as well, since I was not one of the better students in those linguistics courses).

In just the same way, abstruse knowledge about normal environments will typically play no role in our inductive inferences, as can be shown by the fact that we process inductive information just as well even when we lack such abstruse knowledge. This background information is thus epiphenomenal, in the typical case, even in those knowers, such as psychologists and epistemologists, who are in possession of it. And this means that, even for these individuals, it can play no role in what makes them doxastically justified. If one insists, then, on an a priorist account of propositional justification, and an account of doxastic justification which is built upon it, one will be led, once again, to a broad inductive skepticism.

The only way, then, to avoid such skepticism is by allowing one's conception of proper reasoning and proper belief acquisition generally to be informed by an adequate view of what actually goes on in belief acquisition and revision. In doing so, we do not revise our standards downward in order to reassure ourselves that, whatever it is we do when we acquire beliefs, we can come up with some standard which will license it. Rather, our properly informed view about how successful cognition actually works gives us an improved understanding of what is and isn't required to achieve that cognitive success. We have a roughly accurate recognitional capacity for our cognitive successes, as Chisholm suggested. When we put that recognitional capacity to work together with the results of the best available results in experimental psychology, we come to understand just what doxastic justification requires. And with an account of doxastic justification in hand, we come to see that the apsychological notion of propositional justification, which once seemed so attractive, utterly fails to capture the epistemic phenomena which prompted our epistemological theorizing in the first place.

So long as we both view propositional justification as a necessary condition for knowledge, and reject any broad skepticism, we will be forced to accept a psychologized account of propositional justification. There is no role for an apsychological account of propositional justification to play in a non-skeptical theory of knowledge.

V

Those who wish to defend some apsychological notion of propositional justification must thus either endorse a broad skepticism about propositionally justified belief, or defend a notion of propositional justification which is not a necessary condition for knowledge. Let me briefly say something about each of these alternatives.

Throughout the history of philosophy, the threat of skepticism has typically been presented as a motivation for the development of anti-skeptical views about justification and knowledge.[31] Those rare authors who do defend skeptical views are frequently treated by later authors as object lessons of the dangers inherent in accepting the principles which led those authors to their skepticism. In recent analytic epistemology, the presumption against skepticism is typically defended, if it is seen as in need of defense at all, by way of appeals to common sense or intuition. There can be little doubt, after all, that skeptical views are radically at odds with both common sense and our pretheoretical intuitions about justification and knowledge. My own reasons for rejecting skepticism are somewhat different. Every available view about how it is that humans, or, indeed, many other animals, are able to get around in the world in ways which allow them to satisfy their various needs and desires has inevitably appealed to the ways in which knowledge of various features of the environment is implicated in an explanation of successful behavior.[32] It is for this reason that I say that there is a robust phenomenon of knowledge which is worthy of investigation, and it seems to me that it is this very phenomenon which has prompted philosophical theorizing. Skeptical views not only deny the obvious fact that there is such a phenomenon; they thereby present an account of knowledge and justification which is utterly divorced from the very phenomenon which their theories are supposed to illuminate. This, as I see it, is the real cost of rejecting anti-skeptical views in epistemology.

Is there room, however, for an additional notion of justification which is not viewed as a necessary condition for knowledge? Certainly most of those who have defended apsychological accounts of propositional justification have not had this thought in mind, but it is worth exploring nonetheless.

---

[31] John Greco's *Putting Skeptics in Their Place: The Nature of Skeptical Arguments and Their Role in Philosophical Inquiry*, Cambridge University Press, 2000, is representative here.
[32] I have defended this way of thinking about knowledge in *Knowledge and Its Place in Nature*, Oxford University Press, 2002.

There are, after all, various formal accounts which are presented as views of rational ideals for belief, and the talk of rational ideals might suggest two different points relevant to the issue under discussion here. On the one hand, the talk of *rational* ideals may suggest that the target of these investigations is somewhat different from the notion of justification targeted by those epistemologists who view justification as a necessary condition for knowledge. On the other hand, talk of rational *ideals* may suggest that there is little harm should it turn out that these standards are rarely if ever met. But formal accounts are certainly not the only source of views about justification which are not embedded in an account of knowledge. So we will need to return, if only briefly, to the thought that there may be some legitimate notion of propositional justification in addition to the one which plays a role in the theory of knowledge.

There is, I believe, a great deal of theoretical room for such notions. There is, as many have emphasized, an important social practice of giving and asking for reasons,[33] and there can be little doubt that there is a notion of justification at the heart of this practice which is worthy of theoretical investigation. One need not think that being in a dialectical position to defend one's belief against challengers is a necessary condition for knowledge to think that this dialectical notion of justification – the notion of justification at work when we talk about being able to give a justification for our beliefs – is worthy of study. Of course, investigating this particular notion of justification requires an examination of the many different social practices involved in giving and asking for reasons, and it is very much an empirical question as to what the standards implicit in these social practices amount to. Those who are looking for a way of investigating some notion of justification which is susceptible to a priori theorizing will thus need to look elsewhere.

So the real issue here is not simply whether there are other legitimate notions of justification aside from the one involved in an account of knowledge. The issue is whether there is such a notion of justification which is also susceptible to a priori theorizing. The worry I have, of course, as I've indicated above, is that the formal notions which have been offered here, such as Bayesian accounts, while they are certainly worthy of study as formal systems, do not clearly have any epistemological content at all.

---

[33] This has been at the center of Robert Brandom's work for some time. See especially *Making It Explicit: Reasoning, Representing, and Discursive Commitment*, Harvard University Press, 1994. See also Michael Williams, *Problems of Knowledge: A Critical Introduction to Epistemology*, Oxford University Press, 2001.

There can be no question that relieving these accounts of the burden of showing that they serve to define some necessary condition on knowledge does, at least, remove one of their problems. But if these formal accounts are meant, in spite of that, to define some epistemological constraint on belief, work will need to be done to show just how these formal notions pick out genuine epistemological kinds. The notions of propositional and doxastic justification which are necessary conditions for knowledge are, in virtue of that very fact, unquestionably part of epistemology. The notion of knowledge in which they are embedded is one which is not merely a product of stipulation, nor is it one which simply answers to our pre-theoretical intuitions. It is, instead, grounded in a phenomenon which has some real theoretical unity to it, and which is legitimized by its role in explaining successful behavior. The wholly formal notions appealed to by Bayesians, however, have no such grounding, and while this does nothing to undermine their legitimacy as formal systems, it does, I believe, present a substantial challenge to the suggestion that they serve to pick out epistemological kinds. Until that challenge is answered, we have no reason to believe that there is any notion of justification which is entirely apsychological.

VI

Let me summarize. It has been widely held that the notion of doxastic justification, which presents a necessary condition on knowledge, should be explained in terms of a more fundamental notion of propositional justification. Alvin Goldman presented an account which reversed the order of explanation. I have argued that this issue of the order of explanation is a substantive one, and it goes to the very heart of the nature of epistemological theorizing. On traditional accounts, propositional justification is susceptible to a priori theorizing, but if Goldman is right, propositional justification inherits the psychological content of doxastic justification, and it can only be investigated by way of an investigation of contingent features of the psychology of would-be knowers. The notions of justification which serve to define necessary conditions on knowledge do not leave room for any apsychological account of justification.

One might attempt to evade this conclusion by introducing an additional notion of justification which is not among the necessary conditions on knowledge. There are, I have argued, reasons for thinking that this may be a fruitful line of research. At the same time, I have argued that the most promising views of this sort either have psychological content themselves, and thus will also require investigation by way of empirical means, or, alternatively, present merely formal notions which are no part of epistemology.

Goldman's proposal to explain propositional justification in terms of doxastic justification rather than vice versa is thus nothing less than a proposal for a fully psychologized account of some key epistemological notions. If this is the right approach to issues about justification, as I have argued, then reversing the traditional order of explanation, as Goldman proposed, substantially diminishes the role of a priori theorizing in epistemology.[34]

---

[34] I am grateful for comments on a draft of this essay presented at the conference at the College of William and Mary, and especially to Anna-Sara Malmgren, Lisa Miracchi, and Ram Neta.

11

Our Sense of Self

We each have a view of ourselves, ideas about our character, our strengths and weaknesses, the things we might do and might have done, as well as things we simply could not do and could not have done. These views we have about ourselves inform our actions, from the trivial to the most highly consequential. These views we have of ourselves provide us with a sense of our identity.

David Velleman, in the course of arguing that donor conception is wrong,[1] stresses the importance of family history in shaping our self-conception. He is clearly right about this.[2] As Velleman illustrates from examples involving his own family history, one's conception of who one is and what one might be may be shaped in profound ways by one's understanding[3] of one's own family. More than this, Velleman's account of the ways in which his knowledge of family history has shaped his own conception of who he is is anything but idiosyncratic. It is not implausible to think that most, perhaps the vast majority of people, are affected in this way.

Much as I disagree with Velleman's views about donor conception, that will not be the main focus of my remarks here, although I shall have a few things to say about it. I am interested in the extent to which our self-conceptions, shaped, as they are, by our understanding of family history, are genuinely accurate. Velleman stresses the extent to which the stories we tell ourselves about our families and their histories play a role in shaping

---

[1] "Family History," *Philosophical Papers* 34(2005), 357–378. That this is Velleman's conclusion, rather than some weaker claim, is clearly stated at 362 n. 3.
[2] For just one useful source on these issues, see Kate C. McLean, *The Co-Authored Self: Family Stories and the Construction of Personal Identity*, Oxford University Press, 2016.
[3] I use the term "understanding" here advisedly, since talk of one's understanding of family history is not factive, unlike talk of one's knowledge of such history. Velleman often speaks of knowledge here, and the way in which our understanding of family history provides us with self-knowledge, thereby begging the question about the accuracy of the resulting beliefs. Since the issue of accuracy is one of the foci of this essay, I will not simply assume that our beliefs here are correct.

our lives; he is concerned to show just how valuable our understanding of family history is by showing how profound a role it plays in our sense of self. It is worth asking, however, especially if we think that Velleman may be right about the importance we attach to our understanding of family history, and about its very real effects on the conduct of our lives, whether the self-conceptions which are the products of such understanding are typically faithful to the facts. It is not unreasonable to think that a proper assessment of the value of the stories we tell ourselves about family histories may be affected by their accuracy: someone whose self-conception is the product of delusions of grandeur about both his own qualities and the history of his family would hardly provide a model for motivating claims about the ways in which one's views about family history serve as a source of value.

Delusions of grandeur are not, of course, the typical case, but I believe that Velleman has given insufficient attention to the issue of the accuracy of our self-conceptions. My ultimate goal here, however, is not just to address the issue of accuracy. Like Velleman, I am interested in the value that our self-conceptions confer on our lives. The accuracy of these self-conceptions is, in my view, just one important element in understanding the ways in which our self-conceptions affect our lives' value. It is this larger issue of value on which I hope to shed some light.

I

An important part of one's self-conception has to do with one's views about one's own capacities: the kind of life one might successfully pursue or have pursued. Had I not been able to find a job in philosophy, I would probably have gone to law school, and I believe that a career in the law is one in which I might have found some real satisfaction. There are other pursuits which I am confident would not have worked out for me. I do not believe that I could have been a professional athlete of any sort. I began my college career as a mathematics major, thinking that a career in math would be fulfilling, but I found out after just a few semesters that this wasn't possible for me.[4]

Velleman suggests, quite plausibly, that our views on these matters are influenced in important ways by our understanding of family history.

---

[4] My thinking that this kind of career might be open to me may have been prompted, in part, by the knowledge that my father was a very successful mathematics major in college.

> my family-resemblance concept of myself contains much of that self-knowledge by which I am guided in my efforts to cultivate and shape myself. I can articulate a few self-descriptions that indicate some directions of self-cultivation and contra-indicate others ... But many of my aspirations are directed at fulfilling family-resemblance concepts: they are aspirations to be *like that*, where "that" denotes a type for which I have some paradigms or images but no explicit definition. And these aspirations are conditioned and channeled by family-resemblance knowledge as to how someone *like this* might or might not become *like that*. (366)

Even if our view of our own capacities and limitations may be informed by many sources, Velleman plausibly suggests that our knowledge of our own biological relatives can play a powerful role here.

> If I want to know what a person *like this* can make of himself, I can look first at what my parents and grandparents made of themselves, or at the self-cultivation underway on the part of my brothers and cousins. The point is not that I necessarily can or should strive to be whatever my biological relatives have become, but rather that my own experiments-in-living (as Mill called them) are most informatively supplemented by experiments on the part of people who are relevantly like me. Our extended family is, as it were, a laboratory for carrying out experiments-in-living relevant to the lives of people like us. (368)

Let us assume, at least for the sake of argument, that people generally have accurate views about the lives of their relatives, something which, of course, is often not the case at all.[5] Even assuming this, however, just how accurate can we reasonably expect the self-conceptions shaped by these experiments-in-living to be?

Most people who are fortunate enough to be raised by their biological parents know a good deal about them, and at least some knowledge of one's biological grandparents is common as well. It is not at all uncommon, however, to have little knowledge of one's more distant forebears. One may know a good deal about one's own generation, although this knowledge is, of course, sometimes lacking; indeed, not everyone has a large enough family to have a great many cousins or siblings whose lives might inform one. To put it crudely, the number of data points here is likely to be quite small.

The fact that the sample size here is so small is particularly important because any attempt to figure out what one's own capacities are from the

---

[5] For a useful overview of some of the psychological literature on the accuracy of our views of ourselves, see David Dunning, *Self-Insight*, Psychology Press, 2012.

lives one's relatives have led would require a very complicated teasing apart of biological and environmental factors. If one's relatives have pursued a single occupation for several generations, it would be risky, to say the least, to suppose that one is likely to have some special talent for that pursuit. Some distant relative may have fallen into that occupation quite by chance, or through a lack of any real choice in their particular circumstances. Others more recently may have been pushed into that pursuit by parental pressures. None of those relatives need have had any native talent for that pursuit, and even if they did, one certainly needn't have inherited it. Indeed, it would be surprising if many of the choices of this sort which various relatives made were not largely a product of environmental factors, and, in particular, environmental factors which may no longer be present, rather than anything terribly distinctive and attributable to heredity.

Many of us, like Velleman, have parents or grandparents who were born in other countries, in circumstances dramatically different from those we find ourselves in today. The opportunities available to them, in many cases, were utterly unlike anything we currently face. The occupations which my parents pursued and which their parents pursued are, no doubt, quite vivid to me, and I have no doubt that this vividness played a dramatic role in shaping my own self-conception, as vivid data tend to do. But evolutionary biologists know that determining which traits are genuinely heritable is an extraordinarily complicated affair. There is a reason why such biologists base their work on studies of large populations rather than a handful of vivid examples. The extension of evolutionary ideas to the psychological domain in the hands of evolutionary psychologists is exceptionally controversial.[6] What is uncontroversial, however, is that individuals wholly untrained in the workings of evolution, drawing conclusions about their own native talents and capacities on the basis of a tiny sample of their relatives' pursuits, are unlikely to come to any realistic conclusions at all. The vividness of the data and their emotional salience make these ideas loom large in our minds, but they do not contribute to the accuracy of the conclusions we reach.

My point here is not merely that there is a science relevant to the conclusions we draw from family history, namely, evolutionary biology, and most people have little or no knowledge of the relevant science. The same is true, after all, about many different areas of daily life. There is a science devoted to the effects of force on bodies in space, and most

---

[6] For a useful critical discussion of these issues, see David Buller, *Adapting Minds: Evolutionary Psychology and the Persistent Quest for Human Nature*, MIT Press, 2005.

individuals are largely ignorant of the details of that science. In spite of this, we are all well aware that objects which are dropped near the surface of the earth will fall down rather than rise, and we are able to give rough and roughly accurate predictions of the trajectories of many moving bodies. In these cases, however, the accuracy of the beliefs we have which are unaided by science is underwritten by a native folk physics, a set of inferential tendencies which are fairly accurate for many everyday purposes, even if they also produce a great many mistakes as well.[7] In other areas, subject matter–specific native help is not needed to form accurate judgments simply because the target subject matter is relatively easy to comprehend given the kinds of data we are likely to possess and our general intellectual abilities. Accurately understanding one's capacities, strengths and weaknesses, career paths which are likely to be successful, and so on, based on one's beliefs about family history, however, involves neither trivial intellectual skills, given our data, nor native intellectual capacities specially suited to true beliefs on these topics. Without scientific guidance on these topics, and data of a sort which are rarely possessed, true belief is very unlikely to result from our ruminations on family history.

Consider, for example, a child who grows up in very fortunate circumstances, and whose parents and grandparents and great-grandparents all went to college, with many of them obtaining advanced degrees. Compare such a child with one whose family members, for as many generations back as family memory allows, have not completed high school. The first of these children may never have even contemplated the possibility of failing to go to college; the second may not have even thought of going to college as a possibility. Such things are not at all uncommon, and they are of a piece with the ways in which Velleman describes the experiments-in-living which emerge from the laboratory of one's extended family playing a role in shaping one's conception of what one's capacities and talents are and the kind of life that might be open to one. It should be obvious that any adverse judgments about the second child's intellectual capacities on the basis of family history would be completely unjustified, but this is not because Velleman is mistaken in thinking that people tend to form such judgments about their own capacities on just such a basis. Indeed, sadly, Velleman is surely right about this.[8]

---

[7] See, for example, Michael McCloskey, "Intuitive Physics," *Scientific American* 248(1983), 122–130.
[8] Thus, consider these remarks in an obituary in the *New York Times* for the distinguished sociologist and psychotherapist Lillian Rubin:

The data about one's own family thus provide one with an extremely impoverished basis for theorizing about one's talents and capacities, as well as the kind of life which one might lead. The sort of theorizing required for forming accurate judgments about these topics, even if one had a sufficiently large body of data, would involve areas of expertise, in order to reach conclusions that are at all likely to be accurate, which extraordinarily few people have. This does not stop us from reaching conclusions about these topics. It just means that these conclusions are unlikely to be true.

Indeed, this surely understates the problems involved in such inferences. I have been assuming thus far that one's data about family history are themselves accurate, questioning only whether the conclusions one might draw from facts about family history are likely to be true. But the assumption I've been making for the sake of argument – that the data about one's forebears upon which one draws accurately represent one's family history – deserves to be challenged as well. When Velleman discusses his own family history he often uses factive verbs, speaking, for example, of the way in which this history provides him with "self-knowledge" (365). At other times, however, he is quite frank about the extent to which his beliefs about his forebears are a matter of conjecture. "I assume," he says, that his great-grandfather left the Ukraine for certain reasons (358); "I imagine," he says, certain things about the employment possibilities available to his great-grandfather (358). While Velleman often speaks about family history, he also speaks of "family lore" (357), which surely has a less factive flavor, and indeed, he acknowledges that this lore, in his own case, is internally inconsistent (357). Velleman acknowledges, as well, that "the topic of our biological origins is littered with mythical or symbolic thoughts, about blood and bone and such" (362). These are not, to be sure, the kind of factual bases on which one might draw if one were seriously engaged, in the manner of a genealogist, in constructing an accurate family history.

The information about family history which is passed down from parents to children is often, notoriously, not only highly selective and misleading, but inaccurate as well. Parents will often intentionally hide information about relatives which is either embarrassing to them or which they think, rightly or wrongly, might be troubling to their children. It is a

> She graduated from high school at 15 but was 39 before she enrolled in college. By landing a secretarial job straight out of high school, she said, she had fulfilled her family's highest expectations. "For a girl of my generation and class, college was not a perceived option," she wrote in the introduction to *Worlds of Pain*. To her mother, a seamstress, "a daughter who worked at a typewriter in a 'clean' office – yes, this was a high achievement." (July 2, 2014)

rare child indeed who will have an accurate view of the incidence of alcoholism, suicide, or mental illness in their family history, or even the extent to which certain relatives were just plain unpleasant, at least when such information can easily be hidden. It is hardly unusual for family history to be presented through rose-colored glasses, lightly, or at times, heavily edited, for the edification of the listener. Many individuals, understandably, find it difficult to talk about traumatic events in their own lives, failing to inform their children about their dealings with wars, deprivation, or abuse. It would be absurd to suppose that children who are the product of extramarital affairs, or of rape, can count on being given a frank accounting of their origins. If these events, circumstances, and experiences were rare, then it would say little about the typical case. But alcoholism, suicide attempts, both successful and unsuccessful, mental illness, embarrassing characteristics and events, painful circumstances and experiences are, of course, extremely common. The reliability of the data which constitute one's family lore is not just a serious question for that one in a million individual whose family has experienced these things, since such individuals are anything but one in a million. It calls into question the reliability of family lore for all of us.

There are a number of psychological tendencies which are bound to go to work in forming our self-conceptions on the basis of family lore. I have already mentioned the role of vivid data, which play in to a tendency we have to generalize from small bodies of emotionally salient information of just the sort with which family lore and personal interactions with relatives present us.[9] There is also a well-documented tendency to overestimate one's own positive characteristics,[10] a tendency which may frequently be nurtured by one's acquaintance with family history, especially as it is handed down to us. We tend to attribute cross-situational character traits – such as honesty, generosity, and so on – both to ourselves and to others,

---

[9] See, e.g., Richard Nisbett and Lee Ross, *Human Inference: Strategies and Shortcomings of Social Judgment*, Prentice-Hall, 1980, chapter 3. There are circumstances in which this tendency to generalize on the basis of a small sample will be quite reliable, as in cases involving essential properties of natural kinds. (I have discussed these cases in detail in *Inductive Inference and Its Natural Ground*, MIT Press, 1993.) The inferences we are liable to make on the basis of family history, however, are not of this rather special sort.

[10] Nisbett and Ross, op. cit., 196–199; Shelley E. Taylor and J. Brown, "Illusion and Well-Being: A Social Psychological Perspective on Mental Health," *Psychological Bulletin* 103(1988), 193–210; Shelley E. Taylor, *Positive Illusions: Creative Self-Deception and the Healthy Mind*, Basic Books, 1989; David Dunning, Judith Meyerowitz, and Amy Holzberg, "Ambiguity and Self-Evaluation: The Role of Idiosyncratic Trait Definitions in Self-Serving Biases," *Journal of Personality and Social Psychology* 57(1978), 1082–1090; Ziva Kunda, *Social Cognition: Making Sense of People*, MIT Press, 1999, chapter 10.

traits which are unlikely to be implicated in any realistic account of the origins of our behavior.[11] Once we form a conception of our selves, such conceptions tend to be extremely resistant to change in the face of new evidence, aided and abetted by our selective memories, which allow us more easily to recall information which is congruent with our self-conceptions, rather than information which might call them into question.[12] In addition, of course, all of these tendencies play a role in forming the very accounts of family lore which our relatives hand down to us, and which form an important part of the basis for our self-conceptions.

It would thus be a mistake to move very quickly from talk of our knowledge of family lore to talk of our knowledge of actual family history, and to move from there to talk of self-knowledge embodied in our self-conceptions. Our family lore, the beliefs about family history which we form on its basis, and, even more so, the beliefs we form on that basis about our own personal characteristics, strengths and weaknesses, as well as the possibilities which might or might not be open to us, all deserve to be treated with a very large grain of salt. These views we have of ourselves and of our relatives are likely to be filled with a great deal of misleading information, outright error, and wishful thinking. How much real knowledge might be generated by the processes which give rise to these beliefs is very much in question.

II

Just how important is the accuracy of our view of family history, and of our self-conception, to the value of our acquaintance with family lore? Although Velleman presents a good deal of the information about his family lore as fact, and frequently speaks of the self-knowledge to which it leads him, he also, at times, seems quite unconcerned with the accuracy of his beliefs on these matters. Indeed, even when Velleman does, briefly, raise the issue of accuracy, acknowledging that our self-conceptions may, indeed, be inaccurate, it is largely to dismiss the importance of the issue. Thus, for example, Velleman remarks,

---

[11] Lee Ross and Richard Nisbett, *The Person and the Situation*, Temple University Press, 1991; Ziva Kunda, op. cit., chapters 9 and 10; John Doris, *Lack of Character: Personality and Moral Behavior*, Cambridge University Press, 2002.

[12] Nisbett and Ross, op. cit., chapter 8; Lee Ross and Craig A. Anderson, "Shortcomings in the Attribution Process: On the Origins and Maintenance of Erroneous Social Assessments," in *Judgment under Uncertainty: Heuristics and Biases*, Daniel Kahneman, Paul Slovic, and Amos Tversky, eds., Cambridge University Press, 1982, 129–152; Ziva Kunda, op. cit., chapter 5.

> To downplay the symbolic and mythical significance of severing a child's connection to its biological parents is therefore to misrepresent what is really going on, if not because the symbols and stories are literally true then at least because they are truly part of the human psyche. (363)

At another point, he comments,

> How do I know that I have inherited these qualities from Nathan and Golda [Velleman's great-grandparents]? I don't: it's all imaginative speculation. But such speculations are how we define and redefine ourselves, weighing different possible meanings for our characters by playing them out in different imagined stories. In these speculations, family history gives us inexhaustible food for thought. (377)

It would certainly lend a different flavor to Velleman's paper were he to argue, straightforwardly, that inaccurate views about our relatives and ourselves are of such great value that it is simply wrong to have children by way of anonymous donor sperm or egg, thereby cutting such children off from the possibility of erroneous views about themselves by way of inaccurate views of their own family history. But while such a view would have a different flavor to it than the suggestion that it is wrong to cut children off from a knowledge of their own biological family history, and the self-knowledge that results from it, the view which acknowledges the unreliability of our beliefs about family history and our self-conceptions resulting from them is in no way inconsistent. Interestingly, one of the psychologists most noted for work on the inaccuracy of our self-conceptions has herself argued that an overly positive self-conception, one that fails to fit the facts, is an important part of good mental health.[13] Let us therefore ask whether views about one's biological family, and the self-conceptions they give rise to, have the value Velleman ascribes to them, whether they are accurate or not.

Let us grant, for the sake of argument, that beliefs about family history, regardless of their accuracy, provide us with "inexhaustible food for thought" about the possibilities which might be open to us, and the kinds of people that we are. Of course, it is not as if those who are unacquainted with their family histories, for whatever reason, will lack sources of inspiration for ruminations on these matters. One will look in vain in the social psychology literature for evidence that children of closed adoptions, and children who are the product of anonymous sperm and egg donors, are lacking for a self-conception. Role models of all sorts, including adoptive

---

[13] See work cited in Note 10 by Shelley E. Taylor.

parents, family friends, teachers, and figures from history and fiction, may all serve as stimuli for thoughts and beliefs about the kind of person one might be and the possibilities which are open to one. Indeed, even in the case of those who are richly acquainted with their biological relatives, these other sources of inspiration are well known to provide fertile ground for such thinking. Gays and lesbians often note that, on first coming to terms with their sexuality, the role models provided by other gay and lesbian individuals is of tremendous importance in their developing self-conceptions, playing a far more important role than knowledge of family history. The same is true, of course, for a great many individuals who find themselves with personal characteristics of whatever sort which are especially salient and important to them, and which are not represented by other members of their biological families.

This is not to deny, what Velleman rightly points out, that adopted children will often have a profound desire to know about, and meet, their biological parents. But it is important not to mislocate the import of this. While Velleman is right, I believe, to think that these desires deserve our respect and consideration, all his talk of the ways in which our beliefs about our families of biological origin serve as a stimulus for our self-conceptions certainly makes it sound as if the lack of such beliefs will thereby rob us of the possibility of rich imaginative thinking about the lives which might be open to us and the sort of people we might be. And this simply cannot be right. There is ample stimulus for such thinking, however much we may or may not know about our biological origins. The very psychological tendencies described above which serve to provide those who are acquainted with their biological parents with a host of beliefs about the possibilities open to them will go to work on other raw materials to provide a rich basis for the imaginative thought Velleman describes and values so highly. In the case of those who are unacquainted with their biological relatives, one might reasonably think that these imaginative exercises, however compelling to those who engage in them, and however highly valued, will vary a great deal in their reliability. In this respect, however, they do not differ very much from the imaginative exercises of those who are acquainted with their biological relatives.

It is thus revealing that Velleman does not argue that those who are acquainted with some of their ancestors are better able to steer their lives successfully in confronting the many decisions, both small and large, which we all face. Instead, what he argues is that biological family matters loom large in our psyches, whatever role they may play in directing our behavior.[14] Indeed, as Velleman admits, even this claim is not universally true.

> I know that many people have no interest in their ancestry, no sense of kinship with their kin. These people define themselves in terms other than those which are descriptive of their relatives, and they pursue life stories disjoint from their family's history. (377)

But no sooner does Velleman acknowledge this point than he seeks to minimize its importance. "I think that someone who denies having anything in common with his biological relatives," Velleman tells us, "is either speaking figuratively or in denial" (377). And for those who do not find their biological relatives to be the source of the kind of inspiration which Velleman himself finds in his own family history, he remarks,

> Someone who doesn't value what he has in common with his relatives may think that he need never have known them in order to identify and cultivate those aspects of himself which he does value. But I doubt it. This person is likely to have defined himself as different from relatives precisely because they served as ill omens of his possible futures, or at least as foils against which his contrasting qualities could attract his eye. Learning not to be like his relatives has still involved learning from them: if he had never known them, he might well have ended up more like them. (377)

Yes, of course, one's biological relatives may serve as role models, both positive and negative; one may be inspired to try to be like them, or to be different from them. But the same is true, of course, of other people. One may find both positive and negative role models in one's acquaintances of all sorts, whether they are biologically related to one or not. One may have a vivid acquaintance with one's mean Uncle Harry or bitter Aunt Jane and vow, on the basis of that acquaintance, not to be like them. But mean or bitter people, as well as other role models, both negative and positive, are ubiquitous. One would be hard pressed to make out a case for the claim that, absent acquaintance with biological relatives, one would be at a loss for role models of whatever sort. But now the importance of acquaintance with one's biological relatives is becoming harder to make out.

It is worth pointing out, as well, that while Velleman tends to focus on the kinds of positive role models he is fortunate enough to find in his own family, some of the very traits and characters which populate others' family histories may play a role far less constructive than even the negative role

---

[14] Thus, see, for example, the passages quoted in the text above from pages 363 and 377 of Velleman's paper.

models which Velleman considers, individuals who merely serve as useful warnings that one doesn't want to be like *that*. While it is not uncommon to find one's family history inspiring, it is also not uncommon to find features of one's family history tiresome, frightening, demeaning, or overwhelming. Some feel ennobled by the recognition that they are members of a certain family; others feel suffocated by the thought, or depressed, or trapped.[15] Acquaintance with the members of one's family, and with the facts of family history or family lore, is not an unalloyed good. Its role in individuals' psyches is highly variable, which is not surprising, given the high variability in the kinds of families there are. Velleman speaks of children who are raised by neither of their biological parents as ones whose family ties have been "ruptured" (361), a connection "severed" (363, 372), suffering "alienation" from their biological families (374). But for many individuals, connection with their families brings with it a very substantial cost, and it would be unreasonable to suppose that whatever benefits an acquaintance with one's family members may bring will always outweigh those costs. One might reasonably think that the net value of such connection is highly variable, and not always positive.

I have been speaking as if the value of the connection with one's biological relatives consists in the benefits and burdens which such connection provides, the net value consisting then of nothing more nor less than the value of benefits minus burdens. But this may not be the right way to think about this issue. Thus, consider how we should measure the value of a person's life for that person. One might think of the person's life itself as a kind of neutral palette upon which things of positive and negative value are layered. A life need not always be of positive value to the person who lives it if the negative features of the life outweigh the positives. Alternatively, one might think that living itself is of value as well, even apart from the goings-on in that life which are of value.[16] Similarly, one might think about connection with one's biological relatives in just that way. On such a view, connection with those relatives is itself of value, even apart from whatever benefits or burdens it might bring. On this view,

---

[15] A useful counterpoint to Velleman's account of his own family's history, if such is needed, is Ray Monk's biography of Wittgenstein, *Ludwig Wittgenstein: The Duty of Genius*, Jonathan Cape, 1990. Such accounts are hardly a rarity.

[16] Thomas Nagel suggests a view of just this sort in "Death," reprinted in *Mortal Questions*, Cambridge University Press, 1–10:

> The situation is roughly this: There are elements which, if added to one's experience, make life better; there are other elements which, if added to one's experience, make life worse. But what remains when these are set aside is not merely *neutral*: it is emphatically positive. (2)

to lose out on the connection is therefore a real loss, even if a calculation of benefits minus burdens would suggest otherwise.[17]

I must confess that I find such a view rather obscure,[18] and there is certainly nothing in Velleman's paper which suggests a commitment to a view of this sort, let alone a defense of it. Velleman insists that his defense of the importance of biological connections will stick to "realistic and rational considerations" rather than "mystical or symbolic thoughts" (362, and again at 363 and 369). His case for the value of the connection seems to be made entirely on the basis of concrete benefits which the connection is alleged to bring. I will thus continue to focus on these, and assume that the value of the connection is to be assessed, rather prosaically, in terms of benefits minus burdens.

Velleman cites alleged direct benefits not only to the individual who knows his or her biological relatives, but also to those who raise such children, when they know the child's biological relatives (including, of course, the case in which they themselves are the child's biological relatives).

> Information relevant to self-cultivation is also relevant to the rearing of children. And that information is even more consequential for child-rearing, because the growth of children is so dramatic in comparison with what is still possible once the age of self-cultivation has been attained. So much of what perplexes parents has to do with the nature whose unfolding they are trying to foster. How far can the child hope to reach, and in what directions? What is the child unable to help being, and what can it be helped to become? What will smooth its rough edges, and what will just rub against the grain? (370)

There can be no doubt that parents confront all of these questions and more in raising children, and the resources they draw on to address these questions are many and varied. There are numerous parenting guides of all sorts, discussions with friends and other parents, pediatricians, and mental

---

[17] To say that, on this view, losing the connection is always losing something of value is not to say that, all things considered, it is always better to have that connection. Thus, for example, Nagel's view in the article cited above is that life itself is of value, even apart from the good-making experiences it may contain, but he does not hold the view that, all things considered, every life is of positive value. Some lives, on his view, contain so much pain and suffering that it is better to end them than to go on living. Similarly, one might hold that the connection with biological relatives is of value even apart from the good-making experiences it gives rise to, and, at the same time, believe that, in some cases, the bad-making experiences this connection gives rise to are such that one would have been better off without the connection.

[18] This is not because I am attracted to any sort of hedonistic account of value. One needn't think that an account of value need be provided in terms of pleasures and pains alone in order to find the views that life itself is of value, or that connection with biological relatives is itself of value, wholly obscure.

health professionals. Velleman is right to add that one's views about the child's biological heritage will play a role here as well, but, once again, all of the remarks made earlier about our understanding of the influence of such heritage apply. It is doubtful that beliefs formed on the basis of views about biological heritage, with the exception of some views about physical health and a narrow range of mental illnesses,[19] are typically formed in a very reliable manner. Once again, this is not to deny that parents thinking about these issues may often be influenced in a profound way by thinking about the child's biological relatives. The point is just that this tendency is not truth-conducive, especially for the sorts of questions Velleman raises. What we know about the ways in which people form beliefs about character traits[20] thus casts substantial doubt on Velleman's claim that, "The use of anonymously donated gametes can leave not just the child but also its custodial parents in the dark, and in ways that adversely affect their parenting" (370).

It is worth noting as well here that anonymous gamete donation is fully compatible with, and typically goes along with,[21] a frank accounting of the donors' medical histories. Thus, the kind of information which is most useful in self-understanding and in dealing with some of the issues that arise in child rearing need not be, and in typical cases, is not withheld even

---

[19] These are certainly an important exception, although they too must surely be informed by something more than just an acquaintance with the child's biological forebears. Folk views about heritability, even of physical traits, are not known for their reliability. Given sufficient background medical knowledge, knowledge of the medical histories of a child's biological relatives can be of tremendous value, of course, and nothing said here is meant to deny that.

[20] See the sources cited in Notes 7 through 10.

[21] See, for example, the explanation provided by the Sperm Bank of California, which is quite typical: www.thespermbankofca.org/content/why-family-health-history-important-donors. Velleman is no friend of such sperm banks, or the clients who use them. He remarks,

> Frankly, to criticize proponents of gamete donation for overselling the "gift of life" is to credit them with greater moral sensitivity than they generally show. The websites of sperm and egg banks tend to betray no hint that the lives they are helping to create will be the lives of future children whose interests are entitled to consideration. Gamete donation is presented as affecting primarily the parents, by enabling them to "create families." (373)

> One might, with equal fairness, criticize anyone who has purchased a used car by appealing to the dishonesty of used car dealers. The suggestion that we may evaluate the motives and character of individuals by way of the advertisements directed at them is absurd on its face. Further, as far as the advertisers go in this particular case, one might think that the reason their websites "betray no hint that the lives they are helping to create will be the lives of future children whose interests are entitled to consideration" might just be that this point is too obvious to need stating. The reason that gamete donation "is presented as affecting primarily the parents" might well be that advertising directed toward children who don't yet exist is unlikely to be terribly effective. Velleman allows that his remarks in this paper "will no doubt offend some readers" (361). It is passages such as this one which may go a long way toward explaining that reaction.

in the case of anonymous donation. The kind of information which is not provided, and which personal acquaintance with donors would provide, is just the sort that is most likely to lead to beliefs about character and life prospects in unreliable ways. And it is this latter kind of information, rather than the sort that is revealed in medical history, which is the focus of Velleman's discussion throughout.[22] The kind of information and acquaintance which Velleman focuses on is, to be sure, far more evocative and emotionally satisfying than a cold recitation of medical histories, but it is the latter, rather than the former, which is a reliable source of information about the child's likely prospects in life.

It is, indeed, the very evocative nature of information about family history, and personal acquaintance with one's biological relatives, which animates Velleman.

> I am inclined to think that a knowledge of one's origins is especially important to identity formation because it is important to the telling of one's life-story, which necessarily encodes one's appreciation of meaning in the events of one's life ... Organizing events into the form of a story provides an understanding of them distinct from what would be provided by causal explanations. A well constructed story recounts events in such a way as to lead us through a natural sequence of emotions, which is ultimately resolved in an emotional cadence that leaves us knowing how we feel about the events. We know how we feel because we have been through a sequence of feelings that is familiar to our emotional sensibilities; because we have arrived at a conclusory feeling, a state of emotional rest; and because our conclusory feeling takes all of the preceding events into its view. (375)

This contrast between a narrative understanding of our lives and causal explanations seems to be doing a lot of work for Velleman. It deserves some careful attention.

Narrative understandings, on Velleman's view, allow for an "appreciation of meaning," something which, it seems, mere causal explanations do not.[23] Let us consider an example which might be illustrative of this

---

[22] The following passage vividly conveys the sorts of concerns which seem to move Velleman:

> I would not want to have raised my younger son without having known my maternal grandfather, with whom he has so much in common. I would not have understood my older son if I hadn't known his uncles, on both sides. And raising my children without knowing their mother – that would have been like raising them with one eye closed. (370)

[23] One cannot help but be reminded here of Sellars's distinction between "the space of reasons" and "the space of causes." I have discussed that distinction, and the use Sellarsians make of it, in "Reasons, Naturalism, and Transcendental Philosophy," in J. Smith and P. Sullivan, eds., *Transcendental Philosophy and Naturalism*, Oxford University Press, 2011, 96–119.

suggestion. Suppose that Roger has just been fired from his latest job, having suffered through a series of unsatisfying jobs of relatively short duration. He is married, although that too is not going well for him, and he is twice divorced. He takes some time to look back on his life thus far, and he thinks about his family history. His father too suffered through a series of unsatisfying and unsuccessful jobs, and marriages as well, and he sees himself as recapitulating his father's failures. "I'm just doomed to failure," Roger thinks, "just like my old man," and then he remembers something his father used to say. His father had an explanation for his own failures: there was always a woman – one of his wives, a co-worker, a boss – who was responsible. On thinking about this, something clicks, and Roger sees the apparently unconnected events of his own life as "a natural sequence of emotions, which is ultimately resolved in an emotional cadence that leaves [him] knowing how [he] feel[s] about the events." Roger knows how he feels, all right: he's angry at those women, all of them, who are responsible for his failures, just like his father.

Now this is, to be sure, an unattractive narrative, and Roger is someone with a very unattractive personality. But, of course, there are people like this – quite a lot of them – and they too have narratives which provide for them a kind of emotionally satisfying story that makes sense of their lives. Not every story is an uplifting one.

Consider, now, instead, a causal account of certain features of Roger's life. Roger's father was an alcoholic, though Roger never saw that side of him, since his father always hid his drinking from Roger, and Roger too is an alcoholic, though he doesn't see himself that way. In addition, Roger, like his father, suffers from narcissistic personality disorder; neither Roger, nor his father, were ever able to see their own faults very clearly, and both blamed all their failures on nearby others. Roger might well benefit from psychotherapy, treatment for his alcoholism, and medication for depression. The kind of narrative which Roger tells himself, and which seems to him to make sense of his life, is part of his problem.

There's a sense in which this causal explanation of the events in Roger's life fails to assign a meaning to them, while the narrative, instead, does. If the causal explanation is correct, and I'm supposing that it is, then the sequence of events in Roger's life don't have any emotionally satisfying meaning: they're just the meaningless product of some underlying pathologies. If it's an account that gives this sequence of events some emotional resonance that Roger is looking for, the causal story just won't provide it; the false narrative, which is a product of his narcissistic personality disorder, will, instead, fill the bill nicely.

Now not all cases are like this, of course, but when the narrative stories we tell ourselves to make emotional sense of our lives are simply inaccurate, as in Roger's case, I find it hard to see the value of buying into the narrative. Many will tell themselves stories which are more uplifting than Roger's, but uplifting or not, if the narrative is at odds with the facts, then one may be living in a fool's paradise, or, worse still, a hell of one's own making. We shouldn't value these narratives simply because they provide order, whatever order they may provide, and however accurate or inaccurate they may be.

Of course, narratives needn't be at odds with the facts, or an accurate causal account of the features of one's life, and causal accounts need not leave the sequence of events in one's life devoid of meaning. One's choices over an extended period in one's life may be the product of a rational plan, and this may lead to a good deal of emotional satisfaction as the plan develops. There are all sorts of ways in which a rich and satisfying life might proceed. A causal account of such a life does not rob it of its meaning, nor is it emotionally unsatisfying. Some causal accounts are devoid of meaning and unsatisfying, but, of course, this is in part because some lives are devoid of meaning and unsatisfying. When lives are like this, providing a false narrative for them does little to solve the problem.

Velleman's contrast between a narrative story of one's life – which "necessarily encodes one's appreciation of meaning" – and a causal account – which does not – is thus badly overdrawn. Matters are made worse still by the suggestion that knowledge of family history, and personal acquaintance with one's biological relatives, is so extraordinarily instrumental in providing an appreciation of meaning in one's life. As Velleman himself acknowledges, "Adoptees can certainly find meaningful roles for themselves in stories about their adoptive families" (376).[24] Meaningful stories, whether inspired by beliefs derived from biological family lore, from stories about one's adoptive family, or from inspirational fiction, or any manner of other source, are all too easy to come by. Self-

---

[24] At the same time, Velleman suggests that there is something important here that adoptees miss out on. The quoted sentence in the text is followed by this remark:

> Even so, they seem to have the sense of not knowing important stories about themselves, and of therefore missing some meaning implicit in their lives, unless and until they know their biological origins. (376)

As I remarked earlier, one might well think that such a feeling is deserving of consideration, without accepting Velleman's explanation of the import of acquaintance with one's biological relatives and a knowledge of their history.

understanding, however, which requires an accurate account of one's life, is much harder.

To the extent that these narratives we tell ourselves are meant to provide us with self-knowledge, something Velleman alludes to throughout his discussion of these issues, they will need to be at least approximately true, and they had better not depart very far from the accurate causal accounts to which Velleman gives such short shrift. To the extent that we steer our lives and our child-rearing by way of such narratives, an accurate understanding, or at least a roughly accurate understanding, is crucial. Lives guided by self-conceptions which are wholly out of touch with the facts about one's character, the possibilities available to one, and one's interactions with others are unlikely to go well. One should not measure the value of a person's self-conception by the extent to which it provides a coherent and satisfying narrative apart from its contact with the truth. But to the extent that truth matters, acquaintance with one's biological relatives is only one consideration among many, and not one of the more important considerations at that, especially given the unreliability of family lore and the inferences we tend to draw from it.

A clear-eyed look at our self-conceptions and the psychological tendencies which give rise to them must allow that there is a good deal of wishful thinking, hasty generalization, and reliance on tiny pools of information of dubious accuracy which goes into them. There are personality features which play a role in the way in which such self-conceptions are formed which lead to highly non-trivial distortions in our beliefs about ourselves.[25] I am not suggesting that we are wholly ignorant of what we are like; that would be absurd. But it would be equally absurd to take our self-conceptions at face value across the board. These views we have of ourselves are a mix of knowledge and mere fancy, with the ratio of knowledge to fancy being highly variable. The contribution which an acquaintance with family lore provides to real understanding is, as I've argued, far from straightforward.

Velleman wishes to make his case for the importance of contact with biological relatives, as I've noted, in a way which avoids "myth or symbolic thoughts," basing it entirely on "realistic and rational considerations" (362). Judged by these standards, I believe the arguments I have provided here show that he has not succeeded. At the same time, it is important to acknowledge that the standard of "realistic and rational considerations" is

---

[25] I have discussed a number of these features and the ways in which they work in my "Introspection and Misdirection," Chapter 1, and my "What Is It Like to Be Me?," Chapter 2.

not one that Velleman wishes to endorse. After noting that he will confine his argument to just such considerations, Velleman remarks, "My caution in this regard will lead me to overlook many considerations that I see as genuinely meaningful" (362). To the extent that Velleman regards considerations beyond those that are realistic and rational as relevant to an understanding of what is genuinely meaningful, I recognize that the arguments I offer here are ones he is bound to find unconvincing. At the same time, I believe it is still worthwhile to ask what realistic and rational considerations alone suggest on this topic, and it is to that project that I hope to have made some contribution.

III

The issue of the morality of donor conception may now be treated fairly quickly, in the light of the considerations offered thus far. Even those who are convinced by Velleman's arguments that knowledge of one's biological family history, and acquaintance with members of one's biological family, is of real importance should find Velleman's central arguments for the immorality of donor conception extremely unpersuasive.

"Much as we love disadvantaged children," Velleman tells us, "we rightly believe that people should not deliberately create children who they already know will be disadvantaged" (364). If children who are the product of donor conception are not acquainted with at least one of their biological parents, and if this constitutes a disadvantage, as Velleman argues, then people should not create children by way of donor conception. The argument couldn't be more straightforward.

Such an argument, of course, proves far too much. All of us are such that any children we have, even by the most common method of bringing children into being, will inevitably face certain disadvantages. The fact that our medical histories are less than perfectly unblemished, that our characters and personalities are less than ideal, and that the circumstances in which our children will be raised are also less than perfect guarantees that all children will have to cope with disadvantages. In many cases, we know antecedently of some of the disadvantages they will face. Someone might actually endorse such an argument for the conclusion that having children by any means whatsoever is immoral, but this was surely not Velleman's intended conclusion.

Of course, it is not permissible to saddle one's would-be children with just any disadvantage whatsoever. Exactly what is permissible here is, rightly, a subject of real controversy, but I think we can all agree that knowingly bringing into existence a child who will experience nothing but extraordinary pain for an extended period, followed immediately by a painful death, is horribly immoral. If one knows in advance that engaging in unprotected sexual intercourse will bring about the existence of such a child, then it is surely morally required that one abstain from such an act. But nothing in Velleman's case against donor conception suggests that a life without contact with one's biological family is on a par with a life filled with nothing but pain, nor would this be plausible. As Sally Haslanger suggests,[26] one might reasonably think that there is some threshold quality of life here below which one may not permissibly go. Nothing in Velleman's paper even begins to make an argument that a life without contact with, or even knowledge of, one's biological relatives is automatically, or even typically, below such a threshold.

More interesting is Velleman's point that couples who make use of either donor sperm or donor eggs are typically motivated by a desire to have a child who is biologically related to at least one of them. Velleman regards any such motivation as suspect, since it presupposes

> an interest that they choose to further slightly in their own case by creating a person for whom the same interest will be profoundly frustrated. I regard this choice as morally incoherent. (374)

I think that Velleman is right here that such parents do typically value having a biological connection to the child they raise, and this is a motive for their preference for the use of donor gametes over adoption of a child biologically unrelated to them.[27] So, as Velleman sees it, the choice to have a child in this way is incoherent because it both affirms (in the case of the would-be parents) and denies (in the case of the would-be child) the importance of biological ties.[28]

---

[26] "Family, Ancestry and Self: What Is the Moral Significance of Biological Ties?," *Adoption and Culture* 2(2009), 91–122, reprinted in *Resisting Reality: Social Construction and Social Critique*, Oxford University Press, 2012. Haslanger's paper is primarily focused on the implications of Velleman's views for adoption, but the points she makes there are ones with which I am largely sympathetic. Many of her points are complementary to the ones I make here.

[27] This is not, however, the only motivation for such a choice. To note just one other motive: a woman may have a strong desire to experience pregnancy, and to experience giving birth to the child she raises. I agree with Velleman, however, that the desire to have a child with some biological relation to at least one of the parents who will raise the child is typically an important part of the motivation in these cases.

[28] Such parents may view the biological connection as something which is objectively valuable, as Velleman does, but they may also view it as something which is entirely optional, but which they, in fact, value. I will assume that they have the first of these views, since it presents Velleman's argument in a more sympathetic light. Parents who have the latter attitude, however, do not

But such a reconstruction of the motivational source of this kind of choice is extremely unsympathetic. Such parents need not view their own biological connection to a child as important and the child's biological connections as unimportant. They may value both, and choose to use donor gametes because this allows for some connection, both for the parents and for the child. Both may be at a disadvantage, from the parents' perspective, relative to situations in which children are biologically related to both of the parents who raise them, but the would-be parents may rightly think that they have much to offer their child, and that this will allow for the child to have a sufficiently rich and satisfying life. Unless we add the implausible premise from the previous argument, that any disadvantage to one's offspring is unacceptable, there is nothing incoherent in such motivation.

Velleman does also point out that in cases where a couple cannot both serve as biological parents, there is always the option of adopting, if they want children to raise.

> The alternative of adopting an already existing child is often available, and I have argued that it is morally preferable, because it provides a custodial family for a child already and independently destined to be alienated from its biological family. (374)

I certainly understand such a view, and I do not find it obviously unreasonable. But by the same token, it may be morally preferable to adopt rather than to conceive biologically related children of one's own, given the desperate need for good adoptive homes. It is not clear why one should focus here on those who would have children by way of gamete donation, rather than couples both of whom are fertile. One might, moreover, think that adoption in these circumstances, absent a strong independent desire to raise an adopted child, is supererogatory, for both fertile and infertile couples. To say that adoption is morally better, in either case, does not entail that anything less is morally unacceptable.

One final point here is deserving of mention. The only empirical evidence which Velleman offers for his claims about the importance of acquaintance with one's biological relatives is the fact that so many children of closed adoptions are deeply concerned to discover and contact their biological parents (359 n. 1). Velleman suggests that this is best explained by supposing that adoptees value these biological connections

---

even seem to face the problem which Velleman raises, for they may regard it as an open question whether their offspring is likely to share such values.

very highly, and, indeed, that these connections are of great objective value. Human motivation is a complicated thing, and I think it is a mistake simply to assume that adoptees must all share some single overriding motivation for these searches. But it is at least worth considering the possibility that there is another element motivating at least many adoptees who wish to meet their biological family of origin: they may wish to know why it is that they were given up for adoption. It is worth noting in addition that the kinds of concerns which could easily motivate this kind of search might well be far less likely to animate children who are conceived from donated gametes.

Velleman does not provide us with any argument for the immorality of donor conception which is not easily defused.

IV

Let me briefly sum up. Velleman's case for the importance of acquaintance with one's biological relatives, and knowledge of one's biological family, depends on a host of implausible claims about the ways in which such knowledge may enrich one's life. The self-conceptions we form on the basis of such acquaintance and knowledge are often filled with misinformation. While an accurate self-conception may be of tremendous value in guiding one's life, it is not at all clear that the ways in which we make use of family lore reliably contribute to such a conception. We should not take our self-conceptions entirely at face value. There is, to be sure, a certain mythology about the importance of biological connections and the self-understanding that springs from knowing one's biological relatives, but a serious examination of the source of our self-conceptions does not suggest that they are typically reliably formed, especially to the extent that they depend on acquaintance with biological relatives. If this is correct, it is difficult to defend the claim that such self-conceptions are inevitably of great value, and more difficult still to defend, on that basis, the claim that donor conception is immoral.[29]

---

[29] I have profited from comments on an earlier draft of this essay by Brad Skow, as well as discussion of these issues with Robin Harris and Annie Harris-Kornblith. A version of this essay was presented at the University of Colorado, and discussion there was very helpful to me. David Velleman also provided useful comments.

12

Our Rational Nature

It is often claimed that rationality is a distinctive feature of human beings. We are capable, to be sure, of rational belief and action, but in saying that rationality is a distinctive feature of the human species, it is suggested that other animals lack this important capacity. There can be little doubt that there are many other animals that have the capacity to act in ways which reliably satisfy their biologically given needs, and their ability to do this is dependent on their capacity to reliably pick up information about their environment. But these capacities, many believe, fall short of genuine rationality. If all of this is so, the question naturally arises as to what it is that we humans have that other animals lack. What is the special feature of rationality that somehow eludes other animals?

We find this view of rationality throughout the history of philosophy, from Aristotle to the present day. Among contemporary philosophers, Ernest Sosa has given a rich articulation of the view. What is distinctive about human belief acquisition, according to Sosa, is that we, unlike other animals, are responsible for what we believe. In light of this, Sosa defends a view of human knowledge he refers to as *responsibilism*, a view which places this responsibility for what one believes at the center of an understanding of human intellectual capacities in general, and rationality in particular. And when we see the connection between responsibility and rationality, we are led to make a distinction between two fundamentally different sorts of belief.

> At a certain level of abstraction, we can distinguish two sorts of "belief," one implicit and *merely* functional, the other not merely functional but intentional, perhaps even consciously intentional. It is the latter that needs our attention in giving *responsibilism* its proper place in epistemology. This is because our rational nature is most fully manifest in such reasoned choice and judgment. Accordingly, it is consciously, rationally endorsed judgment that is at the focus of the epistemological tradition from the Pyrrhonists through Descartes.[1]

[1] *Judgment and Agency*, Oxford University Press, 2015, 51.

Thus, when I walk across campus thinking about what I will focus on in my seminar next semester, my attention is on philosophy, and not on my surroundings. Nevertheless, I successfully negotiate the various pathways crossing campus, weaving in and out to avoid the many students who are looking down at their cellphones. I consciously entertain thoughts about my seminar, and not about my route across campus, but I am reliably taking in information about the contours of the route, appropriately responsive to the many pitfalls that a walk across campus provides. The beliefs I form along the way about the route are ones which Sosa regards as implicit and merely functional. And this is not where rationality resides.

When I self-consciously think about my coming seminar, however, and self-consciously consider the advantages and disadvantages of taking on various topics, the beliefs I form in the course of my deliberations are what Sosa calls *intentional*. I mentally rehearse the reasons for and against various courses of action, as well as the reasons for and against various beliefs about the effects of those actions. Here, according to Sosa, is where "our rational nature is most fully manifest." And it is this capacity for self-conscious deliberation, both about what to believe and about what to do, that distinguishes us from the other animals.

Sosa is not the only contemporary philosopher to hold such a view. It is widely held that, although other animals register information about their environments, this is something that merely happens to them, given their native biological endowments. We, on the other hand, play an active role in cognition; acquiring beliefs, in the human case, is something that we do, rather than something which merely goes on in us. And that is why we, and not other animals, can be responsible for the beliefs we have. Thus, Paul Boghossian remarks that "the sub-personal transitions of a person's visual system are not ones that we can hold the person *responsible* for, and they are not ones whose goodness or badness enters into our assessments of her *rationality*."[2] Boghossian elaborates further: "It is only if there is a substantial sense in which they are transitions that a thinker *performed* that he/she can be held responsible for them. That is the fundamental reason why such transitions cannot, in and of themselves, amount to reasoning."[3] As Boghossian makes clear, other animals do not reason because they do not play an active role in cognition. Although we do not play an active role in the transitions among our sub-doxastic states, we can play such a role in

---

[2] "Inference, Agency and Responsibility," in M. Balcerak Jackson and B. Balcerak Jackson, eds., *Reasoning: New Essays on Theoretical and Practical Thinking*, Oxford University Press, forthcoming.
[3] "Reasoning and Reflection: A Reply to Kornblith," *Analysis* 76(2016), 50.

transitions among our beliefs. And this is why we, unlike other animals, may be said to reason; why we can be held responsible for our beliefs; and why we, unlike other animals, count as rational.

Like Sosa and Boghossian, Tyler Burge sees a deep connection between the ideas of rationality, agency, and responsibility. As Burge sees it, there is another player which needs to be added to the mix: the first-person concept.

> A being that lacked the first-person concept could be sensitive to the norms of reason, and might (I am conceding for the sake of the argument) even sensitively shape its attitudes according to a conception of good and bad reasons and reasoning. But the agent would lack full conceptualization of what it is doing ... Insofar as *full* intellectual (or any other) responsibility requires the capacity to understand the way norms govern agency and the capacity to acknowledge the responsibility, a being that lacked the first-person concept would not be fully responsible intellectually. It would not have a fully realized rational agency.[4]

So, for Burge, a "fully realized rational agency" is something of which we, but not others animals, are capable.

It is not necessary to continue in this vein. The family of views these philosophers hold, and many others as well,[5] is both familiar and attractive. Human beings are undeniably different from other animals. Our cognitive lives are far more sophisticated than those of other creatures, even if it is also true that the mental sophistication of other animals has often been vastly underestimated. Perhaps most striking is our ability to engage in self-conscious deliberation, a seemingly unique ability in the animal world. Such deliberation seems to have all of the features which Sosa, Boghossian, Burge, and so many others, make note of: we reflectively consider reasons for and against various beliefs and actions; we take responsibility for our beliefs and actions; and we hold others of our species similarly responsible; the manner in which we do this seems essentially to involve our ability to mentally represent not only states of the world, but

---

[4] "Reason and the First Person," in Crispin Wright, Barry Smith, and Cynthia Macdonald, eds., *Knowing One's Own Mind: Essays on Self-Knowledge*, Oxford University Press, 1998, 262.
[5] Similar themes are sounded in Robert Brandom, *Making It Explicit: Reasoning, Representing, and Discursive Commitment*, Harvard University Press, 1994; John Haugeland, *Having Thought: Essays in the Metaphysics of Mind*, Harvard University Press, 1998; Christine Korsgaard, *The Sources of Normativity*, Cambridge University Press, 1996; Eric Marcus, *Rational Causation*, Harvard University Press, 2012; John McDowell, *Mind and World*, Harvard University Press, 1994; Declan Smithies, *The Epistemic Role of Consciousness*, Oxford University Press, 2019; and Michael Williams, *Problems of Knowledge: A Critical Introduction to Epistemology*, Oxford University Press, 2001.

our own mental states as well, in addition to representing these states as our own. We are responsive to reasons, and we are responsive to reasons as reasons.

Those who subscribe to this family of views thus see an examination of the nature of self-conscious deliberation as the key to understanding rationality, and they see the capacity for such deliberation, as well, as the seat of rationality. Animals who lack this capacity may be able to register information about the world reliably. They may even be credited with beliefs. They certainly act in ways which are informed by such informational states. But they do not count as rational. Rational belief formation, on the view under consideration here, is different in kind from the goings-on which occur in non-human minds.

In this essay, I critically examine this view, in part, by bringing together a number of considerations which are raised in various places in the foregoing chapters. In addition, I present a rival picture of rationality, one which does not regard as sub-rational the kind of automatic processing we see in other animals and in ourselves most of the time. More than this, I seek to explain, or rather, explain away, the attraction of the picture of human adults as uniquely rational animals and self-conscious deliberation as the home of rationality.

I

Let us begin with a quick overview of the phenomenology of deliberation. When we deliberate about what to believe, or what to do, we engage in the self-conscious consideration of reasons. Our engagement with reasons qua reasons, on the view under consideration, is the hallmark of rationality.

Consider, once again, my walk across campus, carefully considering various possibilities for my epistemology seminar next semester. I self-consciously consider a number of options: I might teach a seminar on self-knowledge, or a seminar on philosophical methodology, or a course on the epistemology of ethics. I bring to mind some of the advantages and disadvantages of each, and after thinking it through a bit, I settle on one of these options as the best, all things considered. This process of thinking things through, and bringing reasons to mind, seems a paradigm of rationality, quite unlike my automatic and seemingly mindless accommodation to the many students who cross my path in the course of my walk. My choice of seminar topic involves the consideration of reasons as reasons. My choice of a path across campus seems to involve little if any mental engagement; my mind, as we so often put it, is elsewhere.

My self-conscious consideration of reasons involves subvocalized speech. Although I do not actually say words out loud – or at least not typically – my deliberation about what to do and what to believe involves my expressing, subvocally, various sentences in English. I might explicitly entertain the following thoughts, expressing them to myself, subvocally, in English: "What should I do my seminar on next term? I could do something on self-knowledge. Or maybe I could do something on philosophical methodology. Or perhaps I should do something on the epistemology of ethics."

Having enumerated various options, I might then turn to thinking about considerations for and against each of them. Sometimes a single reason, by itself, might seem definitive. As I consider the possibility of teaching a seminar on philosophical methodology, I remember that one of my colleagues taught such a seminar just last term. And as soon as this thought occurs to me, I immediately dismiss the possibility of doing my seminar on methodology. I don't attempt to see whether other reasons in favor might outweigh this concern, and I don't stop to think about whether there are additional reasons why this option is not a good one. This reason, by itself, is sufficient to narrow my search. In the case of the other possibilities, however, I might bring to mind some considerations in favor of each, and considerations against them as well.

One thing I don't do – and I am surely not idiosyncratic in this – is organize my thinking on these issues into simple deductive arguments. When I dismiss the possibility of teaching the seminar on philosophical methodology because a colleague recently taught just such a seminar, I do not explicitly entertain the conditional thought that if a colleague taught such a course, then I shouldn't do such a course again so soon afterward. I could entertain that thought, but I need not. I might simply move directly from the thought that my colleague taught that course to the thought that I shouldn't do so as well, at least as far as the phenomenology of my reasoning goes. And in cases in which the considerations I entertain might form the basis for a good non-deductive argument for the conclusion that I should teach a seminar on some particular topic, I need not explicitly entertain a conditional thought that if such and such conditions hold, then this gives me good even if not decisive reason for thinking that I should teach a particular seminar. My own thinking, at least as it is explicitly represented to me in subvocal speech, is not expressed so pedantically. For better or for worse, the content of my subvocalized reasoning looks enthymematic at best.

These are the kinds of thoughts that pass through my mind as I deliberate; this is how it seems from the first-person perspective. And it is here that Sosa, Boghossian, Burge, and so many others locate the home of rationality.

II

Although these philosophers see self-conscious deliberation as the place where "our rational nature is most fully manifest," this is not to say that the thoughts which I self-consciously entertain when deliberating – the statements I express to myself in subvocal speech – constitute the whole of my rational dealing with the question of what to teach next semester. My sub-vocalized thoughts look like argument sketches rather than full-blown arguments. These argument sketches do not look at all like a "fully realized rational agency." Instead, they need to be filled out a bit if the rationality of my deliberation is to be properly exhibited. The enthymemes of sub-vocal speech need to be augmented so as to properly reflect the very rationality which distinguishes adult human beings from other animals. But where are we to find the additional premises to turn the enthymemes of subvocal speech into paradigms of rationality?

Gilbert Harman faces a similar problem in his approach to the Gettier problem. Harman treats perception as inference to an explanation, despite the fact that no such inference is present to consciousness. If this approach is to succeed, then premises for the argument, absent from conscious thought, need to be found. Here is how Harman deals with an illustrative example.

> A man looks and comes to believe that there is a candle directly before him. There is a candle there; but a mirror intervenes to show the reflection of a candle actually off to one side. The man's belief is justified and true; but he does not know. If his belief is the result of inference, his failure to know is easy to understand. Since inference attempts to find the best total explanatory account, he infers an explanation of the way things look. He infers that it looks to him as if there were a candle before him because there is a candle there and because of the normal connection between the way things look and the way things are. Since that explanation is essential to his conclusion but is false, he does not come to know that there is a candle before him even though his belief is justified and true.[6]

---

[6] *Thought*, Princeton University Press, 1973, 174.

The inference Harman attributes to this ordinary perceiver involves premises which are not self-consciously brought to mind. Nevertheless, we may reasonably attribute belief in these premises to the perceiver, according to Harman, and the inference of which these premises are a part, because this attribution allows us to make sense of the perceiver's belief about the candle. The beliefs missing from consciousness, moreover, are ones, it seems, which any adult human being would endorse, even if they have never self-consciously entertained such thoughts about the normal connection between appearance and reality. Moreover, as Harman urges, this provides a neat solution to the Gettier problem.

Those who see our ability to deliberate self-consciously as the home of rationality may adopt a similar strategy. The thoughts I express to myself in subvocal speech may be enthymematic, but the additional premises needed to turn them into valid deductive arguments or strong non-deductive arguments are easily found. When, for all the first-person perspective shows me, I move directly from the thought that a colleague taught a seminar on philosophical methodology last semester to the thought that I should not teach such a course this coming term, the needed conditional premise which would turn this into a valid argument – that if my colleague taught such a course last semester, then I should not teach such a course this coming term – may nevertheless be attributed to me. It makes sense of my subvocal speech, and it allows us to see my thinking on this matter as rational. Moreover, just as in Harman's example, the missing premise is one which the thinker would endorse if asked, even if that premise was never self-consciously entertained. By attributing beliefs and inference in this manner, we may see the argument sketches which are available from the first-person perspective as offering a glimpse of a deeper rationality. My ability to self-consciously deliberate may be the seat of my rationality, but it is aided and abetted by mental capacities which do not present themselves to consciousness, at least in the ordinary course of events.

These conditional beliefs are not the only ones which are needed to provide a complete picture of the way in which my deliberation rationally addresses the question of what to teach next semester. When thinking about that question, I brought to mind only three candidates for the subject of my coming seminar. But these are not the only subjects I'm capable of teaching! There are, indeed, a very large number of subjects on which I could obviously teach a worthwhile graduate seminar. And there are other subjects, as well, in which I have a real interest, which are worthy, perhaps, of consideration. So the menu of seminars I might teach is considerably longer than three I actually bring to mind in the course of my deliberations. Should we see these other possibilities as playing a role in my choice, despite the fact that they were not consciously considered? We have already seen that a full picture of the rational features of my deliberation is not present to consciousness in the course of my thinking. In order to provide such a picture, do we need to include further possibilities not brought to consciousness, or is it sufficient to fill out the argument sketches consciously considered with additional premises in the manner described by Harman?

I think it is clear that at least some of the possibilities not brought to consciousness must be seen as playing a role in my decision, even if it is very far from clear just how many of these possibilities should be seen as playing such a role. After all, it is not just a coincidence that the possibilities I self-consciously considered were the ones I brought to mind. Some of the courses I'm capable of teaching would be quite far down my list of good choices for next semester, even if they would be perfectly legitimate topics for a seminar. If I only considered topics of this sort, then the best of the topics considered would be far inferior to many of the topics left out of consideration, even if they passed some reasonable threshold of acceptability. A random pick of, say, three possible topics out of the very long list of topics I might teach would not very likely leave me with a menu of seminar topics containing a strong choice. My worry here is not that such randomness is incompatible with optimal choice. Rational as my choice of seminar topic was, I don't assume that it was optimal. But if the topics which come to mind are just randomly brought to mind from the long list of possible topics, it is not remotely clear that the resulting choice of the best among these, or the best among these which exceeds some reasonable threshold, would be a rational one all things considered. The seminar topics I self-consciously considered included topics which were, in fact, serious contenders for my course; many topics which I could have taught, but would have been very bad choices, for one reason or another, were not brought to mind. This cannot just be a coincidence. So, here too, just as in the perceptual case which Harman discusses, it seems there must be features of my rational choice which are not present to consciousness. The options I choose among, in the case described, just present themselves to me; I am unaware of any reasoning that led to considering these possibilities rather than various others. But that menu of options must itself reflect my rational nature, even if no reasoning in putting the menu together was ever present to consciousness. And in this case as well, just as in the move Harman makes in the perceptual case, the missing argumentation needed to justify the menu of choices considered would plausibly be argumentation I would endorse if asked, despite the fact that it is argumentation that did not self-consciously cross my mind. Once again, we see that, even if we view our rational nature as most clearly revealed in self-conscious deliberation, the features that make such deliberation rational must be augmented with mental states and processes which are not present to consciousness.

Nor is the augmentation needed here limited to the adding of premises. Premises and conclusions alone do not make an argument, and when we are considering an agent's rationality, it is not arguments as abstract objects alone which we need to take into account. Rather, we are interested in the inferences which agents actually make. One may come to believe a certain claim, and have available a supply of beliefs which would form the basis for a perfectly sound argument for that claim, but if one does not believe the claim on the basis of the argument, then the existence of such a sound argument is irrelevant to questions about one's rationality. Inference involves some sort of mental transition from premises mentally represented to a conclusion which one accepts. Thus far we have been considering how it is that one finds the stock of premises needed for rational inference, but now we need to consider the mental transition from premises to conclusion which constitute that inference.

Boghossian has focused a good deal of attention on this issue.[7] On Boghossian's view, what is needed to connect premises to conclusion is a mental *taking*, in which one takes the premises to provide support for the conclusion. Without any such taking, Boghossian argues, one just has a series of beliefs passing through one's mind in sequence. It is crucial that one distinguish the notion of a taking from a belief one might have, say, that the premises support the conclusion. Additional beliefs such as this cannot perform the relevant work, for one would still need to know how it is that these beliefs play a role in some sort of mental transition, rather than sit idly by in one's stock of mental representations. Any appeal to beliefs about the relationship between premises and conclusion cannot, as a result, perform the needed work without generating a vicious regress. And once again, just as was the case with the premises needed to fill out the argumentation self-consciously considered in deliberation, the taking of premises to support one's conclusion need not be self-consciously

---

[7] In addition to the papers by Boghossian cited in Notes 2 and 3, see especially "Blind Reasoning," reprinted in his *Content and Justification: Philosophical Papers*, Oxford University Press, 2008, 267–287; "Inference and Insight," *Philosophy and Phenomenological Research* 63(2001), 633–640; and "What Is Inference?," *Philosophical Studies* 169(2014), 1–18.

entertained. At the same time, the suggestion that agents in the situations under discussion do, indeed, take the premises of these arguments to support the conclusions they draw is not one which lacks all grounding in features of the agent: just as in the case of missing premises, agents in the situations described would endorse the claim that their premises support their conclusions if they were asked.

The view that self-conscious deliberation about what to believe and what to do is where our rationality is most fully manifest thus cannot be identified with a view according to which all of the features of one's mental life which make one rational are fully present to consciousness during deliberation. That view is a non-starter, and it is certainly not one which is endorsed by any of the philosophers under discussion here. If the materials present to consciousness during deliberation are to play a central role in explaining our rationality, they will need substantial augmentation.

III

Thus far, we have focused on the ways in which the first-person perspective presents a rather truncated view of the features of our deliberation which make it rational. But this is not the only limitation of the first-person perspective, for the view it offers of deliberation is not only incomplete; it is also inaccurate. And this is where the real problems begin for the view that self-conscious deliberation is the seat of human rationality. We will need, however, to get at these problems indirectly.

Let us return to Harman's example of the man who, failing to realize that he is looking into a mirror, comes to believe that there is a candle in front of him. Harman very plausibly supposes that such a person would believe that how things look to him is a product of "the normal connection between the way things look and the way things are." And Harman goes on to suppose that the man's belief that there is a candle in front of him is a product of inference involving this very belief about the relationship between appearance and reality. That is, Harman is committed to the claim that the belief about the relationship between appearance and reality plays a causal role in the production of the belief about the candle. But there is a problem with any such causal claim. Very young children, who do not have the concepts of appearance and reality, and non-human animals, who similarly lack such conceptual sophistication, make the very same perceptual errors. Lacking the requisite conceptual sophistication, these subjects cannot have the belief which Harman supposes is causally responsible for the production of the belief about the candle. Since these subjects obviously form the belief about the candle without the benefit of some connecting belief about the relationship between appearance and reality, there must be some causal process present in these subjects which allows them to reach the belief about the candle without the benefit of going through the bit of sophisticated argumentation – even subconsciously – which Harman attributes to an adult.

It should not be surprising that natural selection has endowed both young children and many non-human animals with mechanisms of visual information-processing which allow them to acquire beliefs about the world around them even without first acquiring the concepts of appearance and reality. But once we recognize this fact, it seems that we should expect that the very same kind of visual information-processing goes on even in conceptually sophisticated subjects. And what this means is that in the typical cases of perceptual error like the one that Harman imagines, and in normal cases of perception where there is no error at all, any belief about the relationship between appearance and reality plays no role at all in the production of the belief about the world. If our adult subject is questioned about why he believed that there was a candle in front of him, he might appeal, in the face of sufficiently persistent Socratic questioning, to his belief about the relationship between appearance and reality.[8] He might even believe, understandably enough, that this belief explains why he came to believe that there was a candle in front of him. He might believe, that is to say, in the face of persistent Socratic questioning, that his belief about the candle was brought about by the very inference which Harman would have us attribute to him. But if he did come to believe this, he would be mistaken. The belief about the relationship between appearance and reality which sophisticated subjects may have is typically epiphenomenal with respect to the production of perceptual belief. And this will leave those, such as Harman, who wish to fill out the meager phenomenology of deliberation so as to credit subjects with the operation of sophisticated arguments in support of their beliefs without a crucial connecting premise.

My point here is not that there is nothing going on mentally during deliberation which is not present to the first-person perspective. Such a view would be absurd. But Harman's strategy of adding sophisticated premises so as to make the processes of belief-acquisition track subtle

---

[8] Compare the role of Socratic questioning in revealing what it is that justifies our beliefs in Roderick Chisholm's work. See *Theory of Knowledge*, 1st ed., Prentice-Hall, 1966, 24–27; 2nd ed., 1977, 16–18.

argumentation does not present a realistic account of the way in which psychological processes operate. More than this, the fact that adults who deliberate about their reasons for belief may well appeal to such sophisticated argumentation and sincerely believe that such argumentation played a role in their coming to believe as they do does not provide us with good reason to believe that they are correct in this.

What I want to argue is that the difficulties which face Harman's reconstruction of perceptual processing present a problem for those who see our capacity to deliberate as the source of our rationality. As I will argue, these philosophers view deliberation as involving psychological processes which track sophisticated argumentation attributable to the activity of cognitive agents. But just as in the perceptual case which Harman discusses, the sophisticated argumentation which adult human beings are capable of is often epiphenomenal with respect to the processes by which their beliefs are produced, even when such beliefs are formed under conditions of deliberation. Or so I will argue.

IV

The perspective of the deliberating agent provides us with argument sketches in favor of conclusions apparently arrived at as a product of self-conscious consideration of what to believe and what to do. Theorists can easily fill out these enthymematic argument sketches with appropriate missing premises and rules of inference so as to turn them into valid deductive arguments or strong non-deductive arguments. If the material needed to turn the deliverances of self-conscious first-person thought into high-quality argumentation seemed somehow forced – if it seemed implausible that the deliberating agent was actually committed to these missing premises and rules of inference – then the project of locating our rationality in our capacity to deliberate, and explaining this rationality, in turn, by way of good argumentation,[9] would lose all plausibility. But the missing material is not hard to come by, and its attribution to the agent does not seem forced at all. In particular, the agent him- or herself will not only offer up the missing material under appropriate Socratic questioning from others; under conditions of deliberation, where the agent considers

---

[9] I have examined the attempt to explain justification in terms of good argument in "Beyond Foundationalism and the Coherence Theory," *Journal of Philosophy* 77(1980), 597–612, and in my "The Role of Reasons in Epistemology," Chapter 9. See also Anna-Sara Malmgren, "Availability, Goodness, and Argument Structure," manuscript.

the question of what his or her own reasons for belief or action were, the agent will endorse the missing premises and rules of inference as the very ones which played a role in deliberation. And this lends an air of plausibility to the attribution to the agent of a process of inference which tracks the argument sketches augmented in this way.

We have already seen one reason for thinking that this strategy misunderstands the psychological processes by which beliefs and decisions are produced under conditions of deliberation. The fact that young children and non-human animals arrive at the same perceptual beliefs as more sophisticated agents shows that, at least in the case of those unsophisticated believers, the needed additional premises cannot have been playing a role in their belief acquisition. And this, in turn, suggests that it is implausible to think that, even in sophisticated adult humans, the sophisticated content which they are privy to is actually playing a role in their belief acquisition. While they do, indeed, believe the claims which would constitute the missing premises of a good argument for their beliefs, the belief in these sophisticated claims is epiphenomenal with respect to their belief acquisition. And this is so even if these believers think otherwise.

It is important to see, however, that this is a special case of a much more general phenomenon. It has long been understood that we do not have direct cognitive access to psychological processes.[10] When we stop to introspect, when we think about the processes by which we arrived at some belief or some decision, we have the very powerful impression that we have some sort of direct knowledge of our own psychological processes. Such an impression is especially powerful in the case of deliberation, where it seems we can just tell that the goings-on we are so vividly aware of in the deliberative process are effective in guiding and producing our beliefs and actions. What is actually going on, however, is sub-conscious inference. We are reconstructing what our inferential process must have been, and the result of this inferential process of reconstruction is then delivered into

---

[10] See, for example, Richard Nisbett and Timothy Wilson, "Telling More than We Can Know: Verbal Reports on Mental Processes," *Psychological Review* 84(1977), 231–259; Shelley Taylor, *Positive Illusions: Self-Deception and the Healthy Mind*, Basic Books, 1989; Alison Gopnik, "How We Know Our Minds: The Illusion of First-Person Knowledge of Intentionality," *Behavioral and Brain Sciences* 16(1993), 1–15 and 90–101; Timothy Wilson, *Strangers to Ourselves: Discovering the Adaptive Unconscious*, Harvard University Press, 2002; Peter Carruthers, *The Opacity of Mind: An Integrative Theory of Self-Knowledge*, Oxford University Press, 2011; David Dunning, *Self-Insight: Roadblocks and Detours on the Path to Knowing Thyself: Essays in Social Psychology*, Psychology Press, 2012; Joëlle Proust, *The Philosophy of Metacognition: Mental Agency and Self-Awareness*, Oxford University Press, 2013; Quassim Cassam, *Self-Knowledge for Humans*, Oxford University Press, 2014; Hugo Mercier and Dan Sperber, *The Enigma of Reason*, Harvard University Press, 2017.

consciousness as if we were directly aware of the very process which we have attempted to reconstruct.

The evidence for this process of reconstruction is most clear when we examine cases of confabulation. Our beliefs are influenced by a large variety of non-rational factors. Our judgments about the quality of consumer goods laid out upon a table are influenced by the order in which they are placed; we show a pronounced preference for the right-most object.[11] We are susceptible to priming effects so that, for example, our judgments about the motives and character of strangers can be manipulated by exposure to reading material which includes such words as "rude" or "polite."[12] The evaluation of abstracts of scientific papers is influenced by the font in which the abstract is typeset.[13] Moral judgments may be influenced by the smell of the room in which the judgment is elicited.[14] Mere knowledge of the stereotypes of various racial and ethnic groups may influence our judgments, even when we believe the stereotypes to be inaccurate.[15] There is, indeed, an enormous range of non-rational factors which influence our judgments on all manner of topics.[16] What is common to these influences, however, is not only that we are unaware of the fact that they play a role in the beliefs and decisions at which we arrive. In situations where these non-rational factors play a decisive role in influencing our judgments, we sincerely believe that we can tell directly by introspection how we arrived at our beliefs and decisions, and the accounts which subjects offer in these situations portray the subjects as responding exclusively to rational considerations. In a word, we confabulate. We are under an illusion that we can directly introspect the source of our judgments, and the manner in which we arrive at our view of these psychological processes assures that the judgment we reach about them will be that they were rational. The portrait which self-conscious reflection paints

---

[11] Nisbett and Wilson, ibid.
[12] J. A. Bargh, M. Chen, and L. Burrows, "Automaticity of Social Behavior: Direct Effects of Trait Construct and Stereotype Activation on Action," *Journal of Personality and Social Psychology* 71 (1996), 230–244.
[13] Kai Kaspar, Thea Wehlitz, Sara von Knobelsdorff, Tim Wulf, and Marie Antoinette Oktavie von Saldern, "A Matter of Font Type: The Effect of Serifs on the Evaluation of Scientific Abstracts," *International Journal of Psychology* 50(2015), 372–378.
[14] Simone Schnall, Jonathan Haidt, Gerald L. Clore, and Alexander H. Jordan, "Disgust as Embodied Moral Judgment," *Personality and Social Psychology Bulletin* 34(2008), 1096–1109.
[15] For an extensive review of the literature on this subject, see the essays collected in Michael Brownstein and Jennifer Saul, eds., *Implicit Bias and Philosophy*, vol. 1: *Metaphysics and Epistemology*, Oxford University Press, 2016.
[16] For an illuminating discussion of this issue, see Ziva Kunda, *Social Cognition: Making Sense of People*, MIT Press, 1999, chapter 7.

of the psychological processes involved in producing our beliefs and decisions is a portrait of an impressively rational agent, whether the judgments we are reflecting upon were arrived at in a rational manner or not. Reflection portrays us as rational, not because it is in direct cognitive contact with the processes by which our judgments are produced, but rather because it operates in such a manner as to assure that, however our judgments were produced, we will view them as the product of rational factors.

I am not suggesting that we are not ever, or that we are rarely, rational. That introspection portrays us on some occasion as rational, however, is no evidence whatever that we are. I have no doubt that our decisions and beliefs are often rational. The various non-rational factors to which our judgments are susceptible may often play a fairly limited role, even if, on occasion, they are the main causal factors in producing our judgments. But the manner in which introspection portrays the source of our judgments need not reflect the actual source of those judgments, even on those occasions when our judgments are, in fact, rational. That introspection portrays the source of our judgments as residing in argumentation which meets certain logical standards is not evidence that the manner in which our judgments are formed tracks the logical argumentation which introspection so vividly presents to us. Because our introspective judgments about the sources of our beliefs and decisions are due to confabulation, we need to look elsewhere to understand how it is that our judgments are actually produced.

V

There are a number of very different accounts available of the large-scale architecture of the mind. How we should think about the nature of rationality will depend, I believe, on which of these accounts is correct. In order to illustrate this claim, I will very briefly examine three such accounts here.

Let me begin by looking at the picture of cognition offered by Jerry Fodor. According to Fodor, mental content is represented in a language of thought.[17] Thought is linguistically structured, and our cognitive architecture builds in various inferential principles which generate new mental

---

[17] *The Language of Thought*, Thomas Y. Crowell Company, 1975; *The Modularity of Mind*, MIT Press, 1983; *LOT 2: The Language of Thought Revisited*, Oxford University Press, 2008.

contents by way of a responsiveness to the syntactic structure of existing mental contents together with new input.

There are, of course, a great many ways in which this picture may be filled out, and Fodor, of course, has a great deal more to say about it. But it is worth pointing out that if something like this should be correct, it could well be that the identification of inferential justification with the availability of good argument can be defended in rich psychological detail.

Lance Rips has argued, in *The Psychology of Proof*,[18] that the rudiments of a deductive logic may be built in to our cognitive architecture, and just such a claim would be needed to fill out the Fodorian picture. More than this is needed, of course. Some sort of inductive logic is required as well, and I think it's safe to say that no one knows just what such inductive principles might look like. But if the Fodorian picture should prove correct, we can expect that inductive principles are built into our cognitive architecture too.

And now we have what is needed for the proposed identification of inferentially justified belief with belief based on good argument. I will assume – conveniently, I might add – that the principles built into our cognitive architecture are ones which are plausibly viewed as principles of good inference. Fodor's suggestion, that our minds are, in effect, syntactically driven machines, is certainly not plausibly combined with the view that, say, affirming the consequent is hard-wired into our cognitive architecture.

Now it's not as if those epistemologists who have endorsed the traditional view of inferentially justified belief, and of rationality, have typically signed on to Fodor's view of mental representation and mental architecture. On the whole, they have not committed themselves to any particular view about human psychology. But I believe that they should. Some picture such as this is needed, I believe, in order to fund the traditional view of rational belief, and I believe that those who favor this traditional epistemological view should welcome the thought that there could be empirical confirmation for their position.

Of course, the Fodorian view is not without its problems. Indeed, while Fodor shows how modular input systems may be beautifully explained by the language of thought hypothesis, he has far less to say about central systems, which is where belief fixation occurs. Actually, it is worse than this. Fodor argues that central systems must have certain properties – they must be Quinean and isotropic – and such properties fall victim to Fodor's

[18] *The Psychology of Proof: Deductive Reasoning in Human Thinking*, MIT Press, 1994.

First Law of the Nonexistence of Cognitive Science: "the more global (e.g., the more isotropic) a cognitive process is, the less anybody understands it."[19] Fodor thinks, indeed, that we really know nothing at all about central systems, and thus, nothing at all about belief fixation. So, at least at present, the empirical support for the traditional view about inferential justification and rationality is nothing more than a fond hope.

I actually think that things are worse than this. The global features which Fodor assumes must inevitably characterize central systems are ones which seem to raise problems of computational complexity. There could not be a computational device which has the properties Fodor assigns to central systems.[20] But I won't stop to argue for this here. Let me leave it as a mere possibility. Even on Fodor's own sense of the prospects for his account, we are very far from being in a position to endorse it.

At the opposite extreme from Fodor's account of cognitive architecture, we find connectionist views, the modern-day descendant of Hume's view that all of cognition can be explained in terms of association. On one way of thinking about this view, there is no such thing as inferentially justified belief because there is no such thing as inference. Much philosophical work on inference actually begins with the assumption that inference is different in kind from association, and if we simply build this in to our view of inference, eliminationism about inference follows straightforwardly from the connectionist approach. But one needn't have such a narrow view of inferential processes. One might instead think that the right way to understand this view – or at least, one acceptable way to understand it – is that, if it is right, then inference turns out to be quite different than we thought it was.

The connectionist picture not only forces a radical rethinking of inference. It forces, as well, a rethinking of the nature of rationality. Rational belief and action cannot be the product of psychological processes which track valid deductive arguments or good non-deductive arguments, for belief and action are not brought about by processes which track argumentation of any sort. Of course, the connectionist picture does not fit at all well with the way in which belief acquisition and decision are portrayed under conditions of deliberation. But this is not news to connectionists. For all of the reasons discussed above, we should not see the ways in which we seem to acquire beliefs and make decisions as viewed from the first-person perspective as carrying any real weight in psychological theorizing.

---

[19] *The Modularity of Mind*, 107.
[20] For discussion, see Christopher Cherniak, *Minimal Rationality*, MIT Press, 1986, chapter 4.

Connectionist views are not without their problems. They seem incapable of accounting for various systematic features of thought. But given the problems with available alternative views, and given the many mental phenomena which connectionist views do neatly account for, it would, as I see it, be premature to count them out.

Let me briefly mention one final view of cognition: Philip Johnson-Laird's mental models approach.[21] Johnson-Laird's view imparts a good deal more structure to cognition than do connectionist models, without imposing the kind of linguistic structure provided by a language of thought. It provides a conception of inference – if this is the right way to conceive of mental transitions on such a view – which does not leave room for the traditional view of inferentially justified belief as a matter of argument structure. One might combine the mental models approach with a reliabilist view of rational belief, or one might, instead, seek to characterize good-making features of certain models in some other terms. It is safe to say, however, that an account of rationality which fits with Johnson-Laird's picture of mental models will not answer to any traditional view about argument structure.

None of these views is so well supported by current evidence that we can confidently assert that this is the way in which inference, and rationality, should be understood. But that is my point. The discussion of the nature of rationality cannot be pushed forward without a deeper understanding of the architecture of thought. There is a commonsense view of what rational belief and decision must answer to, and this view fits well with the picture of belief and action which the first-person perspective on deliberation presents to us. No doubt, this has a great deal to do with the appeal of the view. But even if we do not have a well-confirmed picture of the large-scale structure of the mind, we know enough now not to be taken in by the way that the first-person perspective presents our thinking to the reflective agent. And this means that we must take seriously the possibility that rational belief and rational action may have a very different etiology, and a very different nature, than they seem to have when we reflect.

VI

What goes on in us when we deliberate seems fundamentally different in kind from what goes on in us when we form beliefs unreflectively. As I remarked at the beginning of this essay, there is a way in which we

---

[21] *Mental Models*, Harvard University Press, 1983.

often describe what goes on when we form beliefs without the benefit of reflection. We say, "My mind was elsewhere," if our attention is focused on one thing – say, a choice of what to teach next semester – when we are unreflectively picking up information about another – perhaps the path across campus that will safely take us where we want to go. Of course, unreflective belief and decision cannot be literally mindless. The mind is engaged in sophisticated information-processing even when our attention is focused on other things. But now the question arises as to whether the mental processes involved under these two conditions are genuinely different in kind. Should we see self-conscious deliberation as the home of rationality, the situation in which our rational nature is most fully manifest, or is our rationality no less present when our attention is elsewhere, and no less fully manifest when our attention is lacking?

I have argued that the picture of our own cognitive processing which is presented to us when we deliberate is deeply misleading, in both what it leaves out and what it includes. We cannot responsibly base an account of our mental processing on the way in which it appears from the first-person point of view. Once we see this, we need to think long and hard about cognitive architecture and the manner in which it constrains a theory of inference, and a theory of rationality as well. The claim that our rational nature should be identified with features of self-conscious deliberation – indeed, with the way in which self-conscious deliberation appears from the first-person point of view – places bets on the outcome of future research which are, at best, premature.

Index

a priori knowledge, 8, 12, 70, 74, 76–77, 89
  empirical refutation, 70–71
  inference and, 75, 188, 190–191
  introspection and, 159
  prima facie case for, 74–76, 83–90
  reasons for belief, 188–190
  recognition by rational intuition, 83–85
  skeptical position, 69–74
  web of belief, 77–80
addiction, 104–105
anchoring effect, 24
animal knowledge, 9, 94–100, 149, 208
  reflective knowledge and, 98–100
animals
  beliefs, 96, 100, 103, 112, 244, 255
  lack of freedom of the will, 95, 105, 152
  lack of normativity, 108
  lack of rationality, 1, 15–16, 95, 243–246
  self-knowledge, 38, 102
  visual perception, 252–253
  See also animal knowledge.
armchair methods, 11–12, 156–159, 161–164, 166–173, 179
  arguments for, 157–158
  as proto-scientific psychology, 168
  concept content and form, 163–164, 167–171
  conceptual analysis and, 167
  empirical alternatives to, 158, 164
  empirical refutation, 167, 171–173
  epistemic responsibility, 166–167
  first-person perspective and, 174–179
  inadequacy of, 159, 162–163, 166
    concept forms and character, 163, 168
    emotion, 164
    memory, 162
    testimonial response, 163
  internalism and, 166
  methodological limits, 173
  physics, 179
  skepticism and, 169
  techniques

  formal modeling, 173
  introspection, 159–161
Armstrong, David, 20, 202

bats, 38, 100
beliefs
  animals, 95–96, 100, 103, 112, 244, 255
  change, 96, 101–104, 192–193
  rational, 79, 100–104
  reason-responsiveness, 111
  Descartes on, 18
  fixation, 57, 151, 195, 199–200, 258
  reason-giving and, 56–57
  reflection as epiphenomenal, 151, 196
  formation, 142, 161, 246
    deliberation and, 148, 151
    empirical study, 137, 194
    first-order (precognitive) processes, 97, 140, 144, 161, 166
    introspection and, 10, 24, 27, 29–31, 160–161
    mental states and, 34
    personal character and, 36
    rationalization and, 53
    reason-giving as epiphenomenal, 56–57, 255
    reflective knowledge and, 96–98
    subconscious factors, 142
    third-person perspective, 137
  implicit vs intentional, 243–245
  philosophical
    epistemic justification, 129
    reflection on, 141
  second-order
    relation to first-order belief, 102–103
  See also justification; reason-giving; reasons for belief.
Boghossian, Paul, 244–245, 248, 251
BonJour, Laurence
  intellectual integrity, 69
  on *a priori* knowledge

262

argument in favor of, 8, 69, 74–76, 83–90
  empiricism leads to skepticism, 80–83
  Quine's web of belief, 76–80
on externalism, 75, 86–87, 208
on induction, 90–93
on justification of belief
  a priori knowledge, 71, 75
  coherentist account, 21–22, 24, 29
  internalism, 138, 165–166, 174–176
  rationalism, 70, 72, 82
Burge, Tyler, 245, 248

Cartesian epistemology, 2–3, 6, 9–10, 20
  impatient, 19–22
  See also coherentism; foundationalism.
Chisholm, Roderick, 21, 204
  anti-skepticism, 210–212
  evidential principles, 62, 205
  on introspection, 160
  on justification, 21, 23–24, 29, 204–205, 209
Christensen, David, 116, 206
cognitive distortions, 5, 36, 38, 44, 63, 153–154
  anchoring effect, 24
  position effect, 22–24, 30
  rationalization and, 52–53, 60–61
  self-understanding and, 36–38
cognitive psychology, 158 *See* psychological research.
coherentism, 3, 21–22, 25, 75
color perception, 42–44
concepts, 163–164, 168
  alignment of philosophical and psychological term, 168–170
  armchair methods, 163–164, 167–171
confabulation, 4, 143–144, 150, 161, 256–257
confirmation bias, 27–28, 143
connectionist, 260
Credulity, Principle of, 62

decision-making, 60, 149, 151–153, 255–257, 259–261
deliberation, 2–3, 16, 148–150, 153, 244
  belief formation and, 16, 148–149, 151, 244
  decision-making and, 151, 153
  doxastic, 194–196
  empirical research, 10–11, 150
  first-person perspective, 11, 148, 151, 248, 252, 254
    argument-sketches, 254–257
    decision-making and, 148, 151
    inaccuracy, 150, 252–254
    incompleteness, 10, 150, 248–252
  rationality and, 16, 194, 244–246, 252, 261
  unreflective belief-formation and, 260–261
  See also decision-making; reflection.

delusions of grandeur, 222
Dennett, Daniel, 30
Descartes, René
  belief formation, 18–19
  epistemological method, 18, 137, 178
  internal-external distinction, 175
  on introspection, 18, 160
    transparency of mental states to, 20, 29, 32, 160, 178
  on reflection, 144
  privileged view of truths of reason, 6
  realism on mental states, 32–33
  rejection of false belief, 19
desires, 105–108
  Frankfurt's account, 104–107
  second-order, 95, 105, 107
disagreement, 55, 113, 132–134, 157
  actual and possible, 118–121, 123
  aesthetic, 124–125
  cases of better judgment, 114
  mathematical, 116–117, 119, 125–126, 130–132
  moral and political, 130–132
  Newcomb Problem, 122–124
  perceptual, 115–116
  philosophy, 114–117, 122, 127, 133–134
  simple cases, 113
discriminatory capacity, 40, 42–43
Dogramaci, Sinan, 139–140, 145–148
donor conception, 221, 229, 234–235, 239–241
  morality of, 239–242
doxastic deliberation, 194–195
  phenomenological account, 194–196
doxastic justification, 14, 201–204, 206–207, 211–212, 219
  propositional justification in terms of, 204, 220
  reliabilist account, 204

Elga, Adam, 117, 130–133
eliminationism, 14, 170, 183, 191, 259
  reasons, 185
empirical research, 77 *See* psychological research.
empiricism, 69–74
  skepticism and, 80–83
  web of belief metaphor, 76–80
epiphenomenal, 11, 56, 151, 216, 253–255
evolutionary biology, 224
experience, subjectivity of, 35–38
experimental philosophy, 159
experimental psychology, 24–25
externalism
  a priori knowledge and, 75
  belief acquisition, 147
  BonJour and, 75, 86–87

externalism (cont.)
  coherentism, 22
  defined, 20
  first-person perspective and, 138–140, 145
  internalism and, 17
  internalism-externalism debate, 114–117, 120, 122, 127–128, 133–134
  introspection and, 146
  justification of belief under, 20–21, 145–148, 174, 208

family history, 222–228
  donor conception and, 221, 229, 234–235, 239–242
  selectivity and inaccuracy, 226
  value of, 228–239
fashion, 124–125
Feldman, Richard, 115, 117, 156–157, 175, 203
feminism, 6, 49, 53, 66–67
first-person perspective, 11
  deliberation and, 11, 148–153, 248–252, 254
    argument-sketches, 254–257
    decision making, 148, 151
    incompleteness, 141, 248–252
  experimental psychology, 140–141
  externalism and, 174
    belief justification, 145–148
  inference and, 145
  limitations, 154–155
    inaccuracy, 141, 195, 252–254
    incompleteness, 141, 248–252
  naturalism and, 136
  primacy of, 136–138, 140, 145, 175, 177
    arguments for, 145, 148
    belief formation and, 140
  reflection and, 154–155, 176, 179
  self-knowledge, 38–39
    advantages, 41
    mental state access from, 40–41, 141, 176–177
    third-person perspective and, 41
Firth, Roderick, 202–204
Fodor, Jerry, 257–259
Foley, Richard, 138–139, 174–177
formal modeling, 173
foundationalism, 21, 25, 75, 160, 187
Frankfurt, Harry, 9, 95, 104–107, 152–153
freedom
  of action, 104
  of the will, 9, 94, 104–105, 152
Frege, Gottlob, 203

Gettier, Ed, 167, 248–249
Gödel, Kurt, 125
Goldman, Alvin, 156, 202, 210

anti-skepticism, 210
  on armchair investigation, 168
  on justification, 202–204, 207–208, 219–220

Hampshire, Stuart, 155
Harman, Gilbert, 191–192, 248–250, 252–254
Harris, Robin, 242
Harris-Kornblith, Annie, 242
Haslanger, Sally, 240
Haug, Matthew, 180
Horowitz, Sophie, 147
hypothesis testing, 27

induction, 90–93, 213, 216
inference
  a priori knowledge and, 75, 188, 190–191
  deductive, 190
  empiricism and, 48, 75
  experimental psychology and, 81, 164, 212–214
  first-person perspective and, 145, 150
  holistic principles, 192–193
  inductive, 90–93, 213, 216
  introspection and, 23–24, 30
  reasons for belief and, 185, 190–191, 196
  reliability, 4
  skepticism about, 48
internalism
  a priori knowledge and, 75
  empirical evidence against, 166
  epistemological priority, 175–179
  externalism and, 17, 165
  first-person perspective and, 138, 145
  internalist-externalist debate, 114–117, 120, 122, 127–129
  introspection and, 165
    fallibility of, 22–26
    unreliability of, 26–29
  justification, 20–21, 75, 115, 138
  justification of belief, 21–22
  propositional justification and, 208
  See also armchair methods; first-person perspective; introspection.
introspection, 4–6, 17–29, 44–48, 159–167, 255–257
  a priori knowledge and, 84
  belief acquisition and, 29–31
  Descartes on, 18–20, 29, 32, 160
  emotion, 164
  externalism and, 20
  incompleteness and inaccuracy of, 84
  internalist account, 21–22
    empirical fallibility of introspection, 22–26
    unreliability of introspection, 26–29
  negative role, 19–20

perception and, 25
positive role, 18–19
skeptical position
  distinguished from perceptual and inferential skepticism, 48
transparency of mental states to, 32
See also armchair methods; first-person perspective; internalism; reflection.

Johnson-Laird, Philip, 212, 260
justification, 20–21, 71, 78, 82, 139–140, 145–147, 169–171, 182–183, 217–220
  a priori, 70, 75, 80, 86, 188, 190
  Descartes on, 19
  externalist accounts, 20–21, 145–148, 174, 208
  meta-justification and, 88–90
  reliabilism, 29, 183–184
  See also doxastic justification; externalism; internalism; propositional justification.

Kahneman, Daniel, 24, 67, 81, 212
Kelly, Thomas, 118–124, 127, 130
Korsgaard, Christine, 9, 95, 108–110, 152–153
Kunda, Ziva, 141–142

logocentrism, 54

Marxism, 66
memory, 150, 162, 170–171, 195
mental models, 260
mental states, 4–6, 32–35, 39–47, 108, 175–177
  beliefs about
    distorted, 4–5
    first vs third-person perspective, 40–42
  internalist accounts
    justification of belief, 176
  introspective access to, 2, 4, 177–178
  introspective knowledge of
    inaccuracy of introspection, 25
    opacity of, 29–31
    skepticism of, 43–48
  objective character, 33
mental taking, 251
Modus Ponens, 190–192
motivations for action, 34, 52, 60, 64, 66, 240

Nagel, Thomas, 33–35, 50, 233
narrative understandings, 235–238
Newcomb Problem, 122–124
normativity, 9, 95, 108, 111, 194
Nozick, Robert, 122

Orenstein, Alex, 77

paranoid personality disorder, 4–5
perception
  animal knowledge and, 96
  beliefs acquired via, 30, 96, 116, 187–189, 255
  color blindness, 42–44
  disagreements, 115–116
  error, 252–253
perspective, 257
philosophy
  as armchair discipline, 157
  disagreement in, 114–117
  experimental, 158
  rationalization in, 62–64
plausibility, 55
position effect, 22–24, 30
propositional justification, 14, 170, 201–211, 216–220
  apsychological, 210, 215–216
    justification as non-necessary epistemic condition, 217–219
    skepticism and, 217
  background knowledge, 215–216
  experimental psychology and, 212–215
  G, 207
  notion of, 207–210, 217
proprioception, 186–187
psychological research, 159
  anchoring effect, 24
  concepts (as term of art), 168–170
  on belief formation, 137, 194
  on first-person perspective, 140–141
  on introspection, 12, 22–26, 163, 165–167, 171–173
  on reasons for belief, 198–199
  position effect, 22–24, 30
  propositional justification and, 212–215

Quine, Willard Van Orman
  BonJour on, 76–80
  epistemological methodology, 80–81
  skepticism and, 61, 80–83
  web of belief metaphor, 77–80

rational argument
  plausibility appeals, 55
  skepticism toward, 53–57
    self-contradiction of, 57–61
rational intuition, 84
  distinguished from belief, 84–85
rational option, 124
rationalism, 69–70, 72, 74, 82, 87
  moderate, 69, 72, 74, 82
  radical, 87
rationality, 68, 258

rationality (cont.)
  as uniquely human faculty, 243
  belief change, 79, 100–104
  first person perspective and deliberation, 248–252
  first-person concept and, 245–246, 252–254
  models
    conectionist, 259–260
    language of thought (Fodor), 257–259
    mental models approach, 260
  phenomenology of deliberation, 246–248
rationalization, 50–59, 61–68, 162
  cognitive distortions and, 52–53, 60–61
  in philosophy, 62–64
  motivations for, 52, 64
    concentration on as distraction from argumentative merit, 64–66
    heterogeneity of, 66
    vested interests as, 66–68
  sincere, 53, 59, 62
reason-giving, 49–50, 52–54, 56–63, 67
  belief fixation and, 56–57
  psychological research, 198–199
  rationalization and, 50–59
  skeptical position
    consequences, 62–68
    motivation analysis, 64–66
  skepticism toward
    as self-contradictory, 57–61
    rationality of, 53–57
  See also rationalization.
reasons for belief
  a priori knowledge and, inferential principles, 190–191
  causal relationship between, 197
  commonsense distinctions, 181–182
  distinct from causes of belief, 181, 193–197
  empirical psychology, 198–199
  epistemological role, 181–184
  inferential principles
    holism, 192–193
  perception and, 187–190
  reasons for belief, 13, 26, 194, 201
  See also belief; justification; reason-giving.
reflection, 8–16, 142–144, 154–155, 174–179, 195–197
  animal and reflective knowledge, 95–100
  belief change and, 100–104
  belief content and, 9, 94–95, 100–101, 110–111, 152–153, 197
  belief formation and, 97–99, 142–144
  freedom of the will and, 104–108

  normativity and, 108–111
reflective knowledge, 9, 94–97, 99
  animal knowledge and, 98–100
  belief acquisition and, 96–98
Reichenbach, Hans, 91
Reid, Thomas, 62
relativity theory, 70
reliabilism, 20, 86, 183–184, 191, 193, 202

science, 80–83
scientia, 3
self-conception, 221
  family history and, 222–228
    value of, 228–239
  narrative and causal understanding, 235–238
  personality and, 238–239
  views on one's own capacities, 222–223, 228
self-knowledge, 149
  animals, 38, 102
  cognitive distortions and, 36–38
  epistemic privilege of first-person perspective, 38–42
  family history and, 223, 226, 228–229, 238
  introspection and, 35–38, 42, 46
  skepticism about, 5, 32, 42, 44
Sellars, Wilfrid, 182, 186–187
Shoemaker, Sydney, 33, 94, 100–104
social psychology, 12 See psychological research.
Sosa, Ernest, 9, 95–96, 149, 177, 208, 243–244
  animal and relfective knowledge, 94–100
  responsiblism, 243–244
Stich, Stephen, 124
Sulloway, Frank, 67

third-person perspective, 137
Turri, John, 201

Velleman, David
  adoption and, 229–230
  child-rearing, 233–234
  donor conception, 221, 234–235, 239–242
  family lore, 226, 228–229
  narrative understandings, 235–238
  relatives as role models, 231
  self-knowledge, 226, 238–239
virtue-reliabilism, 99
volitions, 105 See desires.

wantons, 104–107
Wason, Peter, 27
Williamson, Timothy, 12, 157, 172–173, 180

For EU product safety concerns, contact us at Calle de José Abascal, 56–1º, 28003 Madrid, Spain or eugpsr@cambridge.org.

www.ingramcontent.com/pod-product-compliance
Lightning Source LLC
LaVergne TN
LVHW021803060526
838201LV00058B/3223